Joint Publication 3-0

Joint Operations

11 August 2011

This revised edition of Joint Publication 3-0, *Joint Operations*, reflects the current guidance for conducting joint activities across the range of military operations and is the basis for U.S. participation in multinational operations where the United States has not ratified specific doctrine or procedures. This keystone publication forms the core of joint warfighting doctrine and establishes the framework for our forces' ability to fight as a joint team.

Often called the "linchpin" of the joint doctrine publication hierarchy, the overarching constructs and principles contained in this publication provide a common perspective from which to plan and execute joint operations independently or in cooperation with our multinational partners, other U.S. Government departments and agencies, and intergovernmental and nongovernmental organizations.

As our Nation continues into the 21st century, the guidance in this publication will enable current and future leaders of the Armed Forces of the United States to design, plan, organize, train for, and execute worldwide missions as our forces transform to meet emerging challenges. To succeed, we need adaptive and thinking professionals who understand the capabilities their Service brings to joint operations; how to integrate those capabilities with those of the other Services and interorganizational partners to optimize the strength of unified action; and how to organize, employ, and sustain joint forces to provide national leaders with multiple options for addressing various security threats. Above all, we need professionals imbued with a sense of commitment and honor who will act decisively in the absence of specific guidance.

I challenge all commanders to ensure the widest distribution of this keystone joint publication and actively promote the use of all joint publications at every opportunity. I further challenge you to study and understand the guidance contained in this publication and teach these principles to your subordinates. Only then will we be able to fully exploit the remarkable military potential inherent in our joint teams.

M. G. MULLEN
Admiral, U.S. Navy

PREFACE

1. Scope

This publication is the keystone document of the joint operations series. It provides the doctrinal foundation and fundamental principles that guide the Armed Forces of the United States in joint operations across the range of military operations.

2. Purpose

This publication has been prepared under the direction of the Chairman of the Joint Chiefs of Staff. It sets forth joint doctrine to govern the activities and performance of the Armed Forces of the United States in joint operations, and it provides considerations for military interaction with governmental and nongovernmental agencies, multinational forces, and other interorganizational partners. It provides military guidance for the exercise of authority by combatant commanders and other joint force commanders (JFCs), and prescribes joint doctrine for operations and training. It provides military guidance for use by the Armed Forces in preparing and executing their plans and orders. It is not the intent of this publication to restrict the authority of the JFC from organizing the force and executing the mission in a manner the JFC deems most appropriate to ensure unity of effort in the accomplishment of objectives.

3. Application

a. Joint doctrine established in this publication applies to the joint staff, commanders of combatant commands, subunified commands, joint task forces, subordinate components of these commands, and the Services.

b. The guidance in this publication is authoritative; as such, this doctrine will be followed except when, in the judgment of the commander, exceptional circumstances dictate otherwise. If conflicts arise between the contents of this publication and the contents of Service publications, this publication will take precedence unless the Chairman of the Joint Chiefs of Staff, normally in coordination with the other members of the Joint Chiefs of Staff, has provided more current and specific guidance. Commanders of forces operating as part of a multinational (alliance or coalition) military command should follow multinational doctrine and procedures ratified by the United States. For doctrine and procedures not ratified by the US, commanders should evaluate and follow the multinational command's doctrine and procedures, where applicable and consistent with US law, regulations, and doctrine.

Intentionally Blank

SUMMARY OF CHANGES
REVISION OF JOINT PUBLICATION 3-0, DATED 17 SEPTEMBER 2006
(INCORPORATING CHANGE 2 DATED 22 MARCH 2010)

- **Incorporates a discussion of the *art of joint command*, including new ideas on command-centric leadership and operational design.**

- **Incorporates a new section on *creating shared understanding*, which emphasizes the interaction of information management and knowledge sharing to create an organizational environment of learning that facilitates joint operations.**

- **Consolidates information related to organizing for joint operations in a single Chapter IV.**

- **Consolidates Chapters V, VI, and VII in a single Chapter V.**

- **Reduces redundancies and improves continuity between Joint Publication (JP) 3-0 and JP 1, *Doctrine for the Armed Forces of the United States*.**

- **Reduces redundancies and improves continuity between JP 3-0 and JP 5-0, *Joint Operation Planning*.**

Intentionally Blank

TABLE OF CONTENTS

PAGE

EXECUTIVE SUMMARY ix

CHAPTER I
FUNDAMENTALS OF JOINT OPERATIONS

- Introduction... I-1
- Strategic Environment and National Security Challenges.................................... I-2
- Instruments of National Power and the Range of Military Operations I-4
- Strategic Guidance I-5
- Unified Action I-8
- Levels of War I-12
- Types of Military Operations.. I-14

CHAPTER II
THE ART OF JOINT COMMAND

- Introduction... II-1
- Commander-Centric Leadership II-1
- Operational Art II-3
- Operational Design II-4
- Joint Operation Planning II-5
- Assessment II-9

CHAPTER III
JOINT FUNCTIONS

- Introduction.. III-1
- Command and Control... III-2
- Intelligence III-20
- Fires III-22
- Movement and Maneuver III-27
- Protection III-29
- Sustainment... III-35

CHAPTER IV
ORGANIZING FOR JOINT OPERATIONS

- Introduction... IV-1
- Understanding the Operational Environment IV-1
- Organizing the Joint Force.. IV-6
- Organizing the Joint Force Headquarters IV-10
- Organizing Operational Areas IV-11

Table of Contents

CHAPTER V
JOINT OPERATIONS ACROSS THE RANGE OF MILITARY OPERATIONS

- Introduction V-1

Section A. Types of Military Operations V-3
- Military Operations and Related Missions, Tasks, and Actions V-3

Section B. A Phasing Construct V-5
- Phasing a Joint Operation V-5

Section C. Military Engagement, Security Cooperation, and Deterrence V-9
- Military Engagement, Security Cooperation, and Deterrence V-9
- Typical Operations V-11
- Other Considerations V-18

Section D. Crisis Response and Limited Contingency Operations V-19
- Crisis Response and Limited Contingency Operations V-19
- Typical Operations V-20
- Other Considerations V-29

Section E. Major Operations and Campaigns V-31
- Major Operations and Campaigns V-31
- The Balance of Offense, Defense, and Stability Operations V-35
- Considerations for Shaping V-37
- Considerations for Deterrence V-39
- Considerations for Seizing the Initiative V-43
- Considerations for Dominance V-50
- Considerations for Stabilization V-59
- Considerations for Enabling Civil Authority V-63

APPENDIX
A	Principles of Joint Operations	A-1
B	References	B-1
C	Administrative Instructions	C-1

GLOSSARY
Part I	Abbreviations and Acronyms	GL-1
Part II	Terms and Definitions	GL-5

FIGURE
I-1	Principles of Joint Operations	I-2
I-2	Common Operating Precepts	I-3
I-3	Range of Military Operations	I-5
I-4	Unified Action	I-9
I-5	Relationship Between Strategy and Operational Art	I-13
I-6	Examples of Military Operations	I-15
II-1	Elements of Operational Design	II-5

II-2	Joint Operation Planning Process	II-7
III-1	Command Relationships Synopsis	III-3
III-2	Creating Shared Understanding	III-12
III-3	Risk Management Process	III-16
IV-1	Visualizing the Operational Environment	IV-3
IV-2	The Interconnected Operational Environment	IV-5
IV-3	Notional Joint Force Headquarters and Cross-Functional Staff Organization	IV-10
IV-4	Operational Areas within a Theater	IV-12
IV-5	Contiguous and Noncontiguous Operational Areas	IV-14
V-1	Range of Military Operations	V-1
V-2	Examples of Military Operations	V-4
V-3	Notional Operation Plan Phases versus Level of Military Effort	V-6
V-4	Notional Balance of Offensive, Defensive, and Stability Operations	V-36
V-5	Combinations of Areas of Operations and Linear/Nonlinear Operations	V-53

Intentionally Blank

EXECUTIVE SUMMARY
COMMANDER'S OVERVIEW

- **Presents the Fundamentals of Joint Operations as an Instrument of National Power and as Part of Unified Action**

- **Discusses the Art of Command as It Pertains to Authority, Commander-Centric Leadership, Operational Art of Design, Operational Design, Joint Operations Planning Process**

- **Explains Joint Functions of Command and Control, Intelligence, Fires, Movement and Maneuver, Protection, and Sustainment**

- **Describes Organizing for Joint Operations, Including Organizing the Joint Force Headquarters**

- **Discusses Joint Operations Across the Range of Military Operations**

Fundamentals of Joint Operations

Joint operations is a general term that describes military actions conducted by joint forces or by Service forces employed under command relationships.

Joint Publication (JP) 3-0 is the keystone document in the joint operations series, and is a companion to joint doctrine's capstone JP 1, *Doctrine for the Armed Forces of the United States*. It provides guidance to joint force commanders (JFCs) and their subordinates for planning, preparing, executing, and assessing joint military operations. Although individual Services may accomplish tasks and missions in support of Department of Defense (DOD) objectives, the primary way DOD employs two or more Services (from two Military Departments) in a single operation, particularly in combat, is through joint operations.

Strategic Environment and National Security Challenges

The **strategic environment** is characterized by uncertainty, complexity, and rapid change, which requires persistent engagement. This environment is fluid, with continually changing alliances, partnerships, and new national and transnational threats constantly appearing and disappearing. In addition to traditional conflicts, to include emerging peer competitors, significant challenges continue to include irregular warfare (IW), catastrophic terrorism employing weapons of mass destruction (WMD), and

Executive Summary

threats to disrupt the Nation's ability to project power and maintain its qualitative edge.

The strategic environment presents five broad **national security challenges** likely to require the employment of joint forces in the future.

- A secure US homeland is the Nation's first priority.
- Deterring our adversaries is a US goal.
- Defending national interests requires not only being able to prevail in conflict, but also taking preventive measures to deter potential adversaries who could threaten the vital interests of the United States or its partners.
- Establishing, maintaining, and enhancing security cooperation among our alliances and partners is important to strengthen the global security framework of the United States and its partners.
- As it has in the past, the United States will continue to respond to a variety of civil crises by acting to relieve human suffering and restoring civil functioning, most often in support of civil authorities.

Instruments of National Power and the Range of Military Operations

Our national leaders can use the military instrument of national power in a wide variety of activities, tasks, missions, and operations that vary in purpose, scale, risk, and combat intensity. *Operations* are grouped in three areas that compose the *range of military operation.*

Military Engagement, Security Cooperation, and Deterrence. These are ongoing routine activities that establish, shape, maintain, and refine relations with other nations and domestic civil authorities (e.g., state governors or local law enforcement).

Crisis Response and Limited Contingency Operations. These can be small-scale, limited-duration operations, such as *strikes*, *raids*, and *peace enforcement*, which might include combat depending on the circumstances.

Executive Summary

Strategic Guidance

A combatant commander is the vital link between those who determine national security policy and strategy and the military forces or subordinate joint force commanders (JFCs) who conduct military operations.

Unified Action

Unified action is a comprehensive approach that synchronizes, coordinates, and when appropriate, integrates military operations with the activities of other governmental and nongovernmental organizations to achieve unity of effort.

Levels of War

There are no finite limits or boundaries between these levels, but they help commanders visualize a logical arrangement of operations, allocate resources, and

Major Operations and Campaigns. These are extended-duration, large-scale operations that usually involve combat.

***National strategic direction* provides strategic context** for the employment of the instruments of national power and defines the strategic purpose that guides employment of the military instrument of national power as part of a global strategy. Based on guidance from the President and Secretary of Defense, geographic and functional combatant commanders (CCDRs) develop strategies that translate national and multinational strategic direction into strategic concepts or courses of action to meet joint operation planning requirements.

Whereas the term *joint operations* focuses on the integrated actions of the Armed Forces of the United States in a unified effort, the term *unified action* has a broader connotation. JFCs are challenged to achieve and maintain operational coherence given the requirement to operate in conjunction with interorganizational partners. CCDRs play a pivotal role in unifying joint force actions, since all of the elements and actions that comprise unified action normally are present at the CCDR's level. However, subordinate JFCs also integrate and synchronize their operations directly with the operations of other military forces and the activities of nonmilitary organizations in the operational area to promote unified action.

Three levels of war—strategic, operational, and tactical—model the relationship between national objectives and tactical actions.

Strategic Level. In the context of military operations, strategy develops an idea or set of ideas for employing the instruments of national power in a synchronized and integrated fashion to achieve theater, national, and/or multinational objectives.

Operational Level. The operational level links the tactical employment of forces to national and military strategic objectives.

Executive Summary

assign tasks to the appropriate command.

Tactical Level. Tactics is the employment and ordered arrangement of forces in relation to each other. Joint doctrine focuses this term on planning and executing battles, engagements, and activities at the tactical level to achieve military objectives assigned to tactical units or task forces.

Types of Military Operations

Each military operation may occur simultaneously with or independently of other operations, or multiple operations may overlap.

The United States employs its military capabilities in support of its national security goals in a variety of military operations. Operations such as counterinsurgency (COIN) and counterterrorism are primarily related to IW. Large-scale combat operations associated with traditional warfare typically characterize major operations and campaigns, although the extended nature of some IW will require operations phased over time as a campaign.

The Art of Joint Command

Command is the authority that a commander in the armed forces lawfully exercises over subordinates by virtue of rank or assignment.

While command authority stems from appropriate orders and other directives, **the art of command resides in the commander's ability to use situational leadership to maximize operational performance.** The combination of courage, ethical leadership, judgment, intuition, situational awareness, and the ability to consider contrary views gained over time through training, education, and experience helps commanders make difficult decisions in complex situations.

Commander-Centric Leadership

Historical analysis shows that commander-centric organizations out-perform staff-centric, process-oriented organizations. A commander's perspective of the challenge at hand is broader and more comprehensive than the staff's due to interaction with civilian leaders; senior, peer, subordinate, and supporting commanders; and interorganizational partners. Clear commander's guidance and intent, enriched by the commander's experience and intuition, are common to high-performing units.

Operational Art

Operational art applies to all aspects of joint operations and

***Operational art* is the use of creative thinking by commanders and staffs to design strategies, campaigns, and major operations and organize and employ military forces.** Operational art

Executive Summary

integrates ends, ways, and means, while accounting for risk, across the levels of war.

requires a broad vision, the ability to anticipate, and the skill to plan, prepare, execute, and assess. It helps commanders and their staffs order their thoughts and understand the conditions for victory before seeking battle. Operational art encompasses *operational design*—**the conception and construction of the intellectual framework that underpins joint operation plans and their subsequent execution.**

Operational Design

Operational design supports operational art with a general methodology using elements of operational design for understanding the situation and the problem.

Operational design extends operational art's vision with a creative process that helps commanders and planners answer the ends–ways–means–risk questions. **The commander is the central figure in operational design.** The elements of operational design are individual tools that help the JFC and staff visualize and describe the broad operational approach. Operational art, operational design, and joint operation planning process blend in complementary fashion as part of the overall process that produces the eventual plan or order that drives the joint operation.

Joint Operation Planning

Joint operation planning process underpins planning at all levels and for missions across the range of military operations.

Joint operation planning consists of planning activities associated with joint military operations by CCDRs and their subordinate JFCs in response to contingencies and crises. It transforms national strategic objectives into activities by development of operational products, which include planning for the mobilization, deployment, employment, sustainment, redeployment, and demobilization of joint forces. **Regardless of the commander's level of involvement, certain key planning elements require the commander's participation and decisions.** These include the operational approach, mission statement, commander's planning guidance, commander's intent, commander's critical information requirements, and concept of operations (CONOPS).

Assessment

Continuous assessment helps the JFC and joint force component commanders determine if the joint force is "doing the right things"

Assessment is a process that evaluates changes in the environment and measures progress of the joint force toward mission accomplishment. Assessment begins during mission analysis when the commander and staff consider what to measure and how to measure it **to determine progress toward**

xiii

Executive Summary

(measures of effectiveness) to achieve its objectives, not just "doing things right" (measures of performance).

accomplishing tasks, creating conditions, or achieving objectives. During execution, the commander's staff identifies those key assessment indicators that suggest progress or setbacks in accomplishing tasks, creating effects, and achieving objectives. Assessment actions and measures help commanders adjust operations and resources as required, determine when to execute branches and sequels, and make other critical decisions to ensure current and future operations remain aligned with the mission and military end state.

Joint Functions

Joint functions are related capabilities and activities grouped together to help JFCs integrate, synchronize, and direct joint operations.

Functions that are common to joint operations at all levels of war fall into **six basic groups—command and control (C2), intelligence, fires, movement and maneuver, protection, and sustainment.** The joint functions reinforce and complement one another, and **integration across the functions is essential to mission accomplishment.**

Command and Control

C2 encompasses the exercise of authority and direction by a commander over assigned and attached forces to accomplish the mission. The JFC provides operational vision, guidance, and direction to the joint force.

Intelligence

The intelligence function supports this understanding by providing integrated, evaluated, analyzed, and interpreted information concerning foreign nations, hostile or potentially hostile forces or elements, or areas of actual or potential operations. Intelligence tells JFCs what the enemy is doing, is capable of doing, and may do in the future.

Fires

To **employ fires** is to use available weapons and other systems to create a specific lethal or nonlethal effect on a target. Joint fires are those delivered during the employment of forces from two or more components in coordinated action to produce desired results in support of a common objective. Fires typically produce destructive effects, but various nonlethal ways and means (such as electronic attack) can be employed with little or no associated physical destruction.

Executive Summary

Movement and Maneuver	This function encompasses the disposition of joint forces to conduct operations by securing positional advantages before or during combat operations and by exploiting tactical success to achieve operational and strategic objectives. This function includes moving or deploying forces into an operational area and maneuvering them to operational depths for offensive and defensive purposes. It also includes assuring the mobility of friendly forces.
Protection	The protection function focuses on preserving the joint force's fighting potential in four primary ways. One way uses active defensive measures that protect the joint force, its information, its bases, necessary infrastructure, and lines of communications from an enemy attack. Another way uses passive defensive measures that make friendly forces, systems, and facilities difficult to locate, strike, and destroy. Equally important is the application of technology and procedures to reduce the risk of fratricide. Finally, emergency management and response reduce the loss of personnel and capabilities due to accidents, health threats, and natural disasters.
Sustainment	**Sustainment** is the provision of logistics and personnel services necessary to maintain and prolong operations through mission accomplishment and redeployment of the force. Sustainment provides the JFC with the means to enable freedom of action and endurance and the ability to extend operational reach. Effective sustainment determines the depth to which the joint force can conduct decisive operations, allowing the JFC to seize, retain, and exploit the initiative.

Organizing for Joint Operations

Organizing for joint operations	Organizing for joint operations involves many considerations. Most can be associated in three primary groups related to *organizing the joint force*, *organizing the joint force headquarters (HQ)*, and *organizing operational areas* to help control operations.
Understanding the Operational Environment	The JFC's **operational environment** is the composite of the conditions, circumstances, and influences that

Executive Summary

affect employment of capabilities and bear on the decisions of the commander. It encompasses physical areas and factors (of the air, land, maritime, and space domains) and the information environment (which includes cyberspace). Included within these are enemy, friendly, and neutral systems that are relevant to a specific joint operation. The nature and interaction of these systems will affect how the commander plans, organizes for, and conducts joint operations.

Organizing the Joint Force

Joint forces can be established on a geographic or functional basis.

How JFCs organize their assigned or attached forces directly affects the responsiveness and versatility of joint operations. **The first principle in joint force organization is that JFCs organize forces to accomplish the mission based on their intent and CONOPS.** Unity of command, centralized planning and direction, and decentralized execution are key considerations. JFCs may elect to centralize selected functions within the joint force, but should avoid reducing the versatility, responsiveness, and initiative of subordinate forces. JFCs should allow Service and special operations forces tactical and operational forces, organizations, and capabilities to function generally as they were designed.

Organizing the Joint Force Headquarters

Joint force HQ include those for unified, subunified, and specified commands and joint task forces. While each HQ organizes to accommodate the nature of the JFC's operational area, mission, tasks, and preferences, all generally follow a traditional functional staff alignment (i.e., personnel, intelligence, operations, logistics, plans, and communications). Boards, centers, working groups, and other semipermanent and temporary organizations facilitate cross-functional coordination, synchronization, planning, and information sharing between principal staff directorates. Although these organizations are cross-functional in their membership, they typically fall under the oversight of a principal staff directorate.

Organizing Operational Areas

Except for areas of responsibility, which are assigned in the *Unified Command Plan*, geographic combatant commanders and other JFCs designate smaller operational areas (e.g., joint operations area and area

xvi

JP 3-0

Executive Summary

of operations) on a temporary basis. Operational areas have physical dimensions comprised of some combination of air, land, maritime, and space domains. JFCs define these areas with geographical boundaries, which help commanders and staffs coordinate, integrate, and deconflict joint operations among joint force components and supporting commands.

Joint Operations Across the Range of Military Operations

The range of military operations is another fundamental construct that provides context.

Military operations vary in scope, purpose, and conflict intensity across a range that extends from military engagement, security cooperation, and deterrence activities to crisis response and limited contingency operations and, if necessary, to major operations and campaigns.

Military Operations and Related Missions, Tasks, and Actions

In general, a military operation is a set of actions intended to accomplish a task or mission. Although the US military is organized, trained, and equipped for sustained, large-scale combat anywhere in the world, the capabilities to conduct these operations also enable a wide variety of other operations as well. Examples of military operations include stability operations; civil support; foreign humanitarian assistance (FHA); recovery; noncombatant evacuation (NEO); peace operations (PO); combating WMD; chemical, biological, radiological, and nuclear consequence management; foreign internal defense (FID); counterdrug (CD) operations; combating terrorism; COIN; and homeland defense (HD).

Phasing a Joint Operation

A phase is a definitive stage of an operation or campaign during which a large portion of the forces and capabilities are involved in similar or mutually supporting activities for a common purpose. Phasing, which can be used in any operation regardless of size, helps the JFC organize large operations by integrating and synchronizing subordinate operations. Phasing helps JFCs and staffs visualize, design, and plan the entire operation or campaign and define requirements in terms of forces, resources, time, space, and purpose.

Executive Summary

Military Engagement, Security Cooperation, and Deterrence

Military engagement, security cooperation, and deterrence missions, tasks, and actions encompass a wide range of actions where the military instrument of national power is tasked to support other government agencies (OGAs) and cooperate with intergovernmental organizations (IGOs) (e.g., United Nations, North Atlantic Treaty Organization) and other countries to protect and enhance national security interests, deter conflict, and set conditions for future contingency operations.

Typical Operations of Military Engagement, Security Cooperation, and Deterrence

Engagement activities generally are governed by various directives and agreements and do not require a joint operation plan or operations order for execution.

Even when the US is not conducting limited contingency operations, major operations, or campaigns, numerous routine missions (such as security cooperation) and continuing operations or tasks (such as ensuring freedom of navigation) are occurring under the general heading of *engagement*. Some typical operations of military engagement, security cooperation, and deterrence are: emergency preparedness; arms control, nonproliferation, and disarmament; combating terrorism; DOD support to CD operations; enforcement of sanctions; enforcing exclusion zones; ensuring freedom of navigation and overflight; nation assistance; FID; protection of shipping; show of force operations; support to insurgency; and COIN.

Other Considerations for Military Engagement, Security Cooperation, and Deterrence

Other considerations for military engagement, security cooperation, and deterrence are: interagency, intergovernmental, and nongovernmental organizations (NGOs) and host nation (HN) coordination; information sharing; and cultural awareness.

Crisis Response and Limited Contingency Operations

A limited contingency operation in response to a crisis includes all of those operations for which a JFC must develop an operation plan or operation order. The level of complexity, duration, and resources depends on the circumstances. Included are operations to ensure the safety of American citizens and US interests while maintaining and improving US ability to operate with multinational partners to deter the hostile ambitions of potential aggressors.

Typical Crisis Response and Limited Contingency Operations

Some typical crisis response and limited contingency operations are: NEO; PO; FHA; recovery operations;

Executive Summary

	strikes and raids; and HD and defense support of civil authorities.
Other Considerations for Crisis Response and Limited Contingency Operations	Other considerations for crisis response and limited contingency operations are: duration and end state, intelligence collection, constraints and restraints; force protection, and training.
Major Operations and Campaigns *Campaigns are joint in nature—functional and Service components conduct supporting operations, not independent campaigns.*	When required to achieve national strategic objectives or protect national interests, the US national leadership may decide to conduct a major operation or campaign involving large-scale combat, placing the United States in a wartime state. In such cases, the general goal is to prevail against the enemy as quickly as possible, conclude hostilities, and establish conditions favorable to the HN, the United States, and its multinational partners. A *major operation* is a series of tactical actions, such as battles, engagements, and strikes, and is the primary building block of a campaign. A *campaign* is a series of related military operations aimed at accomplishing a military strategic or operational objective within a given time and space.
The Balance of Offense, Defense, and Stability Operations	Combat missions and tasks can vary widely depending on context of the operation and the objective. Most combat operations will require the commander to balance offensive, defensive, and stability operations. This is particularly evident in a campaign or operation, where combat occurs during several phases and stability operations may occur throughout the campaign or operation. Commanders strive to apply the many dimensions of military power simultaneously across the depth, breadth, and height of the operational area.
Considerations for Shaping	JFCs are able to assist in determining the shape and character of potential future operations before committing forces. In many cases, these actions enhance bonds between potential multinational partners, increase understanding of the region, help ensure access when required, strengthen future multinational operations, and prevent crises from developing.

Executive Summary

Considerations for Deterrence

The *deter* phase is characterized by preparatory actions that indicate the intent to execute subsequent phases of the operation. Deterrence should be based on capability (having the means to influence behavior), credibility (maintaining a level of believability that the proposed actions may actual be employed), and communication (transmitting the intended message to the desired audience) to ensure greater effectiveness. Emphasis should be placed on setting the conditions for successful joint operations in the *dominate* and follow-on phases should deterrence fail.

Considerations for Seizing the Initiative

As operations commence, the JFC needs to exploit friendly advantages and capabilities to shock, demoralize, and disrupt the enemy immediately. The JFC seeks decisive advantage through the use of all available elements of combat power to seize and maintain the initiative, deny the enemy the opportunity to achieve its objectives, and generate in the enemy a sense of inevitable failure and defeat.

Considerations for Dominance

The JFC may designate one component or line of operation (LOO) to be the main effort, with other components providing support and other LOOs as supporting efforts.

During sustained combat operations, JFCs simultaneously employ conventional and special operations forces and capabilities throughout the breadth and depth of the operational area. Some missions and operations (i.e., strategic attack, interdiction, and information operations) continue throughout to deny the enemy sanctuary, freedom of action, or informational advantage. These missions and operations, when executed concurrently with other operations, degrade enemy morale and physical cohesion and bring the enemy closer to culmination.

Considerations for Stabilization

Operations in this phase continue pursuit of the national strategic end state. These operations typically begin with significant military involvement, to include some combat, and then move increasingly toward enabling civil authority as the threat wanes and civil infrastructures are reestablished. As progress is made, military forces will increase their focus on supporting the efforts of HN authorities, OGAs, IGOs, and/or NGOs.

Considerations for Enabling Civil Authority

In this phase, the joint operation normally is terminated when the stated military strategic and/or operational objectives have been met and redeployment of the joint force is accomplished. This should mean that a legitimate civil authority has been enabled to manage the situation without further outside military assistance. In some cases, it may become apparent that the stated objectives fall short of properly enabling civil authority. This situation may require a redesign of the joint operation as a result of an extension of the required stability operations in support of US diplomatic, HN, IGO, and/or NGO efforts.

CONCLUSION

This publication is the keystone document of the joint operations series. It provides the doctrinal foundation and fundamental principles that guide the Armed Forces of the United States in joint operations across the range of military operations.

Intentionally Blank

CHAPTER I
FUNDAMENTALS OF JOINT OPERATIONS

> *"Joint warfare is team warfare."*
>
> **Joint Publication 1, Doctrine for the Armed Forces of the United States**

1. Introduction

a. Joint Publication (JP) 3-0 is the keystone document in the joint operations series, and is a companion to joint doctrine's capstone JP 1, *Doctrine for the Armed Forces of the United States*. It provides guidance to joint force commanders (JFCs) and their subordinates for planning, preparing, executing, and assessing joint military operations. It also informs civilian decision makers and interorganizational partners of fundamental principles, precepts, and philosophies that guide the employment of the Armed Forces of the United States. JP 3-0 describes fundamental keystone constructs—such as *unified action* and *joint functions*—that apply regardless of the nature or circumstances of a specific joint operation. This publication provides a context not only for the joint operations series, but also for other keystone doctrine publications that describe supporting functions and processes.

b. The fundamental purpose of military power is to deter or wage war in support of national policy. In these capacities, military power is a coercive instrument, designed to achieve by force or the threat of force what other means have not. While leaders may employ this power in more benign ways for a variety of important purposes across a wide range of situations, they must understand that these other uses can imperil this Nation's fundamental ability to wage war.

c. Although individual Services may accomplish tasks and missions in support of Department of Defense (DOD) objectives, the primary way DOD employs two or more Services (from two Military Departments) in a single operation, particularly in combat, is through joint operations. ***Joint operations*** is a general term that describes military actions conducted by joint forces and those Service forces employed in specified command relationships with each other, which, of themselves, do not establish joint forces. A ***joint force*** is one composed of significant elements, assigned or attached, of two or more Military Departments operating under a single JFC.

d. **Joint operations doctrine is built on a sound base of warfighting philosophy, theory, and practical experience.** Its foundation rests upon the bedrock principles of war and the associated fundamentals of joint warfare, described in JP 1, *Doctrine for the Armed Forces of the United States*. Joint doctrine recognizes the basic and beneficial effects of unity of command and the synergy that results from the integration and synchronization of military operations in time, space, and purpose. Our leaders employ the Armed Forces of the United States in coordination with the other instruments of national power to advance and defend US values and interests, achieve objectives consistent with national strategy, and conclude operations on terms favorable to the US.

e. **Joint Warfare is Team Warfare.** The synergy that results from the integration and synchronization of Service components' capabilities under a single JFC maximizes the effectiveness and efficiency of the force. The advantage of a joint team extends beyond the operational environment and across the range of military operations. A joint operation does not require that all forces participate in a particular operation merely because they are available; the JFC has the authority and responsibility to tailor forces for the mission at hand.

f. **Principles of Joint Operations.** Since the establishment of the Joint Chiefs of Staff in 1947, joint doctrine has recognized the **nine principles of war**. Subsequent experience from a wide variety of irregular warfare (IW) situations has identified three additional principles—restraint, perseverance, and legitimacy. Together, they comprise the **12 principles of joint operations** (see Figure I-1) as discussed in Appendix A, "Principles of Joint Operations."

g. **Common Operating Precepts.** In addition to the principles of joint operations, ten *common operating precepts* underlie successful joint operations. Listed in Figure I-2, these precepts flow logically from the broad challenges in the strategic environment to the specific conditions, circumstances, and influences in a JFC's operational environment. JP 3-0's text highlights each common operating precept where it applies.

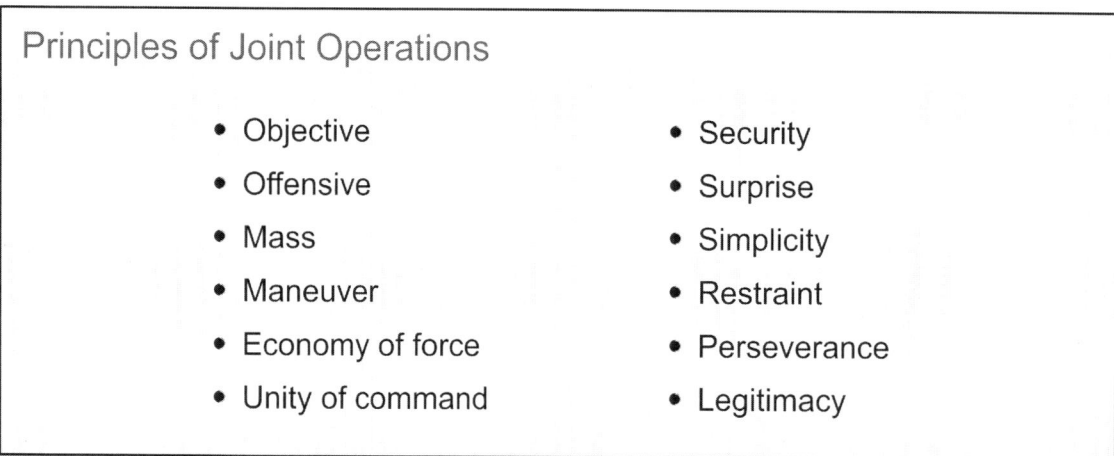

Figure I-1. Principles of Joint Operations

2. **Strategic Environment and National Security Challenges**

a. The strategic environment is characterized by uncertainty, complexity, and rapid change, which requires persistent engagement. This environment is fluid, with continually changing alliances, partnerships, and new national and transnational threats constantly appearing and disappearing. While it is impossible to predict precisely how challenges will emerge and what form they might take, we can expect that uncertainty, ambiguity, and surprise will dominate the course of regional and global events. In addition to traditional conflicts to include emerging peer competitors, significant and emerging challenges continue to include irregular threats, information operations (IO) directly targeting our civilian leadership and population, catastrophic terrorism employing weapons of mass destruction

Fundamentals of Joint Operations

> **Common Operating Precepts**
>
> - Inform domestic audiences and influence the perceptions and attitudes of key foreign audiences as an explicit and continuous operational requirement.
> - Achieve and maintain unity of effort within the joint force and between the joint force and US Government, international, and other partners.
> - Leverage the benefits of operating indirectly through partners when strategic and operational circumstances dictate or permit.
> - Integrate joint capabilities to be complementary rather than merely additive.
> - Avoid combining capabilities where doing so adds complexity without compensating advantage.
> - Focus on operational objectives whose achievement suggests the broadest and most enduring results.
> - Ensure freedom of action.
> - Maintain operational and organizational flexibility.
> - Plan for and manage operational transitions over time and space.
> - Drive synergy to the lowest echelon at which it can be managed effectively.

Figure I-2. Common Operating Precepts

(WMD), and other threats to disrupt the nation's ability to project power and maintain its qualitative edge.

b. The strategic environment presents broad national security challenges likely to require the employment of joint forces in the future. These are not new challenges. They are the natural products of the enduring human condition, but they will exhibit new features in the future. None of these challenges is a purely military problem. Rather, all are national problems calling for the application of all the instruments of national power.

(1) A secure US homeland is the Nation's first priority.

(2) Deterring our adversaries is a US goal. However, winning the Nation's wars remains the preeminent justification for maintaining capable and credible military forces in the event that deterrence should fail.

(3) Defending national interests requires not only being able to prevail in conflict, but also taking preventive measures to deter potential adversaries who could threaten the vital interests of the United States or its partners. These threats could range from direct aggression to less openly belligerent actions that nonetheless threaten vital national interests.

(4) Establishing, maintaining, and enhancing security cooperation among our alliances and partners is important to strengthen the global security framework of the United States and its partners. Security cooperation allows us to proactively take advantage of opportunities and not just react to threats.

Chapter I

(5) As it has in the past, the United States will continue to respond to a variety of civil crises by acting to relieve human suffering and restoring civil functioning, most often in support of civil authorities.

c. Joint operations increasingly occur in urban terrain and in cyberspace. The US homeland and other US interests are potential targets for direct and indirect attack. Adversary actions are likely to follow asymmetric principles. They will avoid "hard" (defended) targets and attack vulnerable ones. Vulnerable targets may include US and partner nation lines of communications (LOCs), ports, airports, staging areas, civilian populations, critical infrastructure, and economic centers. Advances in information technology increase the tempo, lethality, and depth of warfare. Within this environment, maintaining national security and managing the inevitable changes are continuous processes that often preclude simple solutions. These challenges often require well-planned and executed joint operations in conjunction with actions by a variety of other participants. In addition to military forces (including multinational forces) and civilians, there may be a number of interagency partners, intergovernmental organizations (IGOs), nongovernmental organizations (NGOs), and elements of the private sector whose presence or influence can affect the JFC's operations.

For more information on the strategic environment, refer to JP 1, Doctrine for the Armed Forces of the United States. *For more information on interorganizational coordination, refer to JP 3-08,* Interorganizational Coordination During Joint Operations.

3. Instruments of National Power and the Range of Military Operations

a. The various institutions that represent the US instruments of national power face daily challenges within the strategic environment.

b. The routine interaction of the instruments of national power is fundamental to US activities in the strategic environment. The instruments of national power are tools the US uses to apply its sources of power, including its culture, industry, science and technology, academic institutions, geography, and national will. The ability of the United States to advance its national interests is dependent on the effectiveness of the United States Government (USG) in employing the instruments of national power to achieve national strategic objectives. The appropriate governmental officials, often with National Security Council direction, normally coordinate these instruments of national power (diplomatic, informational, military, and economic). The military instrument's role increases relative to the other instruments as the need to compel a potential adversary through force increases.

c. Our national leaders can use the military instrument of national power in a wide variety of activities, tasks, missions, and operations that vary in purpose, scale, risk, and combat intensity. *Operations* are grouped in three areas that compose the *range of military operations* (Figure I-3).

(1) **Military Engagement, Security Cooperation, and Deterrence.** These are ongoing routine activities that establish, shape, maintain, and refine relations with other nations and domestic civil authorities (e.g., state governors or local law enforcement). Many

Fundamentals of Joint Operations

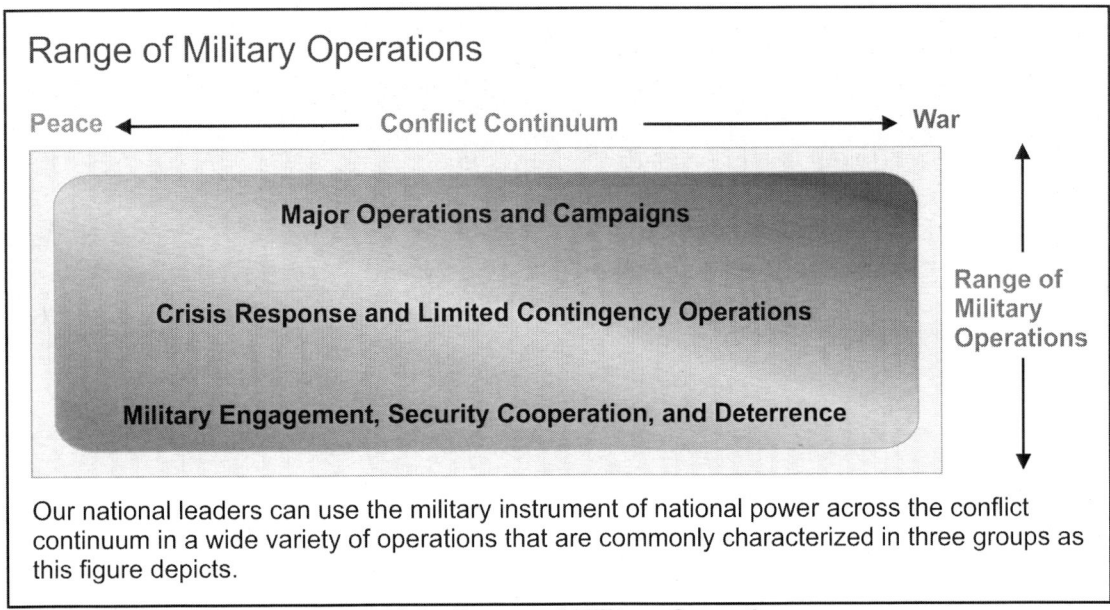

Figure I-3. Range of Military Operations

of these activities occur across the conflict continuum, and will usually continue in areas outside the operational areas associated with ongoing limited contingency operations, major operations, and campaigns.

(2) **Crisis Response and Limited Contingency Operations.** These can be small-scale, limited-duration operations, such as *strikes*, *raids*, and *peace enforcement*, which might include combat depending on the circumstances. Commanders conduct these operations individually, in simultaneous or concurrent groupings, or in conjunction with a major operation or campaign.

(3) **Major Operations and Campaigns.** These are extended-duration, large-scale operations that usually involve combat. A *major operation* is a series of related tactical actions, such as battles, engagements, and strikes. It can be conducted independently or can serve as an important component of a campaign. A *campaign*, in turn, is a series of related major operations. Both campaigns and major operations can achieve strategic or operational objectives, or both, within a given time and space.

For more information on the instruments of national power, refer to JP 1, Doctrine for the Armed Forces of the United States. Refer to Chapter V, "Joint Operations Across the Range of Military Operations," for more information on the types and scope of joint operations.

4. Strategic Guidance

a. ***National strategic direction* provides strategic context** for the employment of the instruments of national power and defines the strategic purpose that guides employment of the military instrument of national power as part of a global strategy. Continuing

Chapter I

assessments of the current and future strategic environment shape our national strategy, goals, and objectives.

(1) In general, the President frames the strategic context by defining national interests and goals in documents such as the *National Security Strategy (NSS)*, Presidential policy directives, executive orders, and other strategic documents in conjunction with additional guidance and refinement from the National Security Council/Homeland Security Council. When the National Security Council and Homeland Security Council work as one, they are referred to as the National Security Staff. The *National Strategy for Homeland Security*, also signed by the President, provides national direction to secure the homeland through a comprehensive framework for organizing the efforts of federal, state, local, and private organizations whose primary functions are often unrelated to national security.

(2) DOD's strategic documents provide amplification to the NSS. The documents outline how DOD will support NSS objectives, and provide a framework for other DOD policy and planning guidance, such as the *Guidance for Employment of the Force (GEF)*, Defense Planning and Programming Guidance, and the Joint Strategic Capabilities Plan.

(3) The President also signs the *Unified Command Plan (UCP)*, which is developed by the Joint Staff. The UCP establishes combatant command (CCMD) missions, responsibilities, and geographic areas of responsibility (AORs). The President approves the contingency planning guidance contained in the GEF, which is developed by the Office of the Secretary of Defense. The GEF provides written policy guidance and priorities to the Chairman of the Joint Chiefs of Staff (CJCS) and combatant commanders (CCDRs) for reviewing and preparing operation plans (OPLANs) and theater campaign plans (TCPs).

b. From this broad strategic guidance, more definitive national, functional, and theater-strategic objectives help focus and refine the context and guide the military's joint operation planning and execution related to a specific crisis or end state. The President and Secretary of Defense (SecDef), through the CJCS, direct national-level support for combatant and subordinate commanders. SecDef, with the CJCS's assistance, continually assesses the relative importance and urgency of various theater operations to determine where to focus US military efforts and when and where the Nation can afford to accept risk. Integrated planning, coordination, and guidance among the Joint Staff, CCMD staffs, Service Chiefs, and other government agencies (OGAs) translate strategic priorities into clear planning guidance, tailored force packages, and sufficient sustainment for the joint force to accomplish its mission.

For more information on national strategic direction, see Presidential Policy Directive 1, Organization of the National Security System, *Chairman of the Joint Chiefs of Staff Instruction (CJCSI) 5715.01B,* Joint Staff Participation in Interagency Affairs, *JP 1,* Doctrine for the Armed Forces of the United States, *and JP 5-0,* Joint Operation Planning.

c. **Strategic communication (SC) is an important component of strategic guidance.** The USG uses SC processes to guide the informational instrument of national power in specific situations. In an ever-changing environment, the communications strategy and success of a joint operation may depend heavily on the sympathy or support of key global audiences. This is especially true for protracted operations. Operations that are concluded rapidly will be much less affected by public opinion even if they are more politically controversial. Through SC, the USG focuses processes and efforts to understand and engage key audiences and create, strengthen, or preserve conditions favorable to advance USG interests, policies, and objectives. This occurs through the use of coordinated information, themes, plans, programs, and actions synchronized with the other instruments of national power. Commanders support USG SC efforts during joint operations primarily through their *communications strategies.* See paragraph 2.l., "Strategic Communication and Communications Strategy," in Chapter III, "Joint Functions," for more information.

For more information on SC, refer to JP 1, Doctrine for the Armed Forces of the United States, *and JP 5-0,* Joint Operation Planning.

   d. **The Combatant Commander's Strategic Role**

      (1) A CCDR is the vital link between those who determine national security policy and strategy and the military forces or subordinate JFCs who conduct military operations. Based on guidance from the President and SecDef, geographic and functional CCDRs develop strategies that translate national and multinational strategic direction into strategic concepts or courses of action (COAs) to meet joint operation planning requirements. **Theater and functional strategies** contain strategic concepts and COAs directed toward securing the objectives of national and multinational policies and strategies through the integrated employment of military capabilities synchronized with the other instruments of national power specific to geographic and functional CCMDs.

      (2) Geographic combatant commanders (GCCs) develop their theater strategies by analyzing events in the operational environment and developing options to set conditions for achieving strategic end states. They translate these options into an integrated set of steady-state engagement, security cooperation, and deterrence activities described in **theater and subordinate campaign plans,** formal products of the Adaptive Planning and Execution (APEX) system. In some cases, a CCDR may be required to develop a global campaign plan. These plans operationalize the CCDR's theater strategy. Contingency plans developed to respond to specific contingencies are treated as branch plans to the campaign plan. Functional combatant commanders (FCCs) develop their functional strategy based on guidance in the UCP and their functional objectives and strategic end states contained in the GEF. FCCs may be responsible for developing functional global or subordinate campaign plans or both. See Chapter V, "Joint Operations Across the Range of Military Operations," for more information on campaign plans.

      (3) In joint operations, the supported CCDR often will have a role in achieving more than one national strategic objective. Some national strategic objectives will be the primary responsibility of the supported CCDR, while others will require a more balanced use of all instruments of national power, with the CCDR in support of other agencies. Supporting CCDRs and their subordinates design their actions to be consistent with the supported commander's strategy. All CCDRs provide strategic direction; assign missions, tasks, forces, and resources; designate objectives; establish operational limitations such as rules of engagement (ROE), constraints, and restraints; and define policies and concepts of operations (CONOPS) to be integrated into OPLANs and operation orders (OPORDs). In

Chapter I

applying military power, CCDRs use the capabilities of assigned, attached, and supporting military forces. They also consider and, when appropriate, integrate the contributions of the other instruments of national power and the capabilities of multinational partners to gain and maintain strategic advantage.

For more information on the strategic environment, strategic guidance, strategy and estimates, and the role of CCDRs, refer to JP 1, Doctrine for the Armed Forces of the United States. *For more information on APEX and joint operation planning, refer to JP 5-0,* Joint Operation Planning.

(4) **Terminating joint operations** is an aspect of the CCDR's functional or theater strategy that links to achievement of national strategic objectives. Based on the President's strategic objectives that compose a desired **national strategic end state,** the supported CCDR can develop and propose **termination criteria**—the specified conditions approved by the President or SecDef that must be met before a joint operation can be concluded. These termination criteria help define the desired **military end state,** which normally represents a period in time or set of conditions beyond which the President does not require the military instrument of national power as the primary means to achieve remaining national objectives. This period or set of circumstances signals a transition from military to civilian lead of subsequent activities. Strategic and operational-level commanders and their staffs consider termination of operations early in planning in a coordinated effort with relevant interorganizational partners. The ability to understand how and when to terminate operations is instrumental to operational design and planning.

For more information on end state and termination, refer to JP 5-0, Joint Operation Planning.

5. Unified Action

a. **General.** Whereas the term *joint operations* focuses on the integrated actions of the Armed Forces of the United States in a unified effort, the term *unified action* has a broader connotation. Unified action has its foundation in national strategic direction, which is governed by the Constitution, federal law, USG policy, international law, and our national interests. Unified action is a comprehensive approach that synchronizes, coordinates, and when appropriate, integrates military operations with the activities of other governmental and NGOs to achieve *unity of effort.* Enabled by *unity of command,* US joint forces have established effective mechanisms to achieve **military** unity of effort. The goal of unified action is to achieve a similar level of unity of effort with external partners, as Figure I-4 shows. This publication uses the term *interorganizational partners* to refer collectively to USG departments and agencies; state, territorial, local, and tribal agencies; foreign military forces and government agencies; nongovernmental agencies; and the private sector. This aligns with the term and definition of *interorganizational coordination* established in JP 3-08, *Interorganizational Coordination During Joint Operations.*

COMMON OPERATING PRECEPT

Achieve and maintain unity of effort within the joint force and between the joint force and interorganizational partners.

Fundamentals of Joint Operations

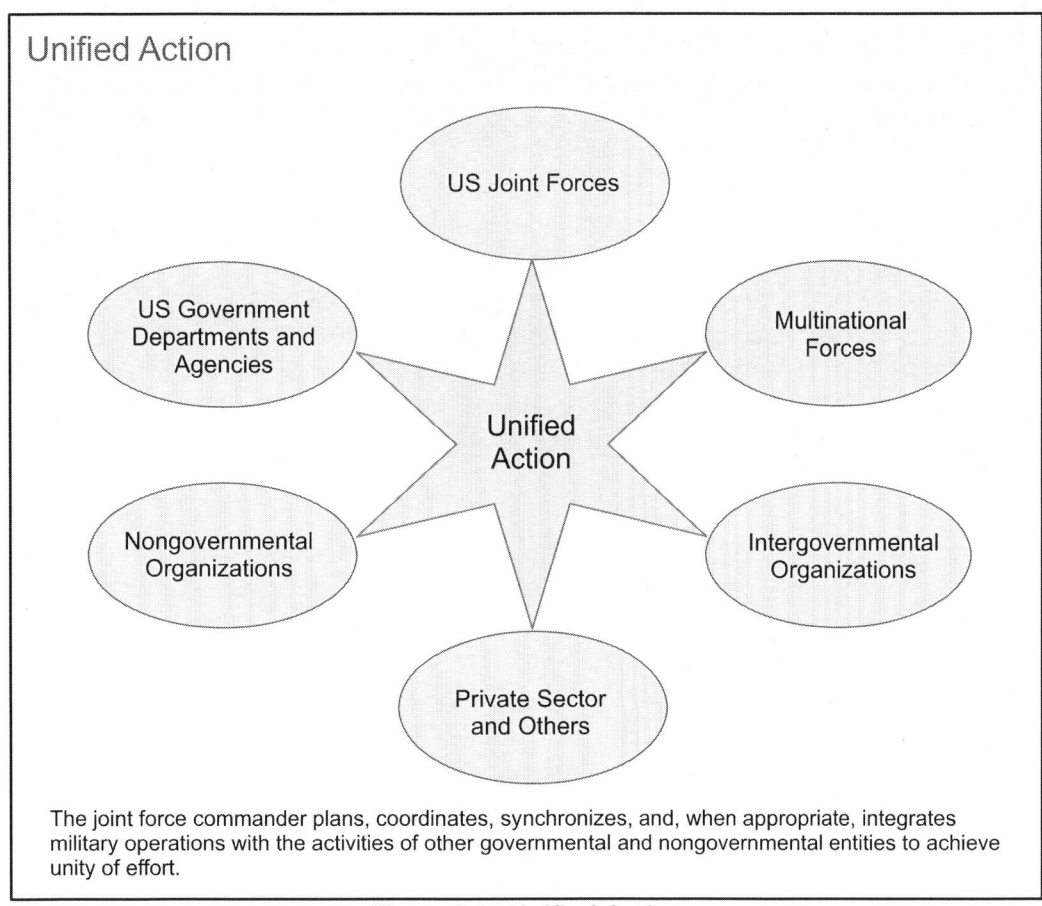

Figure I-4. Unified Action

b. **The JFC's Role.** JFCs are challenged to achieve and maintain operational coherence given the requirement to operate in conjunction with interorganizational partners. CCDRs play a pivotal role in unifying joint force actions, since all of the elements and actions that comprise *unified action* normally are present at the CCDR's level. However, subordinate JFCs also integrate and synchronize their operations directly with the operations of other military forces and the activities of nonmilitary organizations in the operational area to promote unified action.

c. **Multinational Participation in Unified Action**

(1) **General.** Joint forces must be prepared to plan and execute operations with forces from other nations within the framework of an alliance or coalition under US or other-than-US leadership. However, US forces often will be the predominant and most capable force within an alliance or coalition and can be expected to play a central leadership role. The military leaders of contributing member nations must emphasize common objectives as well as mutual support and respect. Cultivation and maintenance of personal relationships between counterparts are fundamental to achieving success. Language and communications differences, cultural diversity, historical animosities, and the varying capabilities of allies and multinational partners are among the many factors that complicate the integration and synchronization of their activities during multinational operations. Likewise, differing

Chapter I

national obligations derived from international treaties and agreements and national legislation complicate multinational operations. Regardless of other members' treaty obligations or their lack of participation in a treaty, US forces will remain bound by US treaty obligations.

(2) **Command and Control of US Forces. By law, the President retains command authority over US forces.** This includes the authority and responsibility to effectively plan for, organize, coordinate, control, employ, and protect these forces. Nevertheless, the President may deem it prudent or advantageous (for reasons such as maximizing military effectiveness and ensuring unified action) to place specific US forces under the control of a foreign commander to achieve specified military objectives. Even when operating under the operational control (OPCON) of a foreign commander, US commanders will maintain the capability to report separately to higher US military authorities.

(3) **Command and Control Structures.** Alliances typically have developed command and control (C2) structures, systems, and procedures, with the predominant contributing nation providing the allied force commander. Staffs are integrated, and subordinate commands often are led by senior representatives from member nations. Shared doctrine, standardization agreements, close military cooperation, and robust diplomatic relations characterize alliances. Coalitions are less standardized and may adopt a parallel or lead-nation C2 structure or a combination of the two. In a *parallel command construct,*

Commanding officer of 1st Battalion, 5th Marine Regiment, whose mission is to conduct counterinsurgency operations in partnership with the Afghan national security forces in southern Afghanistan, greets Afghan national army generals during a key leader engagement involving Afghan national army soldiers and local Nawa District officials at Patrol Base Jaker in Afghanistan's Helmand province.

nations retain control of their deployed forces and operate under their own doctrine and procedures, and in a ***lead nation command*** *construct,* the nation providing the preponderance of forces and resources typically provides the commander of the coalition force. These command structures also can exist simultaneously within a coalition.

For more information on unified action with respect to multinational participation, refer to JP 1, Doctrine for the Armed Forces of the United States. *For more information on all aspects of multinational operations, refer to JP 3-16,* Multinational Operations. *For more information on multinational logistics, refer to JP 4-08,* Logistics in Support of Multinational Operations. *For North Atlantic Treaty Organization (NATO) specific doctrine ratified by the United States, see Allied Joint Publication (AJP)-01(C),* Allied Joint Doctrine, *and AJP-3(A),* Allied Doctrine for Joint Operations.

   d. **Interorganizational Coordination in Unified Action**

      (1) **General.** CCDRs and subordinate JFCs often operate with interorganizational partners. The nature of interagency coordination demands that JFCs and planners consider the contribution of other instruments of national power and recognize which agencies can best contribute toward achieving objectives. DOD may support other agencies during some operations, but US military forces will remain under the DOD command structure. Federal lead agency responsibility may be prescribed by law or regulation, Presidential directive, policy, or agreement among or between agencies. Even then, because of its resources and well-established planning methods, the joint force will likely provide significant support to the lead agency.

      (2) **Civil-Military Integration**

         (a) Military operations will require some level of civil-military integration. The degree of integration depends on the mission, objectives, and interests involved. Presidential directives guide participation by all USG departments and agencies in such operations. Military leaders work with the other members of the national security team to promote unified action. The agencies' different and sometimes conflicting policies, procedures, decision-making processes, organizational cultures, and nature and extent of resourcing complicate this interface.

         (b) **Integration and coordination among the military force and interorganizational counterparts are much less rigid than military C2.** Some organizations may have policies that conflict with those of the USG, particularly those of the US military. Formal agreements, robust liaison, and information sharing with interorganizational partners are processes that should facilitate common understanding, coordination, and support mission accomplishment. Information sharing with NGOs and the private sector may be more restrictive, but options such as the joint interagency coordination group (JIACG) and civil-military operations center (CMOC) are available to the JFC to facilitate interorganizational coordination and information sharing. DOD, in collaboration with USG departments and agencies, and state, local, and tribal governments use the unifying structures and procedures provided by the National Response Framework (NRF) and the National Incident Management System in order to prepare for, plan, coordinate, and

Chapter I

respond to natural and man-made disasters in the US and its territories. Similar structures and processes, incorporating the capabilities and interests of foreign partners, can be incorporated into disaster-response and civil affairs (CA) in connection with US operations in foreign countries.

For more information on interorganizational coordination, refer to JP 3-08, Interorganizational Coordination During Joint Operations. *For more information on civil-military operations (CMO) and the CMOC, refer to JP 3-57,* Civil-Military Operations.

> **COMMON OPERATING PRECEPT**
>
> **Leverage the benefits of operating indirectly through partners when strategic and operational circumstances dictate or permit.**

e. The intent of unified action is not that the US must lead every operation, since our country will not be able to respond directly to every crisis. Also, any large-scale employment of US military forces abroad invites political repercussions simply because it is the US that is acting. Some international parties will oppose almost any US military commitment, no matter how limited or benign, solely to restrain the exercise of American power. In such circumstances, friendly surrogates assisted by US joint forces may be able to conduct operations and achieve mutually agreeable objectives when the direct employment of US forces would be objectionable or infeasible. In other instances, such as counterinsurgency (COIN), eventual success may depend on the indigenous government demonstrating its own sovereign power, and the overt exercise of power by US forces may ultimately be counterproductive. JFCs may increasingly find it advantageous or necessary to pursue operational and strategic objectives by enabling and supporting such partners, whether friendly nations, international organizations, or some other entity.

6. **Levels of War**

a. **General.** Three levels of war—strategic, operational, and tactical—model the relationship between national objectives and tactical actions. There are no finite limits or boundaries between these levels, but they help commanders visualize a logical arrangement of operations, allocate resources, and assign tasks to the appropriate command. Echelon of command, size of units, types of equipment, and types and location of forces or components may often be associated with a particular level, but the strategic, operational, or tactical purpose of their employment depends on the nature of their task, mission, or objective. For example, intelligence and communications satellites, previously considered principally strategic assets, are also significant resources for tactical operations. Likewise, tactical actions can cause both intended and unintended strategic consequences, particularly in today's environment of pervasive and immediate global communications. Figure I-5 depicts general relationships between strategy, operational art, and tactics and between leaders who typically focus at these levels.

Fundamentals of Joint Operations

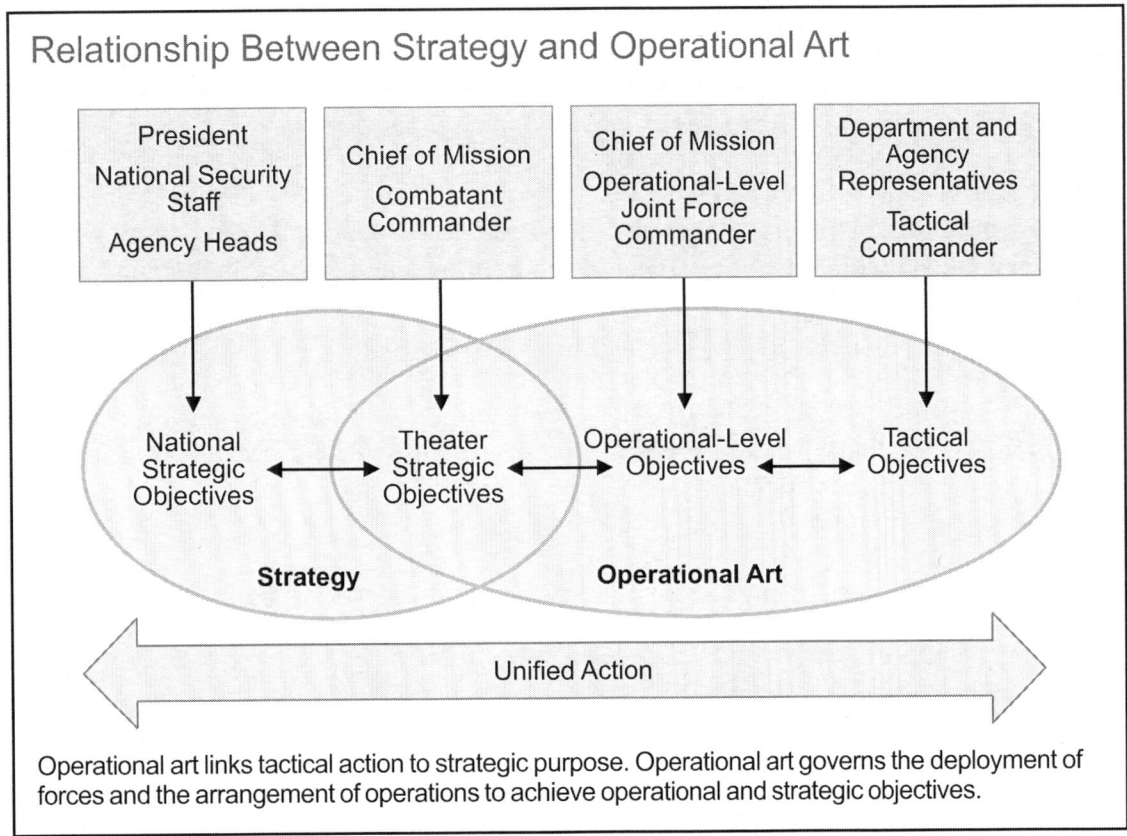

Figure I-5. Relationship Between Strategy and Operational Art

b. **Strategic Level.** In the context of military operations, strategy develops an idea or set of ideas for employing the instruments of national power in a synchronized and integrated fashion to achieve theater, national, and/or multinational objectives. Through development of strategy (such as the NSS and *National Military Strategy*), a nation's leader, often as a committee member with other nations' leaders, determines national or multinational strategic objectives and guidance to develop and use national resources to achieve these objectives. The President, aided by the National Security Staff, establishes policy and national strategic objectives. SecDef translates these into strategic military objectives that facilitate theater strategic planning. CCDRs usually participate in strategic discussions with the President and SecDef through the CJCS and with allies and multinational members. Thus the CCDR's strategy is an element that relates to both US national strategy and operational-level activities within the theater. Military strategy, derived from national policy and strategy and informed by doctrine, provides a framework for conducting operations.

c. **Operational Level**

(1) The operational level links the tactical employment of forces to national and military strategic objectives. **The focus at this level is on the design, planning, and execution of operations using *operational art*:** the application of creative imagination by commanders and staffs—supported by their skill, knowledge, and experience—to design strategies, campaigns, and major operations and organize and employ military forces. JFCs and component commanders use operational art to determine how, when, where, and for

I-13

Chapter I

what purpose major forces will be employed and to influence the adversary's disposition before combat. Operational art governs the deployment of those forces and the arrangement of operations to achieve operational and strategic objectives.

(2) Many factors will affect relationships between leaders at these levels. For example, the primary Service and functional component commanders of a joint force do not plan tactical actions in a vacuum; they and their staffs collaborate with the operational-level JFC in planning the joint operation. This collaboration facilitates the components' tactical planning and execution. Likewise, the operational-level JFC and staff typically collaborate with the CCDR on framing theater strategic objectives as well as tasks that the CCDR eventually will assign to the subordinate joint force. In some cases, such as in the 1991 Operation DESERT STORM, the CCDR will not form a subordinate joint force and will direct both operational-level and theater strategic actions. In this instance, the CCDR's component commanders assume a greater operational-level role, while their subordinates focus on tactical execution.

d. **Tactical Level.** Tactics is the employment and ordered arrangement of forces in relation to each other. Joint doctrine focuses this term on planning and executing battles, engagements, and activities at the tactical level to achieve military objectives assigned to tactical units or task forces (TFs). An engagement can include a wide variety of noncombat tasks and activities and combat between opposing forces normally in a short-duration action. A battle consists of a set of related engagements. Battles typically last longer, involve larger forces, and normally affect the course of a campaign. Forces at this level generally employ various tactics to achieve their military objectives.

7. **Types of Military Operations**

a. The United States employs its military capabilities in support of its national security goals in a variety of military operations (Figure I-6). Operations generally involve military action or the accomplishment of a strategic, operational, or tactical, service, training, or administrative military mission. Operations such as COIN and counterterrorism (CT) are primarily related to IW. Encounters between friendly and enemy forces in IW seldom amount to more than tactical engagements. Insurgents, terrorists, and other IW actors rarely mass in sufficient numbers to fight battles. However, IW can occur in conjunction with large-scale traditional operations as well. Large-scale combat operations associated with traditional warfare typically characterize major operations and campaigns, although the extended nature of some IW will require operations phased over time as a campaign. Each military operation may occur simultaneously with or independently of other operations, or multiple operations may overlap. Additionally, each may have different root causes and objectives.

b. With a significant array of available Service capabilities—supplemented as required by specialized joint or other capabilities—joint forces can be designed, organized, equipped, and trained to accomplish a wide variety of military operations such as those in Figure I-6. The nature of objectives and the magnitude of tasks and requirements will determine if a joint force headquarters (HQ) and joint operations are necessary or if a single-Service force can accomplish the mission. Chapter V, "Joint Operations Across the Range of Military

Operations," describes various types of joint operations and considerations in the context of the three broad areas that compose the range of military operations.

Examples of Military Operations

- Stability operations
- Civil support
- Foreign humanitarian assistance
- Recovery
- Noncombatant evacuation
- Peace operations
- Combating weapons of mass destruction
- Chemical, biological, radiological, and nuclear consequence management
- Foreign internal defense
- Counterdrug operations
- Combating terrorism
- Counterinsurgency
- Homeland defense

Figure I-6. Examples of Military Operations

Intentionally Blank

CHAPTER II
THE ART OF JOINT COMMAND

> *"When all is said and done, it is really the commander's coup d'oeil, his ability to see things simply, to identify the whole business of war completely with himself, that is the essence of good generalship."*
>
> **Carl von Clausewitz**
> **On War**

1. Introduction

a. ***Command*** is the authority that a commander in the armed forces lawfully exercises over subordinates by virtue of rank or assignment. Accompanying this authority is the responsibility to effectively organize, direct, coordinate, and control military forces to accomplish assigned missions. Command includes responsibility for health, welfare, morale, and discipline of assigned personnel.

b. While command authority stems from appropriate orders and other directives, **the art of command resides in the commander's ability to use situational leadership to maximize operational performance.** The combination of courage, ethical leadership, judgment, intuition, situational awareness, and the ability to consider contrary views gained over time through training, education, and experience helps commanders make difficult decisions in complex situations. The desired result is the conscious and skillful exercise of command authority through visualization, decision making, and leadership. Effective decision making combines judgment and visualization with information; it requires knowing if to decide, when to decide, and what to decide quickly enough to maintain the initiative over the adversary. Information management (IM), knowledge sharing, an understanding of the operational environment, and a sound battle rhythm facilitate decision making.

c. This chapter discusses factors related to "commander-centric" leadership, and then focuses on operational art and processes that help the commander make decisions during planning and execution.

2. Commander-Centric Leadership

a. Historical analysis shows that commander-centric organizations out-perform staff-centric, process-oriented organizations. A commander's perspective of the challenge at hand is broader and more comprehensive than the staff's due to interaction with civilian leaders; senior, peer, subordinate, and supporting commanders; and interorganizational partners. Clear commander's guidance and intent, enriched by the commander's experience and intuition, are common to high-performing units. Employing the "art of war," which has been the commander's central historical *command* role, remains critical in the contemporary complex environment regardless of technological and informational improvements in *control*—the "science of war." Successful commanders can strike a balance between the "art of war" (human interaction) and the "science of war" (technological solutions) by emphasizing the inherently human aspects of warfare.

b. The C2 function is commander-centric and network-enabled to facilitate initiative and decision making at the lowest appropriate level. Although we have grown used to communicating freely without fear of jamming or interception, natural phenomena or an adaptive enemy may rapidly negate technology advantages. This is especially true at the lower echelons. If a commander loses reliable communications, he must have subordinates who can act without instructions. *Mission command*—a key component of the C2 function described in Chapter III, "Joint Functions"—is the conduct of military operations through decentralized execution based upon mission-type orders. Successful mission command demands that subordinate leaders at all echelons exercise disciplined initiative and act aggressively and independently to accomplish the mission. They focus their orders on the purpose of the operation rather than on the details of how to perform assigned tasks. They delegate decisions to subordinates wherever possible, which minimizes detailed control and empowers subordinates' initiative to make decisions based on understanding what the commander wants rather than on constant communications. Essential to mission command is the thorough understanding of the *commander's intent* at every level of command. See paragraph 5.e., "Key Planning Elements," for a discussion of commander's intent as a key planning element.

c. Commanders should engage other leaders to build personal relationships and develop trust and confidence. Developing these relationships is a conscious collaborative act rather than something that just happens. Commanders build trust through words and actions and continue to reinforce it not only during actual operations, but also during training, education, and practice. Trust and confidence are essential to synergy and harmony, both within the joint force and also with our interorganizational partners. Commanders also may engage other political, societal, and economic leaders and other influential people in the operational environment who are potentially key to the joint force's success. This engagement not only supports mission accomplishment, but is also essential to continuity of the commander's communications strategy themes and messages. The JFC ensures that subordinate commanders understand the importance of key leader engagement and encourages them to extend the process to lower levels, as appropriate, based on the mission and communications strategy requirements.

d. Commanders should provide subordinate commands with sufficient time to plan, particularly in a crisis action planning situation. They do so by issuing a warning order to subordinates at the earliest opportunity and by collaborating with other commanders, agency leaders, and multinational partners (as appropriate) to ensure a clear understanding of the commander's mission, intent, guidance, and priorities. Commanders resolve command-level issues that are beyond the staff's authority. Examples of such issues include the close-hold, compartmented planning that occurs with some sensitive operations, and the continuing challenge of incorporating interorganizational partners in the joint operation planning process (JOPP) given their potentially limited capabilities and restricted access to some information.

e. Commanders collaborate with their seniors to resolve differences of interpretation of higher-level objectives and the ways and means to accomplish these objectives. A commander might tend to expect that the higher HQ has correctly described the operational environment, framed the problem, and devised a sound approach to achieve the best solution.

Strategic guidance can be vague, and the commander must interpret and clarify it for the staff. While national leaders and CCDRs may have a clear strategic perspective of the problem, subordinate JFCs and their component commanders often have a better perspective of the situation at the operational level. Both perspectives are essential to a sound solution. During a commander's decision cycle, subordinate commanders should aggressively share their perspective with senior leaders with the intent to resolve issues at the earliest opportunity.

COMMON OPERATING PRECEPT

Integrate joint capabilities to be complementary rather than merely additive.

---

f. The essential skill of a JFC is the ability to match the mission of each Service component to its capabilities. Each component's mission should also create a complementary synergy with that of the others. This enables the actions of each component to enhance the capabilities and limit the vulnerabilities of the others. Achieving this complementary synergy requires more than just understanding the particular capabilities and limitations that each component brings to the operation. The JFC must also be able to visualize operations holistically, identify the preconditions that enable each component to optimize its own contribution, and then determine how the other components might help to produce them. The JFC must be willing to compare alternative component missions and mixes solely from the perspective of combined effectiveness, unhampered by Service parochialism. But this approach also requires mutual trust among commanders that the missions assigned to components will be consistent with their intrinsic capabilities and limitations; that those capabilities will not be risked for insufficient overall return; and that components will execute their assignments.

g. The JFC executes a commander-centric approach to leadership using operational art and design, joint operation planning, rigorous assessment of progress toward objectives, and timely decision making. The remainder of this chapter discusses these key areas.

3. Operational Art

a. ***Operational art* is the use of creative thinking by commanders and staffs to design strategies, campaigns, and major operations and organize and employ military forces.** It is a thought process that uses skill, knowledge, experience, and judgment to overcome the ambiguity and uncertainty of a complex environment and understand the problem at hand. Operational art also promotes unified action by encouraging JFCs and staffs to consider the capabilities, actions, goals, priorities, and operating processes of interorganizational partners, while determining objectives, establishing priorities, and assigning tasks to subordinate forces. It facilitates the coordination, synchronization, and, where appropriate, integration of military operations with those of interorganizational partners, thereby promoting unity of effort.

b. Operational art requires a broad vision, the ability to anticipate, and the skill to plan, prepare, execute, and assess. It helps commanders and their staffs order their thoughts and

Chapter II

understand the conditions for victory before seeking battle. Without operational art, campaigns and operations would be sets of disconnected events. Operational art governs the deployment of forces and the arrangement of operations to achieve military operational and strategic objectives.

c. The commander is the central figure in operational art, not only due to education and experience, but also because the commander's judgment and decisions are required to guide the staff throughout joint operation planning and execution. Commanders draw on operational art to mitigate the challenges of complexity and uncertainty, leveraging their knowledge, experience, judgment, and intuition to generate a clearer understanding of the conditions needed to focus effort and achieve success. Operational art supports the effective exercise of command by enabling a broad perspective that deepens understanding and visualization. Commanders compare similarities of the existing situation with their own experiences or history to distinguish the unique features that require innovative or adaptive solutions. They understand that each situation requires a solution tailored to the context of the problem. Through the application of operational art, commanders seek innovative, adaptive options to solve complex problems.

d. Operational design requires the commander to encourage discourse and leverage dialogue and collaboration to identify and solve complex, ill-defined problems. To that end, the commander must empower organizational learning and develop methods to determine if modifying the operational approach is necessary during the course of an operation. This requires continuous assessment, evaluation, and reflection that challenge understanding of the existing problem and the relevance of actions addressing that problem.

e. Operational art applies to all aspects of joint operations and integrates ends, ways, and means, while accounting for risk, across the levels of war. Among the many considerations, operational art requires commanders to answer the following questions.

(1) What are the **objectives and desired end state?** (Ends)

(2) What **sequence of actions** is most likely to achieve those objectives and end state? (Ways)

(3) What **resources** are required to accomplish that sequence of actions? (Means)

(4) What is the likely **chance of failure or unacceptable results** in performing that sequence of actions? (Risk)

f. Operational art encompasses *operational design*—**the conception and construction of the intellectual framework that underpins joint OPLANs and their subsequent execution.** Together, operational art and operational design strengthen the relationship between strategy and tactics.

4. Operational Design

a. *Operational design* extends operational art's vision with a creative process that helps commanders and planners answer the ends–ways–means–risk questions. Operational design supports operational art with a general methodology using elements of operational design for understanding the situation and the problem. The methodology helps the JFC and staff to understand conceptually the broad solutions for attaining mission accomplishment and to reduce the uncertainty of a complex operational environment. The elements of operational design (Figure II-1) are individual tools that help the JFC and staff visualize and describe the broad operational approach. These operational design elements are useful throughout JOPP.

   b. Commanders and staffs can use operational design when planning any joint operation. Notwithstanding a commander's judgment, education, and experience, the operational environment often presents some situations so complex that they defy complete understanding. Nor does such complexity lend itself to coherent planning. Bringing adequate order to complex problems to facilitate further detailed planning requires an iterative dialogue between commanders and staff. Rarely will members of the staff recognize an implicit operational approach during their initial analysis of the operational environment and tasks from higher HQ. Successful development of the approach requires continuous analysis, learning, and discourse between commander, staff, and other subject matter experts. The challenge is even greater when the JFC considers the intended and unintended consequences of both military and interorganizational actions within the joint operations area (JOA), the perceptions and plans of those partners, the expectations of the local populace and host nation (HN) government, and the regional and global implications.

   c. Operational art, operational design, and JOPP blend in complementary fashion as part of the overall process that produces the eventual plan or order that drives the joint operation. Effective operational design results in more efficient detailed planning and increases the chances of mission accomplishment.

For more information on operational art and the details of operational design, refer to JP 5-0, Joint Operation Planning.

5. Joint Operation Planning

   a. Joint operation planning consists of planning activities associated with joint military operations by CCDRs and their subordinate JFCs in response to contingencies and crises. It

---

Elements of Operational Design

- Termination
- Military end state
- Objective
- Effects
- Center of gravity
- Decisive point
- Lines of operation and lines of effort
- Direct and indirect approach
- Anticipation
- Operational reach
- Culmination
- Arranging operations
- Forces and functions

Figure II-1. Elements of Operational Design

transforms national strategic objectives into activities by development of operational products, which include planning for the mobilization, deployment, employment, sustainment, redeployment, and demobilization of joint forces. It ties the military instrument of national power to the achievement of national security goals and objectives and is essential to securing desired strategic end states during peacetime and war. Planning begins with the end state in mind, providing a unifying purpose around which actions and resources are focused.

b. Joint operation planning occurs within APEX, which is the department-level system of joint policies, processes, procedures, and reporting structures. APEX is supported by communications and information technology that is used by the joint planning and execution community (JPEC) to monitor, plan, and execute mobilization, deployment, employment, sustainment, redeployment, and demobilization activities associated with joint operations. APEX formally integrates the planning activities of the JPEC and facilitates the JFC's seamless transition from planning to execution during times of crisis. The integration of joint operation planning with interagency and multinational partners begins with national strategic direction. APEX activities span many organizational levels, but the focus is on the interaction between SecDef and CCDRs, which ultimately helps the President and SecDef decide when, where, and how to commit US military forces. The interactive and collaborative process at the national level guides the way in which planning and execution occurs throughout the Armed Forces.

c. Based on understanding gained through the application of operational design, more detailed planning takes place within the steps of JOPP. JOPP is an orderly, analytical process, which consists of a set of logical steps to analyze a mission; develop, analyze, and compare alternative COAs; select the best COA; and produce a plan or order. Through JOPP, planners effectively translate the commander's planning guidance into a feasible COA and CONOPS by which the joint force can achieve its assigned mission and military end state. This, in turn, links tactical actions, through operational planning and execution, to the accomplishment of national strategic objectives in support of the strategic end state. Planners align actions and resources in time and space to complete the plan. In doing so, they must take into account the details of force requirements, force availability, task organization, and sustainment and deployment concepts. They should also take into account the capacity and objectives of the other instruments of national power, risk, and functional elements of the plan (i.e., personnel, intelligence, logistics).

d. **JOPP underpins planning at all levels and for missions across the range of military operations.** It applies to both supported and supporting JFCs and to component and subordinate commands when they participate in joint planning. Together with operational design, JOPP facilitates interaction between the commander, staff, and their HQ throughout planning. JOPP helps commanders and their staffs organize their planning activities, share a common understanding of the mission and commander's intent, and develop effective plans and orders. Figure II-2 shows the primary steps of JOPP.

e. **Key Planning Elements.** Commanders typically participate in planning to the greatest extent possible from early operational design through approval of the plan or order. **Regardless of the commander's level of involvement, certain key planning elements**

require the commander's participation and decisions. These include the operational approach, mission statement, commander's planning guidance, commander's intent, commander's critical information requirements (CCIRs), and CONOPS.

(1) **Operational Approach.** The operational approach is a commander's description of the broad actions the force must take to achieve the desired military end state. It is the commander's visualization of how the operation should transform current conditions into the desired conditions at the end state—the way the commander wants the operational environment to look at the conclusion of operations. The operational approach is based largely on an understanding of the operational environment and the problem facing the JFC. Once the JFC approves the approach, it provides the basis for beginning, continuing, or completing detailed planning. The JFC and staff should continually review, update, and modify the approach as the operational environment, end state, or problem change.

(2) **Mission Statement.** The joint force's *mission* is what the joint force must accomplish. It is described in the *mission statement,* which is a sentence or short paragraph that describes the organization's essential task (or set of tasks) and purpose—a clear statement of the action to be taken and the reason for doing so. The mission statement—approved by the commander—contains the elements of who, what, when, where, and why; but seldom specifies how. It forms the basis for planning and is included in various products such as the planning guidance and as paragraph 2 (Mission) of the completed OPLAN or order. Clarity of the joint force mission statement and its understanding by subordinates are essential to success.

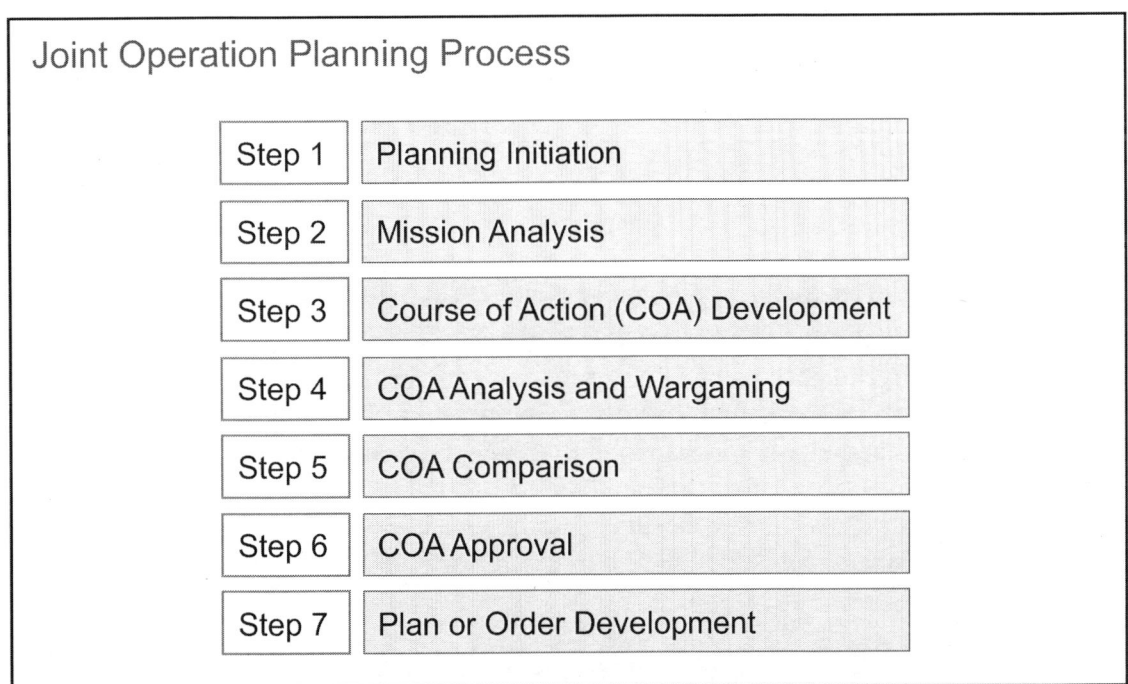

Figure II-2. Joint Operation Planning Process

Chapter II

(3) **Commander's Planning Guidance.** JFCs guide the joint force's actions throughout planning and execution. However, the staff and component commanders typically expect the JFC to issue *initial guidance* soon after receipt of a mission or tasks from higher authority and provide more detailed *planning guidance* after the JFC approves an operational approach. This guidance is an important input to subsequent mission analysis, but the completion of mission analysis is another point at which the JFC may provide updated planning guidance that affects COA development.

(4) **Commander's Intent.** *Commander's intent* is the commander's clear and concise expression of what the force must do and the conditions the force must establish to accomplish the mission. It is a succinct description of the commander's visualization of the entire operation and what the commander wants to accomplish. Commander's intent supports mission command and allows subordinates the greatest possible freedom of action. It provides focus to the staff and helps subordinate and supporting commanders act to achieve the commander's desired results without further orders once the operation begins, even when the operation does not unfold as planned. Successful command demands that subordinate leaders at all echelons exercise disciplined initiative and act aggressively and independently to accomplish the mission within the commander's intent. Subordinates' emphasis is on timely decision making, understanding the higher commander's intent, and clearly identifying the subordinates' tasks necessary to achieve the desired end state. Well-crafted commander's intent improves subordinates' ability to act effectively in fluid, chaotic situations.

(5) **Commander's Critical Information Requirements.** CCIRs are elements of friendly and enemy information the commander identifies as critical to timely decision making. They focus IM and help the JFC and staff assess the operational environment. The CCIR list is normally a product of mission analysis, and JFCs add, delete, and update CCIRs throughout an operation.

(6) **Concept of Operations.** The CONOPS, included in paragraph 3, (Execution) of the plan or order, describes how the JFC intends to integrate, synchronize, and phase actions of the joint force components and supporting organizations to accomplish the mission, including potential branches and sequels. The CONOPS typically is a detailed extension of the operational approach, but incorporates modifications based on updated information and intelligence gained during planning as well as the JFC's approved COA. The staff writes (or graphically portrays) the CONOPS in sufficient detail so that subordinate and supporting commanders understand their mission, tasks, and other requirements and can develop their supporting plans accordingly. The CONOPS also provides the basis for developing the concept of fires, concept of intelligence operations, and concept of logistic support, which also are included in the final OPLAN or OPORD.

COMMON OPERATING PRECEPT

Ensure freedom of action.

f. **Freedom of Action.** The JFC must maintain freedom of action throughout the operation. Of necessity, freedom of action must extend beyond the JFC's operational area. For example, operational reach—the distance and duration across which a joint force can successfully employ military capabilities—can extend far beyond the limits of a JFC's JOA and is inextricably tied to lines of operation (LOOs). So the joint force must protect LOOs to ensure freedom of action. Likewise, the C2 and intelligence functions depend on operations within cyberspace. Losing the capability to operate effectively in cyberspace can greatly diminish the JFC's freedom of action. While various actions (such as computer network defense [CND] and the consideration of branches to current operations) contribute individually to freedom of action, operational design and joint operation planning are the processes that coherently link these actions. Thus the JFC and staff must consider freedom of action from the outset of operational design and must be alert to indicators during operations that freedom of action is in jeopardy.

For more information on JOPP, refer to JP 5-0, Joint Operation Planning. *For more information on fires and joint fire support planning, refer to JP 3-09,* Joint Fire Support, *and JP 3-60,* Joint Targeting. *For more information on intelligence support and planning, refer to JP 2-0,* Joint Intelligence, *and other intelligence series publications. For more information on logistic planning, refer to JP 4-0,* Joint Logistics, *and other logistics series publications.*

6. Assessment

a. **Assessment is a process that evaluates changes in the environment and measures progress** of the joint force toward mission accomplishment. **Commanders continuously** assess the operational environment and the progress of operations, compare them to their initial visualization, understanding, and intent, and adjust operations based on this analysis. Staffs monitor key factors that can influence operations and provide the commander timely information needed for decisions. **The CCIR process is linked to the assessment process** by the commander's need for timely information to support decision making. Commanders devise ways to continually update their understanding of the operational environment and assess their progress toward achieving assigned objectives without mistaking activity for progress.

b. Assessment begins during mission analysis when the commander and staff consider what to measure and how to measure it **to determine progress toward accomplishing tasks, creating conditions, or achieving objectives.** During planning and preparing for an operation, for example, the staff assesses the joint force's ability to execute the plan based on available resources and changing conditions in the operational environment. During the early mission analysis process, the commander and staff begin to devise indicators of progress that will be incorporated in the plan or order and used during execution. Certain assessment indicators act as triggers during the operation to help the commander determine the necessity to revise the original design approach.

c. During execution, the commander's staff identifies those key assessment indicators that suggest progress or setbacks in accomplishing tasks, creating effects, and achieving

Chapter II

objectives. Assessment actions and measures help commanders adjust operations and resources as required, determine when to execute branches and sequels, and make other critical decisions to ensure current and future operations remain aligned with the mission and military end state. Normally, the operations directorate of a joint staff (J-3), assisted by the intelligence directorate of a joint staff (J-2), is responsible for coordinating assessment activities. The chief of staff facilitates the assessment process and the determination of CCIRs by incorporating them into the HQ's battle rhythm. Various elements of the JFC's staff use assessment results to adjust both current operations and future planning.

d. Actions by friendly forces, the HN and population, adversary, and neutral diplomatic, informational, and economic entities in the operational environment can affect military actions and objectives. When relevant to the mission, the commander must determine how to assess results of these actions to include relevant information on the civil environment. This typically requires collaboration with other agencies and interorganizational partners—preferably within a common, accepted process—in the interest of unified action. Many of these organizations may be outside the JFC's authority. Accordingly, the JFC should grant some joint force organizations (CA directorate/CMOC) authority for direct coordination with key outside organizations—such as USG interagency elements from the Departments of State or Homeland Security, national intelligence agencies, intelligence sources in other nations, and other CCMDs—to the extent necessary to ensure timely and accurate assessments.

e. **Levels of War and Assessment**

(1) Assessment occurs at all levels and across the range of military operations. Even in operations that do not include combat, assessment of progress is just as important and can be more complex than traditional *combat assessment*. **As a general rule, the level at which a specific operation, task, or action is directed should be the level at which such activity is assessed.** To do this, JFCs and their staffs consider assessment ways, means, and measures during planning, preparation, and execution. This properly focuses assessment and collection at each level, reduces redundancy, and enhances the efficiency of the overall assessment process.

(2) Assessment at the operational and strategic levels is typically broader than at the tactical level (e.g., combat assessment), and uses measures of effectiveness (MOEs) and measures of performance (MOPs) that support strategic and operational mission accomplishment. Assessment at these levels concentrates on broader tasks, conditions, objectives, and progress toward the military end state. **Continuous assessment helps the JFC and joint force component commanders determine if the joint force is "doing the right things" (MOE) to achieve its objectives, not just "doing things right" (MOP).**

(3) Tactical-level assessment uses MOEs and MOPs to evaluate **task accomplishment.** The results of tactical tasks are often physical in nature, but also can reflect the impact on specific functions and systems. Tactical-level assessment may include assessing progress by phase lines; destruction of enemy forces; control of key terrain, peoples, or resources; and other tasks. Assessment of results at the tactical level helps commanders determine operational and strategic progress, so JFCs must have a

comprehensive, integrated assessment plan that links assessment activities and measures at all levels.

(4) ***Combat assessment*** is an example of a tactical-level assessment and a term that can encompass many tactical-level assessment actions. Combat assessment typically focuses on determining the results of weapons engagement (with both lethal and nonlethal capabilities), and thus is an important component of joint fires and the joint targeting process (see JP 3-60, *Joint Targeting*). **Combat assessment is composed of three related elements: battle damage assessment, munitions effectiveness assessment, and reattack recommendations or future targeting.** However, combat assessment methodology also can be applied by joint force functional and Service components to other tactical tasks not associated with joint fires (e.g., disaster relief delivery assessment, relief effectiveness assessment, and future relief recommendations).

For more information on assessment, refer to JP 5-0, Joint Operation Planning.

Intentionally Blank

CHAPTER III
JOINT FUNCTIONS

> "US military power today is unsurpassed on the land and sea and in the air, space, and cyberspace. The individual Services have evolved capabilities and competencies to maximize their effectiveness in their respective domains. Even more important, the ability to integrate these diverse capabilities into a joint whole that is greater than the sum of the Service parts is an unassailable American strategic advantage."
>
> **Admiral M. G. Mullen**
> **Chairman of the Joint Chiefs of Staff**
> **Capstone Concept for Joint Operations, January 2009**

1. Introduction

a. This chapter discusses joint functions, related tasks, and key considerations. **Joint functions are related capabilities and activities grouped together to help JFCs integrate, synchronize, and direct joint operations.** Functions that are common to joint operations at all levels of war fall into **six basic groups—C2, intelligence, fires, movement and maneuver, protection, and sustainment.** Some functions, such as C2 and intelligence, apply to all operations. Others, such as fires, apply as the JFC's mission requires. A number of subordinate tasks, missions, and related capabilities help define each function, and some could apply to more than one joint function.

b. The joint functions reinforce and complement one another, and **integration across the functions is essential to mission accomplishment.** For example, joint fires can enhance the protection of a joint security area (JSA) by dispersing or disrupting enemy assets threatening the JSA. Likewise, ground forces can improve their protection by using intelligence to alter movement or maneuver so that enemy ambushes or other hazards are avoided. In any joint operation, the JFC can choose from a wide variety of joint and Service capabilities and combine them in various ways to perform joint functions and accomplish the mission. The OPLAN or OPORD describes how the JFC uses military capabilities (i.e., organizations, people, and systems) to perform tasks associated with each joint function. However, forces and other assets are not characterized by the functions for which the JFC is employing them. Individual Service capabilities often can support multiple functions simultaneously or sequentially while the joint force is executing a single task. For example, capabilities employed in the air domain typically accomplish tasks that support all six functions in a single combat operation. Just as component commanders integrate activities across functions to accomplish tasks and missions, the JFC and staff do likewise for the joint force. Various factors complicate the JFC's integration challenge, such as competing demands for high-priority capabilities and the fact that joint force components have different function-oriented approaches, procedures, and perspectives. The synchronization, coordination, and/or integration of military operations with the activities of interorganizational partners to achieve unity of effort are key to success, and military forces need to work competently in this environment while properly supporting the lead agency, department, or organization.

Chapter III

c. While information operations (IO) is not a separate function, the JFC and staff apply the IO core, supporting, and related capabilities across the joint functions and independently in some cases. Some IO capabilities are offensive in application, such as computer network attack (CNA). Operations security (OPSEC) is an example of a defensive capability, and relates to the protection function. Regardless of these alignments, integration and synchronization across IO capabilities and actions is essential to many aspects of joint operations. For example, the commander and staff integrate public affairs (PA) and the commander's defense support to public diplomacy (DSPD) with other IO actions to enable the commander's communications strategy.

For a more detailed discussion of IO, see JP 3-13, Information Operations.

2. **Command and Control**

a. C2 encompasses the exercise of authority and direction by a commander over assigned and attached forces to accomplish the mission. The JFC provides operational vision, guidance, and direction to the joint force. The **C2 function** encompasses a number of tasks, including the following:

(1) Establish, organize, and operate a joint force HQ.

(2) Command subordinate forces.

(3) Prepare and, when required, modify plans, orders, and guidance.

(4) Establish appropriate command authorities among subordinate commanders.

(5) Assign tasks and operational areas as needed.

(6) Prioritize and allocate resources.

(7) Manage risk.

(8) Communicate and maintain the status of information.

(9) Assess progress toward accomplishing tasks, creating conditions, and achieving objectives.

(10) Coordinate and control the employment of joint lethal and nonlethal capabilities.

(11) Coordinate, synchronize, and when appropriate, integrate joint operations with the operations and activities of interorganizational partners.

(12) Conduct PA from the operational area.

b. **Command** includes both the authority and responsibility to effectively use available resources to accomplish assigned missions. Command at all levels is the art of motivating and directing people and organizations into action to accomplish missions. The C2 function supports an efficient decision-making process. Enabled by timely intelligence, surveillance, and reconnaissance (ISR), the goal is to **provide the ability to make decisions and execute those decisions more rapidly and effectively than the adversary.** This decreases risk and allows the commander more control over the timing and tempo of operations.

> *"The key is not to make quick decisions, but to make timely decisions."*
>
> **General Colin Powell
> Chairman of the Joint Chiefs of Staff
> 01 October 1989–30 September 1993**

   c. **Command Authorities.** JFCs exercise command authorities (i.e., combatant command [command authority] {COCOM}, OPCON, tactical control [TACON], and support) delegated to them by law or senior leaders and commanders over assigned and attached forces. *Command relationships* is another term for these authorities. JP 1, *Doctrine for the Armed Forces of the United States*, provides details on each authority, and Figure III-1 summarizes their relationships. Unity of command in joint operations is maintained through the application of the various command relationships as follows.

Command Relationships Synopsis

Combatant Command (Command Authority)

(Unique to Combatant Commander)

- Planning, programming, budgeting, and execution process input
- Assignment of subordinate commanders
- Relationships with Department of Defense agencies
- Directive authority for logistics

Operational control when delegated

- Authoritative direction for all military operations and joint training
- Organize and employ commands and forces
- Assign command functions to subordinates
- Establish plans and requirements for intelligence, surveillance, and reconnaissance activities
- Suspend subordinate commanders from duty

Tactical control when delegated

Local direction and control of movements or maneuvers to accomplish mission

Support relationship when assigned

Aid, assist, protect, or sustain another organization

Figure III-1. Command Relationships Synopsis

Chapter III

(1) COCOM is the nontransferable command authority established by Title 10, United States Code (USC), Section 164, exercised only by commanders of unified or specified CCMDs unless otherwise directed by the President or SecDef. COCOM, which cannot be delegated, is the authority of a CCDR to perform those functions of command over assigned forces involving organizing and employing commands and forces, assigning tasks, designating objectives, and giving authoritative direction over all aspects of military operations, joint training, and logistics necessary to accomplish the missions assigned to the command. COCOM should be exercised through the commanders of subordinate organizations. Normally this authority is exercised through subordinate JFCs and Service and/or functional component commanders. COCOM provides full authority to organize and employ commands and forces as the CCDR considers necessary to accomplish assigned missions. In crisis response and combat, or where critical situations require changing the normal logistic process, the CCDRs' logistic authority enables them to use all logistic capabilities of all forces assigned and attached to their commands as necessary to accomplish their mission. Under peacetime conditions, the CCDR will exercise logistic authority consistent with the peacetime limitations imposed by legislation, DOD policy or regulations, budgetary considerations, local conditions, and other specific conditions prescribed by SecDef or CJCS.

(2) *Operational control* is inherent in COCOM and may be delegated within the command. OPCON is command authority that may be exercised by commanders at any echelon at or below the level of CCMD to perform those functions of command over subordinate forces involving organizing and employing commands and forces, assigning tasks, designating objectives, and giving authoritative direction necessary to accomplish the mission. OPCON includes authoritative direction over all aspects of military operations and joint training necessary to accomplish missions assigned to the command. This authority should be exercised through the commanders of subordinate organizations, normally through subordinate JFCs and Service and/or functional component commanders. OPCON normally provides full authority to organize commands and forces and to employ those forces as the commander in operational control considers necessary to accomplish assigned missions; it does not, in and of itself, include authoritative direction for logistics or matters of administration, discipline, internal organization, or unit training.

(3) *Tactical control* is inherent in OPCON. TACON is command authority over assigned or attached forces or commands, or military capability or forces made available for tasking, that is limited to the detailed direction and control of movements or maneuvers within the operational area necessary to accomplish missions or tasks assigned. TACON may be delegated to, and exercised at any level at or below the level of CCMD. TACON provides sufficient authority for controlling and directing the application of force or tactical use of combat support assets within the assigned mission or task. Commanders may delegate TACON to subordinate commanders at any echelon at or below CCMD and may exercise TACON over assigned or attached forces or military capabilities or forces made available for tasking. TACON does not provide organizational authority or authoritative direction for administrative and logistic support or discipline (Uniform Code of Military Justice authority); the commander of the parent unit continues to exercise those responsibilities unless the establishing directive specifies otherwise. Except for special operations forces

Joint Functions

(SOF), functional component commanders typically exercise TACON over military capabilities or forces made available for tasking.

(4) **Support.** Establishing support relationships between components (as described in JP 1, *Doctrine for the Armed Forces of the United States)*, is a useful option to accomplish needed tasks. **The JFC can establish support relationships among all functional and Service component commanders,** such as for the coordination of operations in depth involving the joint force land component commander (JFLCC) and the joint force air component commander (JFACC). Within a joint force, the JFC may designate more than one supported commander simultaneously, and components may simultaneously receive and provide support for different missions, functions, or operations. For instance, a joint force special operations component commander (JFSOCC) may be supported for a direct-action mission while simultaneously supporting a JFLCC for a raid. Similarly, a joint force maritime component commander (JFMCC) may be supported for a sea control mission while simultaneously supporting a JFACC to achieve air superiority over the operational area.

(5) **Other authorities** granted to commanders, and to subordinates as required, include ***administrative control, coordinating authority,* and *direct liaison authorized.*** JP 1, *Doctrine for the Armed Forces of the United States,* outlines the specific details for each command relationship.

> **COMMON OPERATING PRECEPT**
>
> **Avoid combining capabilities where doing so adds complexity without compensating advantage.**

(6) The perceived benefits of "jointness" do not occur naturally just by virtue of C2 relationships. The integration necessary for effective joint operations requires explicit effort, can increase operational complexity, and will require additional training, technical and technological interoperability, liaison, and planning. Although effectiveness typically is more important than efficiency in joint operations, the JFC and component commanders must determine when the potential benefits of joint integration cannot compensate for the additional complicating factors. Synergy is a means to greater operational effectiveness, not an end in itself. The joint operations principle simplicity is always a key consideration.

d. **Control is inherent in command.** To control is to manage and direct forces and functions consistent with a commander's command authority. Control of forces and functions helps commanders and staffs compute requirements, allocate means, and integrate efforts. Control is necessary to determine the status of organizational effectiveness, identify variance from set standards, and correct deviations from these standards. Control permits commanders to acquire and apply means to support the mission and develop specific instructions from general guidance. Control provides the means for commanders to maintain freedom of action, delegate authority, direct operations from any location, and integrate and synchronize actions throughout the operational area. Ultimately, it provides commanders a means to measure, report, and correct performance.

> **COMMAND RELATIONSHIPS DURING OPERATION IRAQI FREEDOM**
>
> In December 2002, representatives from United States Central Command (USCENTCOM) and United States European Command (USEUCOM) met in Stuttgart, Germany to discuss Operation IRAQI FREEDOM (OIF). The two broad issues were organizing the operational area and coordinating the command relationships for all OIF phases.
>
> The USCENTCOM OIF theater of operations would by necessity cross the Unified Command Plan (UCP) designated USCENTCOM and USEUCOM areas of responsibility (AORs) boundary. Specifically, the land and airspace of Turkey was recognized for its potential to contribute to opening a northern line of operation.
>
> Discussions over the potential options for organizing the OIF operational area led to an agreement not to request a temporary change in the UCP modifying the AORs, but to rely on the establishment of appropriate command relationships between the two combatant commanders (CCDRs).
>
> Discussions over the potential command and control options led to the decision to establish a support relationship between USCENTCOM (supported) and USEUCOM (supporting). This relationship was established by the Secretary of Defense. It enabled the development of coherent and supporting campaign plans.
>
> In the campaign design and plan, USEUCOM retained tactical control for the coordination and execution of operational movement (i.e., reception, staging, onward movement, and integration); intelligence, surveillance, and reconnaissance; logistic and personnel support; and protection in support of USCENTCOM forces transiting the USEUCOM AOR; specifically Turkey. Once USCENTCOM-allocated joint forces were positioned and prepared to cross the Turkish–Iraqi border (to commence offensive operations) operational control would be given to USCENTCOM.
>
> Maintaining UCP AOR boundaries and the establishment of an umbrella support relationship between the CCDRs with conditional command authorities exercised over the participating forces based on their readiness and operation phase provided a workable solution to the integration and employment of joint forces on the boundary of two AORs.
>
> Various Sources

e. **Area of Operations and Functional Considerations**

(1) **Command and Control in an Area of Operations. The land and maritime force commanders are the supported commanders within their designated areas of operations (AOs).** Through C2, JFLCCs and JFMCCs integrate and synchronize movement and maneuver with intelligence, fires, protection, and sustainment and the supporting IO

Joint Functions

activities. To facilitate this integration and synchronization, they have the authority to designate target priority, effects, and timing of fires within their AOs.

(a) Synchronization of efforts within land or maritime AOs with theater- and/or JOA-wide operations is of particular importance. To facilitate synchronization, the JFC establishes priorities that will guide or inform execution decisions throughout the theater and/or JOA, including within the land and maritime force commander's AOs. The JFACC is normally the supported commander for the JFC's overall air interdiction effort, while JFLCCs and JFMCCs are supported commanders for interdiction in their AOs.

(b) In coordination with the JFLCCs and JFMCCs, other commanders designated by the JFC to execute theater- or JOA-wide functions have the latitude to plan and execute these JFC-prioritized operations within land and maritime AOs. Commanders executing such a mission within a land or maritime AO must coordinate the operation to avoid adverse effects and fratricide. If those operations would have adverse impact within a land or maritime AO, the commander assigned to execute the JOA-wide functions must readjust the plan, resolve the issue with the land or maritime component commander, or consult with the JFC for resolution.

(2) **Command and Control of Space Operations.** A supported JFC normally designates a space coordinating authority (SCA) to coordinate joint space operations and integrate space capabilities. Based on the complexity and scope of operations, the JFC can either retain SCA or designate a component commander as the SCA. The JFC considers the mission, nature, and duration of the operation; preponderance of space force capabilities made available, and resident C2 capabilities (including reachback) when selecting the appropriate option. The **SCA** is responsible for coordinating and integrating space capabilities in the operational area and has primary responsibility for joint space operations planning, to include determining space requirements within the joint force. The SCA normally will be supported by assigned or attached embedded space personnel. There are established doctrinal processes for articulating requirements for space force enhancement products. These processes are specifically tailored to the functional area they support and result in prioritized requirements. Thus the SCA typically has no role in prioritizing the JFC's day-to-day space force enhancement requirements. The SCA gathers operational requirements that may be satisfied by space capabilities and facilitates the use of established processes by joint force staff to plan and conduct space operations. Following coordination, the SCA provides the JFC a prioritized list of recommended space requirements based on joint force objectives. To ensure prompt and timely support, the supported CCDR and Commander, United States Strategic Command (CDRUSSTRATCOM), may authorize direct liaison between the SCA and applicable United States Strategic Command (USSTRATCOM) component(s). Joint force component commands should communicate their requirements to the SCA or designated representative to ensure that all space activities are properly integrated and synchronized.

For detailed guidance on C2 of space operations, refer to JP 3-14, Space Operations.

(3) **Command and Control of Joint Air Operations.** The JFC will normally designate a JFACC and assign responsibilities. The JFACC's responsibilities normally

Chapter III

include, but are not limited to organizing the staff, planning, coordinating, and monitoring joint air operations, and the allocation and tasking of joint air operations forces based on the JFC's CONOPS and air apportionment decision. The JFC may designate the JFACC as the supported commander for strategic attack, air interdiction, and airborne ISR (among other missions) who is responsible to the JFC for planning, coordinating, executing, and assessing these missions. **When the JFC designates a JFACC, the JFC also normally designates the JFACC as the area air defense commander (AADC) and airspace control authority (ACA)** because the three functions are so integral to one another. When appropriate, the JFC may designate a separate AADC or ACA. In those joint operations where separate commanders are designated, close coordination is essential for unity of effort, prevention of fratricide, and deconfliction of joint air operations.

(a) **Airspace Control Authority.** The JFC is ultimately responsible for airspace control in the operational area. The ACA, in conjunction with the Service and functional components, coordinates and integrates the use of the airspace under the JFC's authority. The ACA develops guidance, techniques, and procedures for airspace control and for the coordination required among units within the operational area. The ACA establishes an airspace control system (ACS) that is responsive to the JFC's needs, integrates ACS with the HN, and coordinates and deconflicts user requirements. The airspace control plan (ACP) and airspace control order (ACO) express how the airspace will be used to support mission accomplishment. The ACA develops the ACP and, after JFC approval, distributes it throughout the operational area and to all supporting airspace users. The ACP begins with the distribution of the ACO, and is executed when components and users comply with the ACO as described in JP 3-30, *Command and Control for Joint Air Operations*.

(b) **Area Air Defense Commander.** The AADC is responsible for defensive counterair (DCA) (which includes both air and missile threats) operations. The AADC must identify those volumes of airspace and control measures that support and enhance DCA operations, identify required airspace management systems, establish procedures for systems to operate within the airspace, and ensure they are incorporated into the ACS. During complex operations or campaigns conducted in a large theater of operations, the AADC may recommend and the JFC may choose to divide the JOA into separate air defense regions, each with a regional air defense commander who could be delegated responsibilities and decision-making authority for DCA operations within the region.

f. **Command and Control System.** JFCs exercise authority and direction through a C2 system, which consists of the facilities, equipment, communications, staff functions and procedures, and personnel essential for planning, preparing for, monitoring, and assessing operations. The C2 system must enable the JFC to maintain communications with higher, supporting, and subordinate commands in order to control all aspects of current operations while planning for future operations.

(1) The joint force staff is the linchpin of the C2 system, since the JFC understands, plans, directs, and controls most aspects of operations through the staff's expertise and efforts.

Joint Functions

(2) **Liaison** is an important aspect of C2. Commanders may exchange liaison teams or individuals between higher, supporting, and subordinate commands as required. Liaison personnel generally represent the interests of the sending commander to the receiving commander, but can greatly promote understanding of the commander's intent at both the sending and receiving HQ; they should be assigned early during joint operation planning. Liaison officers (LNOs) from supporting to supported commanders are particularly essential in determining needs and coordinating supporting actions.

(3) **Control and Coordination Measures.** JFCs establish various maneuver and movement control, airspace coordinating, and fire support coordination measures to facilitate effective joint operations. These measures include boundaries, phase lines, objectives, coordinating altitudes to deconflict air operations, air defense areas, operational areas, submarine operating patrol areas, no-fire areas, and others as required.

For additional guidance on C2 of air operations, refer to JP 3-30, Command and Control for Joint Air Operations. *For additional guidance on control and coordination measures, refer to JP 3-09,* Joint Fire Support, *and JP 3-52,* Joint Airspace Control. *See Military Standard-2525C,* Common Warfighting Symbology, *for additional guidance on the use and discussion of graphic control measures and symbols for the joint force.*

(4) **Communications and ISR systems** provide communications, ISR, targeting, and ballistic missile warning. The precision, speed, and interoperability with which these systems operate improve access to the information available to all command levels, thereby enhancing a common perspective of the operational environment. Effective command at varying operational tempos requires timely, reliable, secure, interoperable, and sustainable communications. Communications and ISR planning increases options available to JFCs by providing the communications sensor systems necessary to collect, process, store, protect, and disseminate information at decisive times. These communications and sensor systems permit JFCs to exploit tactical success and facilitate future operations.

(a) **Communications System Planning.** The mission and structure of the joint force determine specific information flow and processing requirements. These requirements dictate the general architecture and specific configuration of the communications system. Therefore, communications system planning must be integrated and synchronized with joint operation planning. Through effective communications system planning, the JFC is able to apply capabilities at the critical time and place for mission success.

(b) Communications system planning considers, and when appropriate, accommodates communications links with interorganizational partners. Interoperability and communications security planning with these partners is essential to ensure secure communications protect sensitive information. Routine communications and backup systems may be disrupted, and civil authorities might have to rely on available military communications equipment. Communications system planning also must consider termination of US involvement and procedures to transfer communications system control to another agency such as the United Nations (UN). Planning should consider that it may be

Chapter III

necessary to leave some communications resources behind to continue support of the ongoing effort.

(c) Use of ISR capabilities for domestic non-intelligence activities is known as **incident awareness and assessment.** All requests for imagery or other intelligence support for areas within the United States are subject to USG intelligence oversight regulations and Department of Defense Directive (DODD) 5240.1, *DOD Intelligence Activities*. DOD intelligence component capabilities, resources, and personnel as a rule may not be used for activities other than foreign intelligence or counterintelligence (CI), unless that use is specifically approved by SecDef. In addition, to ensure compliance with the Posse Comitatus Act requests for direct DOD support to civilian law enforcement agencies are closely reviewed and processed separately for approval.

For additional guidance on the communications and ISR systems support, refer to JP 2-01, Joint and National Intelligence Support to Military Operations, *JP 6-0,* Joint Communications System, *and North American Aerospace Defense Command and United States Northern Command Instruction 14-3,* Domestic Imagery.

g. **Network Operations**

(1) Network Operations (NETOPS) is the DOD-wide operational, organizational, and technical capabilities for operating and defending DOD information networks. NETOPS includes, but is not limited to, enterprise management, net assurance, and content management. DOD information networks situational awareness is gained through the operational and technical integration of enterprise management and defense actions and activities across all levels of command.

(2) CDRUSSTRATCOM is the supported commander for global NETOPS and synchronizes planning for cyberspace operations. US Cyber Command is a subunified command subordinate to USSTRATCOM and directs the operations and defense of specified DOD information networks. It is capable of conducting full-spectrum military cyberspace operations to enable US freedom of action in cyberspace and enable actions in other domains and deny the same to our adversaries. CDRUSSTRATCOM also is a supported commander for nonglobal NETOPS and provides support to affected CCMDs, Services, and DOD agencies. OGAs also may provide support per intra-governmental agreements.

For additional guidance on NETOPS, refer to JP 6-0, Joint Communications System.

h. **Commander's Critical Information Requirements**

(1) **CCIRs are elements of information that the commander identifies as being critical to timely decision making.** CCIRs help focus IM and help the commander assess the operational environment and identify decision points during operations. **CCIRs belong exclusively to the commander.** The CCIR list is normally short so that the staff can focus its efforts and allocate scarce resources. But the CCIR list is not static; JFCs add, delete, adjust, and update CCIRs throughout an operation based on the information they need for decision making. At a minimum, CCIRs should be reviewed and updated during each phase of the operation.

(2) **Categories.** Priority intelligence requirements (PIRs) and friendly force information requirements (FFIRs) constitute the total list of CCIRs.

(a) **PIRs** focus on the enemy or adversary and the operational environment and drive intelligence collection and production requirements. All staff sections can recommend potential PIRs that they believe meet the JFC's guidance. However, the joint force J-2 has overall staff responsibility for consolidating PIR nominations and for providing the staff recommendation to the commander. JFC-approved PIRs are automatically CCIRs. PIRs are continuously updated as they are addressed during the intelligence collection and production efforts. PIRs are reviewed during the transition of each operational phase to ensure they are still relevant.

For more information on PIRs, see JP 2-0, Joint Intelligence.

(b) **FFIRs** focus on information the JFC must have to assess the status of the friendly force and supporting capabilities. All staff sections can recommend potential FFIRs that they believe meet the JFC's guidance. The plans directorate of a joint staff (J-5) typically has overall staff responsibility for consolidating FFIR nominations and for providing the staff recommendation to the commander during planning prior to execution. During execution, the joint force J-3 is responsible for consolidating these nominations and providing the recommendation for FFIRs that relate to current operations. However, the J-5 remains responsible for consolidating nominations and recommending FFIRs related to the future plans effort. JFC-approved FFIRs are automatically CCIRs.

i. **Battle Rhythm.** The HQ battle rhythm is its daily operations cycle of briefings, meetings, and report requirements. A stable battle rhythm facilitates effective decision making, efficient staff actions, and management of information within the HQ and with higher, supporting, and subordinate HQ. The commander and staff should design a battle rhythm that minimizes meeting requirements while providing the necessary venues for command and staff interaction internal to the joint force HQ and with subordinate commands. Joint and component HQ's battle rhythms should be synchronized to accommodate operations in multiple time zones and the battle rhythm needs of higher, subordinate, and adjacent commands. Other factors such as planning, decision, and operating cycles (i.e., intelligence collection, targeting, and air tasking order cycles) influence the battle rhythm. Further, meetings of the necessary staff organizations must be synchronized. The chief of staff normally manages the joint force HQ's battle rhythm. When coordinating with civilian USG departments and agencies, the joint force HQ should consider that those organizations often have limited capabilities and restricted access to some information.

j. **Creating Shared Understanding.** In one sense, decisions are the most important products of the C2 function, because they guide the force toward objectives and mission accomplishment. Commanders and staff require not only information to make these decisions, but also the knowledge and understanding that results in the wisdom essential to sound decision making (Figure III-2).

Chapter III

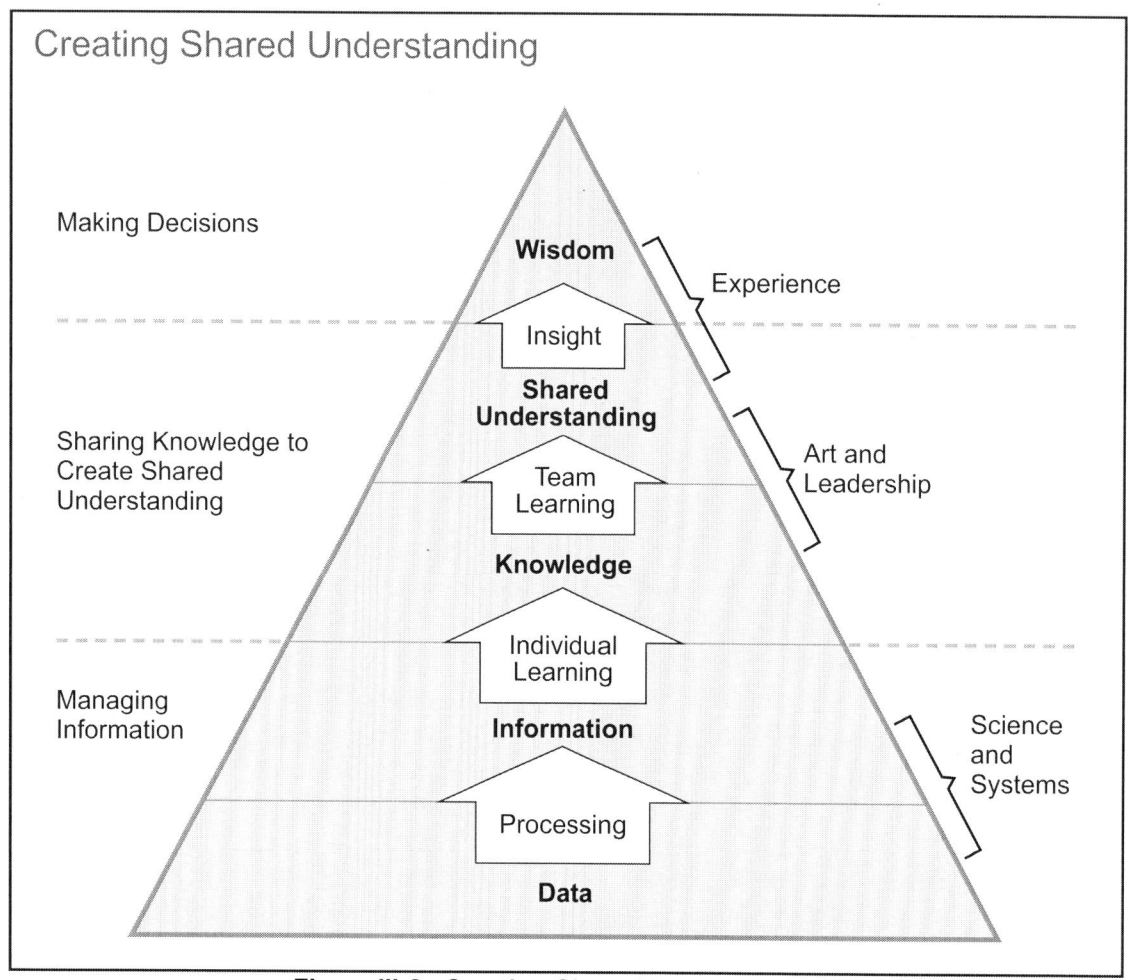

Figure III-2. Creating Shared Understanding

(1) ***Information management*** is an essential process that receives, organizes, stores, controls, and secures an organization's wide range of data and information in a manner that facilitates availability to relevant users, while concurrently preventing inadvertent disclosure of sensitive or proprietary information. IM is important for the commander's battle rhythm and the development and sharing of information to increase both individual and collective knowledge. Effective IM improves the speed and accuracy of information flow and supports execution through reliable communications. The process is used to manage the organization's information resources and optimize access to information by all who need it. As the key joint force staff integrator, the chief of staff may be responsible for managing the IM process, while the communications system directorate of a joint staff ensures the operation and connectivity of the supporting C2 communication systems and processes. Many joint HQ will also have an IM officer and an IM plan. HQ may also form a joint IM board to serve as a focal point for information oversight and coordination. HQ's standard operating procedures (SOPs) normally will describe specific IM procedures and responsibilities. IM feeds the development and sharing of knowledge-based information products.

For further guidance on IM, refer to JP 6-0, Joint Communications System, *and JP 3-33,* Joint Task Force Headquarters.

(2) **Knowledge sharing** complements the value of IM with processes to create an organizational culture that encourages and rewards knowledge and information sharing to achieve shared understanding. It supports *team learning* activities and a supporting environment. While information can be collected, processed, and stored as structured or unstructured content, such as in reports and databases, knowledge is acquired through a cognitive process and exists in the minds of individuals. **The knowledge sharing that occurs is best characterized as an activity within a *learning environment,* rather than defined as a purely systematic process with inputs and outputs.**

(a) For example, the free exchange of ideas between the commander and staff that should typify early operational design is an activity that shares the individual knowledge of numerous functional experts, modifies and increases their collective knowledge, and promotes shared understanding. In a similar way, the after-action sessions that a commander conducts with subordinate commanders and staff during and following an operation create an environment of learning in which participants share knowledge and increase their collective understanding. Knowledge and understanding occur better through interaction, whether in person or virtual, than through reading and assimilating various products.

(b) Certain products are particularly relevant to knowledge sharing. For example, *commander's intent* is a knowledge-based product that commanders use to share their insight and direction with the joint force. The intent creates shared purpose and understanding, provides focus to the staff, and helps subordinate and supporting commanders act to achieve objectives without further orders, even when operations do not unfold as planned. Likewise, lessons-learned databases are knowledge-based products that help users avoid previous mistakes and adopt proven best practices. These databases exemplify how the marriage of IM and decision-support processes can improve future operations by sharing knowledge gained through experience.

(3) Specific IM, knowledge-sharing, and other collaborative processes and products vary across joint commands based on the commander's needs and preferences. The HQ SOP should specify these procedures and products and describe the relationship between IM, knowledge sharing, and the HQ battle rhythm.

(4) **Collaboration**

(a) Effective collaboration enhances C2 by sharing knowledge and aiding the creation of shared understanding. Although the value of face-to-face interaction is indisputably preferred, capabilities that improve long-distance, asynchronous collaboration among dispersed forces can enhance both planning and execution of joint operations. One has to consider, however, the added risk as long-distance collaboration may create a critical vulnerability that an adversary can exploit. These capabilities not only can improve efficiency and common understanding during routine, peacetime interaction among participants, they also can enhance combat effectiveness during time-compressed operations associated with both combat and noncombat operations.

Chapter III

(b) A collaborative environment is one in which participants are encouraged to solve problems and share information, knowledge, perceptions, ideas, and concepts in a spirit of mutual cooperation that extends beyond the requirement to coordinate with others. In joint operations, commanders and staffs tend to collaborate due to an established common purpose. However, collaboration can be enhanced when personnel understand the value of leveraging social networks, establishing trusted relationships, and sharing knowledge. This is particularly important in relationships with interorganizational partners, since their objectives and perceptions of the desired end state will not always coincide with the military's.

(c) **Collaborative Capabilities.** Collaborative capabilities can enable planners and operators worldwide to build a plan without being colocated. Collaboration also provides planners with a "view of the whole" while working on various sections of a plan, which helps them identify and resolve planning conflicts early. Commanders can participate more readily in COA analysis even when away from the HQ, with the potential to select a COA without the traditional sequential briefing process. The staff can post plans and orders on interactive web pages or portals for immediate use by subordinate elements (e.g., as facilitated by automated machine-to-machine interfaces or "publish and subscribe" mechanisms). Collaborative capabilities require effective and efficient processes, trained and disciplined users, and a usable collaborate tool infrastructure. A fully functioning electronic collaborative environment requires more than just **collaborative capabilities** that help participants share and protect **information and knowledge.** A second component of this environment is **infrastructure**—the various information systems on which the tools reside and the networks that link these systems. The C2 systems, networks, and collaborative tools and participants need **procedures**—based on accepted theory and practice and established to meet joint force needs—that enable exchanges of knowledge and information. The full benefit of these capabilities is realized only with a fourth component—**users** who are trained to use the tools and systems and educated to understand the advantages and power of a collaborative environment.

(d) **Information Sharing.** The sharing of information with relevant USG agencies, foreign governments and security forces, interorganizational partners, NGOs, and members of the private sector, has proved vital in recent operations. Commanders at all levels should determine and provide guidance on what information needs to be shared with whom and when. DOD information should be appropriately secured, shared, and made available throughout the information life cycle to appropriate mission partners to the maximum extent allowed by US laws and DOD policy. Commanders, along with their staffs, need to recognize the criticality of the information-sharing function at the outset of complex operations and not as an afterthought.

For additional guidance on collaboration and related capabilities, refer to CJCSI 6715.01B, Joint Operational Employment of Virtual Collaboration, and JP 6-0, Joint Communications System.

k. **Risk Management.** Risk is inherent in military operations. Risk management is the process of identifying, assessing, and controlling risks arising from operational factors and making decisions that balance risk cost with mission benefits. Risk management is a

Joint Functions

function of command and a key planning consideration. Risk management helps commanders preserve lives and resources, avoid or mitigate unnecessary risk, identify feasible and effective control measures where specific standards do not exist, and develop valid COAs. Risk management does not inhibit a commander's flexibility and initiative; remove risk altogether (or support a zero-defects mindset); dictate a GO/NO-GO decision to take a specific action; sanction or justify violating the law; or remove the necessity for SOPs. Risk management is relevant at all levels of war, across the range of military operations, and through all phases of an operation and its branches and sequels. To alleviate or reduce risk, commanders may take a variety of actions, such as changing the CONOPS, changing the plan for employment of operational fires, or executing a branch to the original plan.

(1) **Safety** is crucial to successful operations and the preservation of military power. High-tempo operations may increase the risk of injury and death due to mishaps. Command interest, discipline, risk mitigation measures, education, and training lessen those risks. The JFC reduces the chance of mishap by conducting risk assessments, assigning a safety officer and staff, implementing a safety program, and seeking advice from local personnel. Safety planning factors could include geospatial and weather data, local road conditions and driving habits, uncharted or uncleared mine fields, and special equipment hazards.

(2) To assist in risk management, commanders and their staffs may develop or institute a risk management process tailored to their particular mission or operational area. Figure III-3 is a generic model that contains the likely elements of a risk management process.

l. **Strategic Communication and Communications Strategy**

(1) The term *strategic communication,* an aspect of strategic guidance, applies to USG-level department and agency activities. CCDRs are the primary interface for implementing SC in the context of their theater strategies and during specific joint operations. The US military plays an instrumental role in SC, primarily through IO, PA, and DSPD. SC considerations affect every military operation and are essential when the focus is on gaining and maintaining the support of the relevant population as is common in IW.

(2) **Integral to joint operation planning,** CCDRs and subordinate JFCs develop ***communications strategies*** to nest with and support USG SC plans, programs, and actions and influences key audiences. The JFC designs the communications strategy to provide intent, objectives, thematic guidance, and the process by which IO, PA, and other SC-related means coordinate and integrate their efforts and ensure consistency of messages, activities, and operations to the lowest level. The JFC's communications strategy synchronizes and, when appropriate, integrates communications-related activities across subordinate and supporting commands and with interorganizational partners. The OPLAN or OPORD supplements the communications strategy with additional guidance and tasks as necessary. In particular, the strategy and plan or order synchronize and integrate the JFC's primary supporting capabilities and actions of PA, IO, and DSPD to achieve the strategy's objectives. The typical communications strategy for a specific operation contains at least a *narrative, themes, messages, visual products, supporting activities, and key audiences.* These

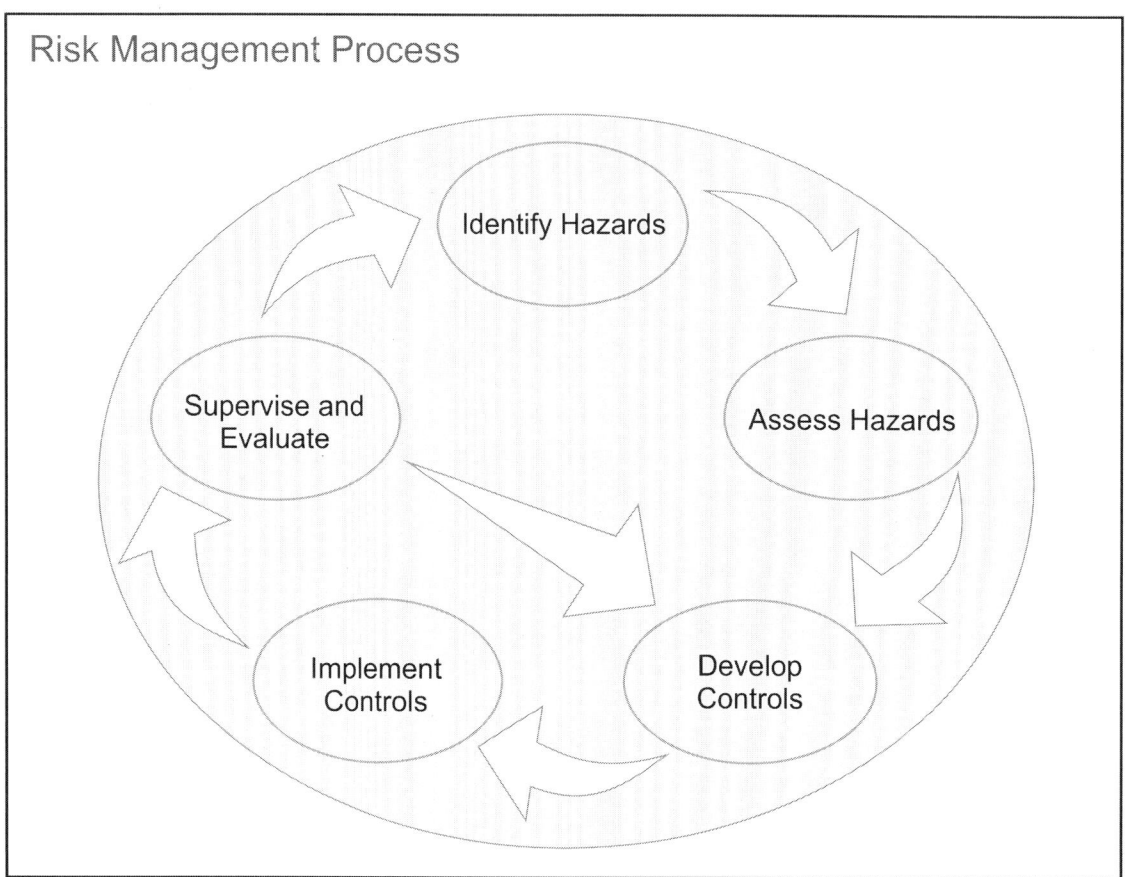

Figure III-3. Risk Management Process

elements, in conjunction with specific tasks in the plan or order, help guide and regulate joint force actions when communicating and interacting with the local populace, interorganizational partners, and the media, and they support other relevant objectives.

(a) The Narrative. This is the overarching expression of the context, reason, and desired results associated with the CCDR's communications strategy or a specific joint operation. The narrative enables understanding for external stakeholders whose perceptions, attitudes, beliefs, and behaviors are relevant to the operation.

(b) Themes. The communications strategy typically contains two or more themes, which are distinct, unifying ideas or intentions that support the narrative and are designed for broad application to achieve specific objectives. A subordinate JFC's communications strategy themes normally nest under the GCC's communications strategy themes and support the overarching narrative.

(c) Messages. These are narrowly focused communications that support a specific theme. They are typically directed at a specific audience to create a specific effect.

For additional guidance on PA and IO support to SC and communications strategy, refer to JP 3-61, Public Affairs, *and JP 3-13,* Information Operations. *Also see JP 5-0,* Joint Operation Planning, *for information on SC-related planning.*

m. **Key Leader Engagement.** Most operations require commanders and other leaders to engage key local and regional leaders in order to affect their attitudes and gain their support. **Building relationships to the point of effective engagement and influence usually takes time.** Commanders can be challenged to identify key leaders, develop appropriate messages, establish meaningful dialogue, and determine other effective ways and means of delivery, especially in societies where interpersonal relationships are paramount. Interaction opportunities with friendly and neutral leaders could include face-to-face meetings, town meetings, and community events. Understanding cultural context, cognitive orientation patterns, and communication methods is essential. The J-2's joint intelligence preparation of the operational environment (JIPOE) should include identification of key enemy and neutral leaders, and well as key friendly leaders who are not in the commander's usual sphere of influence. However, the entire staff should identify leaders relative to their functional areas as part of JIPOE.

n. **Public Affairs.** PA are the public information, command information, and community engagement activities directed toward both the external and internal publics with interest in DOD. Joint PA plans, coordinates, and synchronizes US military public information activities and resources in order to support the commander's communications strategy and operational objectives through the distribution of truthful, timely, and factual information about joint military activities. PA contributes to the achievement of military objectives, by countering adversary misinformation and disinformation through the publication of accurate information. PA also assists OPSEC by educating the media on the implications of premature release of information or the inadvertent release of classified or sensitive information. PA advises the JFCs on the possible impact of military operations and activities within the public information realm.

(1) The speed and methods with which people and organizations can collect and convey information to the public makes it possible for the world populace to quickly become aware of an incident. Internet sites, social media, text messages, and cellular telephones are some of the means through which potential adversaries engage audiences worldwide in the information environment. This instantaneous, unfiltered and often incomplete, intentionally biased, or factually incorrect information provided via satellite and the Internet makes planning and effective execution of PA essential.

(2) The JFC should develop a PA plan relevant to the mission that addresses both current and future operations. This plan should minimize adverse effects upon the joint operation from inaccurate media reporting/analysis, violations of OPSEC, and promulgation of disinformation and misinformation. Well-planned PA support is important in every phase of operations. PA plans should provide for open, independent reporting and anticipate and respond to media queries. These plans should provide the maximum disclosure allowed with minimum delay and create an environment between the JFC and reporters that encourages balanced coverage of operations. An effective plan provides proactive ways to communicate information about an operation and fulfills the US military's obligation to keep the American public informed while maintaining requisite OPSEC.

(3) **Communication Coordination.** Commanders and their staffs should integrate communication activities throughout planning and execution to establish consistency in

intent, actions, and information disseminated about those actions. While audiences and intent at times differ, the JFC, through the communications strategy and JOPP, coordinates planning for PA, IO, CMO, and DSPD to establish and reinforce consistent themes and messages.

(4) PA and IO activities directly support military objectives; counter adversary propaganda, misinformation, and disinformation; and deter adversary actions. Although both PA and IO plan and execute public information activities and conduct media analysis, IO may differ with respect to audience, scope, and intent. As such, they are governed by separate procedures. JFCs ensure appropriate coordination between PA and IO activities consistent with the DOD principles of information, policy, or legal limitation and security.

For additional guidance on PA, refer to JP 3-61, Public Affairs.

o. **Civil-Military Operations.** CMO establish, maintain, influence, or exploit relations between military forces, governmental and nongovernmental civilian organizations and authorities, and the civilian populace to facilitate military operations and consolidate and achieve the commander's objectives. CMO may include activities and functions normally the responsibility of the local, regional, or national governments. CMO are conducted to minimize civil-military friction and threats from the civil component, maximize support for operations, and meet the commander's legal obligations and moral responsibilities to the civilian populations within the operational area. These activities may occur prior to, during, or after other military actions. They also may occur, if directed, in the absence of other military operations. CMO are an inherent command responsibility.

For additional guidance on CMO, refer to JP 3-57, Civil-Military Operations.

p. **Military Deception.** Military deception (MILDEC) includes actions executed to deliberately mislead adversary decision makers as to friendly military capabilities, intentions, and operations, thereby causing the adversary to take specific actions (or inactions) that will contribute to the accomplishment of the friendly mission. The intent is to cause adversary commanders to form inaccurate impressions about friendly force dispositions, capabilities, vulnerabilities, and intentions; misuse their ISR assets; and/or fail to employ combat or support units to their best advantage. As executed by JFCs, MILDEC targets adversary leaders and decision makers through the manipulation of adversary intelligence collection, analysis, and dissemination systems. MILDEC depends on intelligence to identify appropriate deception targets, to assist in developing a credible story, to identify and orient on appropriate receivers (the readers of the story), and to assess the effectiveness of the deception effort. Deception requires a thorough knowledge of opponents and their decision-making processes. During the formulation of the CONOPS, planners determine how the JFC wants the adversary to act at critical points in the operation. Those desired adversary actions then become the MILDEC objective. MILDEC is focused on causing the opponents to act in a desired manner, not simply to be misled in their thinking.

For additional guidance on MILDEC, refer to JP 3-13.4, Military Deception.

> **MILITARY DECEPTION IN THE YOM KIPPUR WAR, 1973**
>
> On 6 October 1973, the Egyptian 3rd Army surprised the Israeli Defense Force by attacking across the Suez Canal. Egyptian forces gained a significant foothold in the Sinai and began to drive deeper until a determined defense and counterattack drove them back.
>
> To achieve the initial surprise, Egyptian forces conducted deception operations of strategic, operational, and tactical significance to exploit Israeli weaknesses. At the strategic level, they conveyed the notions that they would not attack without both a concerted Arab effort and an ability to neutralize the Israeli Air Force, and that tactical preparations were merely in response to feared Israeli retaliation for Arab terrorist activity. At the operational level, Egyptian forces portrayed their mobilization, force buildup, and maneuvers as part of their annual exercises. Egyptian exercises portraying an intent to cross the canal were repeated until the Israelis became conditioned to them and therefore did not react when the actual attack occurred. At the tactical level, Egyptian forces expertly camouflaged their equipment, denying information to Israeli observers and creating a false impression of the purpose of the increased activity.
>
> For their part, Israeli forces were overconfident and indecisive at the operational and strategic levels. In spite of the deception, tactical observers reported with increasing urgency that the Egyptian buildup and activity were significant. Their reports caused concern, but no action. Egyptian forces exploited these vulnerabilities and timed the attack to occur on Yom Kippur, the Jewish Day of Atonement, when they perceived the response of Israeli forces would be reduced.
>
> As a result of their deception efforts, synchronized with other operations of the force, Egyptian forces quickly and decisively overwhelmed Israeli forces in the early stages of the Yom Kippur War.
>
> **Various Sources**

q. **Language, Regional, and Cultural Expertise.** Language skills, regional knowledge, and cultural awareness enable effective joint operations. Deployed joint forces must be capable of understanding and effectively communicating with native populations, local and national government officials, and coalition partners. Supporting this capability should be an understanding of the regional and local culture, economy, politics, religion, and customs. Lessons learned from Operation IRAQI FREEDOM (OIF) and Operation ENDURING FREEDOM (OEF) proves that these force-multiplying capabilities can save lives and are integral to mission accomplishment. Consequently, commanders will integrate foreign language and regional expertise capabilities in contingency, security cooperation, and supporting plans, and provide for them in support of daily operations and activities.

For specific planning guidance and procedures regarding language and regional expertise, refer to CJCSI 3126.01, Language and Regional Expertise Planning.

Chapter III

For additional and more detailed guidance on C2 of joint forces, refer to JP 1, Doctrine for the Armed Forces of the United States.

For additional guidance on C2 of air, land, or maritime operations, refer to JP 3-30, Command and Control for Joint Air Operations; *JP 3-31,* Command and Control for Joint Land Operations; *and JP 3-32,* Command and Control for Joint Maritime Operations.

For additional guidance on C2 of special operations (SO), refer to JP 3-05, Special Operations, *and JP 3-05.1,* Joint Special Operations Task Force Operations.

3. Intelligence

a. **Understanding the operational environment is fundamental to joint operations.** The intelligence function supports this understanding by providing integrated, evaluated, analyzed, and interpreted information concerning foreign nations, hostile or potentially hostile forces or elements, or areas of actual or potential operations. Intelligence tells JFCs what the enemy is doing, is capable of doing, and may do in the future. These assessments are important to acting inside the enemy's decision cycle. Thus, intelligence must be sufficiently detailed and timely to satisfy the commander's decision-making needs.

b. Intelligence identifies enemy capabilities, helps identify enemy and friendly centers of gravity (COGs), projects probably enemy COAs, and assists in planning friendly force employment. The process also attempts to identify what the enemy is able to discern about friendly forces. Intelligence provides assessments that help the JFC decide which forces to deploy; when, how, and where to deploy them; and how to employ them in a manner that accomplishes the mission. The process helps JFCs and their staffs visualize the operational environment and achieve information superiority. During all activities, the operational environment can produce casualties due to disease and combat or noncombat injuries. Intelligence provides information that helps decision makers devise protection measures to mitigate these threats.

c. **Joint Intelligence Preparation of the Operational Environment**

(1) JFCs use a broad range of supporting capabilities to develop a current intelligence picture or to conduct an analysis of adversary systems. These supporting capabilities include combat support agencies and national intelligence agencies (e.g., National Security Agency, Central Intelligence Agency, Defense Intelligence Agency, National Geospatial-Intelligence Agency [NGA]). A national intelligence support team provides the J-2 with the means to integrate national intelligence capabilities into a comprehensive intelligence effort designed to support the joint force. J-2 should integrate these supporting capabilities with the efforts of the joint intelligence center. Liaison personnel from the various agencies provide access to the entire range of capabilities resident in their agencies and can focus those capabilities on the JFC's intelligence requirements.

(2) At the advent of a crisis or other indication of potential military action, JFCs examine available intelligence estimates. As part of the JIPOE process, JFCs focus intelligence efforts to determine or confirm enemy COGs and refine estimates of enemy capabilities, dispositions, intentions, and probable COAs within the context of the current

situation. They look for specific indications and warning of imminent enemy activity that may require an immediate response or an acceleration of friendly decision cycles.

For additional guidance on intelligence support to joint operations, refer to the JP 2-0 series.

d. The **intelligence function** encompasses the following intelligence process components:

(1) Planning and direction, to include managing CI activities that protect against espionage, sabotage, and assassinations.

(2) Collection of data.

(3) Processing and exploitation of collected data to produce relevant information.

(4) Analysis of information and production of intelligence.

(5) Dissemination and integration of intelligence with operations.

(6) Evaluation and feedback regarding intelligence effectiveness and quality.

e. **Key Considerations**

(1) **Responsibilities. JFCs and their component commanders are the key players in planning and conducting intelligence tasks.** Commanders are more than just consumers of intelligence. They are ultimately responsible for ensuring that intelligence is fully integrated into their plans and operations. They are also responsible for distributing intelligence and information to subordinate commands, and when appropriate, to interorganizational partners through established protocols and systems. Commanders establish the operational and intelligence requirements and continuous feedback needed to ensure optimum intelligence support to operations. This interface is essential to support the commander, to support operational planning and execution, to avoid surprise, to assist friendly deception efforts, and to assess the results of operations.

(2) **Surveillance and Reconnaissance.** Surveillance and reconnaissance are important elements of the intelligence function that support information collection across the range of military operations. JFCs require wide-area surveillance of the operational area that is focused on planned collection requirements and has sufficient flexibility to respond to time-sensitive and operationally emerging requirements. Commanders will also require persistent surveillance of specific targets that they determine are mission essential and support guidance and intent. Computer network exploitation is a form of surveillance and reconnaissance conducted in cyberspace that involves the use of computer networks to gather data from target or adversary automated information systems or networks.

(3) **CI and Human Intelligence (HUMINT).** JFCs rely on intelligence acquired through CI and HUMINT capabilities and throughout all phases of joint operations. CI and HUMINT both use human sources to collect information, and while their activities may at

Chapter III

times be overlapping, each has its own distinct purpose and function. CI support is essential to protecting the force and must be fully integrated into operation planning and execution.

For additional information on CI, refer to Secret JP 2-01.2, Counterintelligence and Human Intelligence in Joint Operations.

For additional guidance on the intelligence function, refer to JP 2-0, Joint Intelligence; *JP 2-01,* Joint and National Intelligence Support to Military Operations; *and other subordinate JPs that address intelligence support to targeting, CI, HUMINT, geospatial intelligence (GEOINT), and JIPOE.*

4. Fires

a. To **employ fires** is to use available weapons and other systems to create a specific lethal or nonlethal effect on a target. Joint fires are those delivered during the employment of forces from two or more components in coordinated action to produce desired results in support of a common objective. Fires typically produce destructive effects, but various nonlethal ways and means (such as electronic attack [EA]) can be employed with little or no associated physical destruction. This function encompasses the fires associated with a number of tasks, missions, and processes, including:

(1) **Conduct joint targeting.** This is the process of selecting and prioritizing targets and matching the appropriate response to them, taking account of command objectives, operational requirements, and capabilities.

(2) **Provide joint fire support.** This task includes joint fires that assist joint forces to move, maneuver, and control territory, populations, airspace, and key waters.

(3) **Countering air and missile threats.** This task integrates offensive and defensive operations and capabilities to attain and maintain a desired degree of air superiority and force protection. These operations are designed to destroy or negate enemy aircraft and missiles, both before and after launch.

(4) **Interdict enemy capabilities.** Interdiction diverts, disrupts, delays, or destroys the enemy's military surface capabilities before they can be used effectively against friendly forces, or to otherwise achieve their objectives.

(5) **Conduct strategic attack.** This task includes offensive action against targets—whether military, political, economic, or other—which are selected specifically in order to achieve strategic objectives.

(6) **Employ IO Capabilities.** This task focuses on military actions involving the use of electronic warfare (EW) and military information support operations (MISO). It can involve targeting key leaders and influential groups to affect their decision-making processes.

(7) **Assess the results of employing fires.** This task includes assessing the effectiveness and performance of fires as well as their contribution to the larger operation or

objective. For more guidance on assessment, refer to paragraph 6, "Assessment," of Chapter II, "The Art of Joint Command."

b. **Key Considerations.** The following are key considerations associated with the above tasks.

(1) **Targeting** supports the process of linking the desired effects of fires to actions and tasks at the component level. Commanders and their staffs must consider strategic and operational objectives, the potential for fratricide and other undesired fires effects, and legal limitations (e.g., constraints and restraints) when making targeting decisions. Successful integration of IO considerations into the targeting process is important to mission accomplishment in many operations.

(a) **Oversight.** JFCs may task their staff to accomplish broad targeting oversight functions or may delegate the responsibility to a subordinate commander. **Typically, JFCs organize joint targeting coordination boards (JTCBs).** If the JFC so designates, a JTCB may be either an integrating center for this effort or a JFC-level review mechanism. In either case, it should be composed of representatives from the staff, all components and, if required, their subordinate units. The primary focus of the JTCB is to ensure target priorities, guidance, and the associated desired results link to the JFC's objectives. Briefings conducted at the JTCB should focus on ensuring that all components and applicable staff elements coordinate and synchronize targeting efforts with intelligence and operations.

(b) **Delegation of Joint Targeting Process Authority.** The JFC is responsible for all aspects of the targeting process, and may conduct joint targeting at the joint force HQ level or authorize a component commander to do so. The JFC normally appoints the deputy JFC or a component commander to chair the JTCB. When the JFC does not delegate targeting authority and does not establish a JTCB, the JFC performs this task at the joint force HQ with the assistance of the J-3. In this instance, the JFC may approve the formation within the J-3 of a joint fires element to provide recommendations to the J-3. The JFC ensures that this process is a joint effort involving applicable subordinate commands. Whoever the JFC authorizes to plan, coordinate, and deconflict joint targeting must possess or have access to a sufficient C2 infrastructure, adequate facilities, joint planning expertise, and appropriate intelligence.

For additional targeting guidance, refer to JP 3-60, Joint Targeting.

(c) **Air Apportionment.** In the context of joint fires, air apportionment is part of the targeting process. Air apportionment is how the JFACC ensures the weight of joint force air effort is consistent with the JFC's intent and objectives. After consulting with other component commanders, the JFACC recommends air apportionment to the JFC, who makes the air apportionment decision. The JFACC's rationale for the recommendation may include priority or percentage of effort based on the JFC's CONOPS, specific tasks for which air assets are essential, and other factors such as the component commanders' joint fires requirements. Following the JFC's air apportionment decision, the JFACC allocates and tasks the capabilities/forces made available.

For additional guidance on air apportionment, refer to JP 3-30, Command and Control for Joint Air Operations.

(2) **Joint fire support** includes joint fires that assist air, land, maritime, and SOF to move, maneuver, and control territory, populations, airspace, and key waters. Joint fire support may include, but is not limited to, fixed- and rotary-wing aircraft capabilities, naval surface fire support, artillery, mortars, rockets, and missiles, as well as nonlethal effects of some EA, space control operations, and other nonlethal capabilities. Integration and synchronization of joint fires and joint fire support with the fire and maneuver of the supported force are essential.

For additional guidance on joint fire support, refer to JP 3-09, Joint Fire Support.

(3) **Countering Air and Missile Threats**

(a) The JFC normally seeks to gain and maintain air superiority as quickly as possible to allow friendly forces to operate without prohibitive interference from adversary air threats. Air superiority is achieved through the counterair mission, which integrates both offensive counterair (OCA) and DCA operations from all components to counter the air and missile threat. These operations may use aircraft, surface-to-surface and surface-to-air missiles, artillery, SOF, ground forces, and EA. US military forces must be capable of countering the air and missile threat from initial force projection through redeployment of friendly forces. Missiles represent a particularly difficult and dangerous threat because of their proliferation, advances in missile technologies (perhaps coupled with WMD), and the often fleeting nature of adversary missile targets. Unmanned aircraft are a new challenge to US air defenses, as many systems have smaller radar cross sections and fly at much slower speeds than manned aircraft making them much harder to detect. Close coordination and synchronization between DCA and OCA operations to counter the missile threat is essential. DCA (both air and missile defense) is essential to the protection function described in paragraph 6, "Protection."

(b) **OCA** operations are the preferred method of countering theater air and missile threats. OCA consists of offensive measures to destroy, disrupt, or neutralize enemy aircraft, missiles, launch platforms, and their supporting structures and systems both before and after launch, but as close to the source as possible. Ideally, joint OCA operations will prevent the launch of, or destroy enemy aircraft and missiles and their supporting infrastructure prior to launch. OCA includes attack operations, fighter sweep, fighter escort, and suppression of enemy air defenses.

For additional guidance on air superiority and countering air and missile threats, refer to JP 3-01, Countering Air and Missile Threats.

(4) **Interdiction**

(a) Interdiction is a powerful tool for JFCs. Interdiction operations are actions to divert, disrupt, delay, or destroy the enemy's military surface capability before it can be used effectively against friendly forces, or to otherwise achieve objectives. Air interdiction is conducted at such distance from friendly forces that detailed integration of each air mission with the fire and movement of friendly forces is not required. The JFC is responsible for the planning and synchronization of the overall interdiction effort in the assigned operational area. The JFACC normally is the supported commander for the JFC's overall air interdiction effort, while JFLCCs and JFMCCs are supported commanders for interdiction in their AOs.

(b) At the direction of appropriate authorities, forces engaged in homeland defense (HD) or defense support of civil authorities (DSCA) may perform interdiction against specific targets. For example, military forces also provide DSCA to US departments or agencies responsible for domestic law enforcement interdiction activities when requested and approved by SecDef or the President. These activities include actions to divert, disrupt, delay, intercept, board, detain, or destroy, as appropriate, suspect vessels, vehicles, aircraft, people, and cargo. Federal law and DOD policy impose limitations on the types of support that the US military may provide and what type of military mission (e.g., HD or DSCA) is being conducted.

See DODD 5525.5, DOD Cooperation with Civilian Law Enforcement Officials, *for more information on DSCA to domestic law enforcement interdiction activities.*

(c) Many elements of the joint force can conduct interdiction operations. Air, land, maritime, and SOF can conduct interdiction operations as part of their larger or overall mission. For example, naval expeditionary forces charged with seizing and securing a lodgment along a coast may include the interdiction of opposing land and maritime forces inside the amphibious objective area (AOA) as part of the overall amphibious plan.

(d) JFCs may choose to employ interdiction as a principal means to achieve an objective (with other components supporting the component leading the interdiction effort). For example, one of the JFC's objectives associated with the seize initiative phase of an operation might be to prevent the enemy's navy from interfering with friendly force sea transit through a choke point in the operational area. The JFC might task the JFACC to accomplish this through an interdiction effort supported by SOF. Interdiction during warfighting is not limited to any particular region of the operational area, but generally is conducted forward of or at a distance from friendly surface forces. Likewise, military interdiction that supports HD is guided and restricted by domestic law to a greater extent than other interdiction. Joint interdiction can be planned to create tactical, operational-level, or strategic advantages for the joint force, with corresponding adverse effects on the enemy. Interdiction deep in the enemy's rear area can have broad operational effects; however, deep interdiction may have a delayed effect on land, maritime, and selected SO. Interdiction closer to land, maritime, and joint SOF will have more immediate operational and tactical effects. Thus, JFCs vary the emphasis upon interdiction operations and surface maneuvers, depending on the strategic and operational situation confronting them.

(e) Counter threat finance (CTF) incorporates efforts to interdict money that funds terrorism, illegal narcotics networks, weapons proliferation, espionage, and other activities that generate revenue through trafficking networks. Illicit finance networks represent a critical vulnerability of state and non-state adversaries threatening US national security. Employing CTF activities are the means to detect, counter, contain, disrupt, deter,

> **AIR INTERDICTION DURING OPERATION IRAQI FREEDOM**
>
> During Operation IRAQI FREEDOM, most of the effort against Iraqi ground troops was focused on Republican Guard divisions and on a handful of stalwart regular divisions that formed part of the defensive ring south of Baghdad.
>
> One prominent air interdiction success story involved the Iraqi Republican Guard's redeployment of elements of the Hammurabi, Nebuchadnezzar, and Al Nida divisions after 25 March 2003 to the south of Baghdad toward Karbala, Hillah, and Al Cut. Their road movements were steadily bombed by US Air Force A-10s and B-52s (dropping 500-pound bombs) and British Tornados. An Iraqi commander concluded that their movement south had been one of the Iraqi regime's major errors because it exposed the Republican Guard to coalition air power and resulted in large casualty figures.
>
> **SOURCE: Project on Defense Alternatives Briefing Memo #30**
> **Carl Conetta, 26 September 2003**

or dismantle these illicit financial networks. Monitoring, assessing, analyzing, and exploiting financial information are key support functions for CTF activities.

For more guidance on joint interdiction operations, refer to JP 3-03, Joint Interdiction.

(5) **Strategic Attack.** A strategic attack is a JFC-directed offensive action against a target—whether military, diplomatic, economic, or other—that is specifically selected to achieve national or military strategic objectives. The JFC should consider conducting strategic attacks, when feasible. These attacks seek to weaken the adversary's ability or will to engage in conflict or continue an action and as such, could be part of a campaign, major operation, or conducted independently as directed by the President or SecDef. Additionally, these attacks may achieve strategic objectives without necessarily having to achieve operational objectives as a precondition. Suitable targets may include but are not limited to enemy strategic COGs. All components of a joint force may have capabilities to conduct strategic attacks.

(6) **IO Capabilities in Support of Fires**

(a) **CNA** disrupts, denies, degrades, or destroys information resident in computers and computer networks (relying on the data stream to execute the attack), or the computers and networks themselves.

(b) **EA** involves the use of electromagnetic (EM) energy, directed energy, or antiradiation weapons to attack personnel, facilities, or equipment with the intent of degrading, neutralizing, or destroying adversary combat capability. The effects of EA can be lethal or nonlethal. EA can be used against a computer when the attack occurs through the electromagnetic spectrum (EMS), while CNA attacks using the data stream through the network or by physical destruction. Integration and synchronization of EA with maneuver, C2, and other joint fires are essential.

(c) **MISO.** MISO convey selected information and indicators to foreign audiences to influence their emotions, motives, and objective reasoning, and ultimately induce or reinforce foreign attitudes and behavior favorable to the originator's objectives. MISO provide a nonlethal capability to craft messages using a variety of print, audio, audio-visual, and electronic media, which can then be delivered by air, land, and sea-based means or through cyberspace to select target audiences. MISO have strategic, operational, and tactical applications and must be considered early in planning to ensure maximum effectiveness. MISO are central to the achievement of objectives, so the JFC should address the approval authorities for MISO during planning to ensure integration and unity of effort between MISO, civil support (CS), and supporting IO.

For additional guidance on EA, refer to JP 3-13.1, Electronic Warfare.

For additional guidance on MISO, refer to JP 3-13.2, Military Information Support Operations. *MISO support to non-US military is outlined in DODD S-3321-1,* Overt Psychological Operations Conducted by the Military Services in Peacetime and in Contingencies Short of Declared War (U).

(7) **Limiting Collateral Damage.** Collateral damage is an important consideration at all levels of command. Collateral damage is unintentional or incidental injury or damage to persons or objects that would not be lawful military targets based on the operational limitations existing at the time and does not violate the law of war so long as it is not excessive in relation to the concrete and direct military advantage anticipated from the attack. Under the law of war, the balancing of military necessity in relation to collateral damage is known as the principle of *proportionality*. Limiting collateral damage will not only reduce the requirement to address civilian claims but may help better support friendly and HN actions to influence the population and reduce the magnitude of stability operations required.

(8) **Nonlethal Capabilities.** Nonlethal capabilities can generate effects that limit collateral damage, reduce risk to civilians, and may reduce opportunities for adversary propaganda. They may also reduce the number of casualties associated with excessive use of force, limit reconstruction costs, and maintain the good will of the local populace.

5. Movement and Maneuver

a. This function encompasses the disposition of joint forces to conduct operations by securing positional advantages before or during combat operations and by exploiting tactical success to achieve operational and strategic objectives. This function includes moving or deploying forces into an operational area and maneuvering them to operational depths for offensive and defensive purposes. It also includes assuring the mobility of friendly forces. The **movement and maneuver function** encompasses a number of tasks including:

(1) Deploy, shift, regroup, or move joint and/or component force formations within the operational area by any means or mode (i.e., air, land, or sea).

Chapter III

(2) Maneuver joint forces to achieve a position of advantage over an enemy.

(3) Provide mobility for joint forces to facilitate their movement and maneuver without delays caused by terrain or obstacles.

(4) Delay, channel, or stop movement and maneuver by enemy formations. This includes operations that employ obstacles (i.e., countermobility), enforce sanctions and embargoes, and conduct blockades.

(5) Control significant areas in the operational area whose possession or control provides either side an operational advantage.

b. **Movement to Attain Operational Reach**

(1) Forces, sometimes limited to those that are forward-deployed or even multinational forces formed specifically for the task at hand, can be positioned within operational reach of enemy COGs or decisive points to achieve decisive force at the appropriate time and place. *Operational reach* is the distance and duration across which a joint force can successfully employ its military capabilities. At other times, mobilization and deployment processes can be called up to begin the movement of reinforcing forces from the continental United States (CONUS) or other theaters to redress any unfavorable balance of forces and to achieve decisive force at the appropriate time and place. Alert may come with little or no notice.

(2) JFCs must carefully consider the movement of forces and whether to recommend the formation and or movement of multinational forces. At times, movement of forces can contribute to the escalation of tension, while at other times its deterrent effect can reduce those tensions. Movement of forces may deter adversary aggression or movement.

For more information on deployment process, refer to JP 3-35, Deployment and Redeployment Operations.

c. **Maneuver is the employment of forces in the operational area through movement in combination with fires to achieve a position of advantage in respect to the enemy.** Maneuver of forces relative to enemy COGs can be key to the JFC's mission accomplishment. Through maneuver, the JFC can concentrate forces at decisive points to achieve surprise, psychological effects, and physical momentum. Maneuver also may enable or exploit the effects of massed or precision fires.

(1) The principal purpose of maneuver is to place the enemy at a disadvantage through the flexible application of movement and fires. The goal of maneuver is to render opponents incapable of resisting by shattering their morale and physical cohesion (i.e., their ability to fight as an effective, coordinated whole) by moving to a point of advantage to deliver a decisive blow. This may be achieved by attacking enemy forces and controlling territory, airspace, populations, key waters, and LOCs through air, land, and maritime maneuvers.

(2) There are multiple ways to attain positional advantage. A naval expeditionary force with airpower, cruise missiles, and amphibious assault capability, within operational reach of an enemy's COG, has positional advantage. In like manner, land and air expeditionary forces that are within operational reach of an enemy's COG and have the means and opportunity to strike and maneuver on such a COG also have positional advantage. Maintaining full-spectrum superiority contributes to positional advantage by facilitating freedom of action. See Chapter V, "Joint Operations Across the Range of Military Operations," paragraph 14.f, "Full-Spectrum Superiority."

(3) At all levels of war, successful maneuver requires not only fire and movement but also agility and versatility of thought, plans, operations, and organizations. It requires designating and then, if necessary, shifting the main effort and applying the principles of mass and economy of force.

(a) At the strategic level, deploying units to and positioning units within an operational area are forms of maneuver if such movements seek to gain positional advantage. Strategic maneuver should place forces in position to begin the phases or major operations of a campaign.

(b) At the operational level, maneuver is a means by which JFCs set the terms of battle by time and location, decline battle, or exploit existing situations. Operational maneuver usually takes large forces from a base of operations to an area where they are in position to achieve operational objectives. The objective for operational maneuver is usually a COG or decisive point.

(4) JFCs should consider various ways and means to help maneuver forces attain positional advantage. For example, SOF may expose vulnerabilities through special reconnaissance and attack the enemy at tactical, operational, and strategic levels through direct action or using indigenous or surrogate forces. Additionally, the planning of CA and use of an effective IO program may minimize civilian interference with operations as well as the impact of military operations on the populace.

6. Protection

a. The protection function focuses on preserving the joint force's fighting potential in four primary ways. One way uses active defensive measures that protect the joint force, its information, its bases, necessary infrastructure, and LOCs from an enemy attack. Another way uses passive defensive measures that make friendly forces, systems, and facilities difficult to locate, strike, and destroy. Equally important is the application of technology and procedures to reduce the risk of fratricide. Finally, emergency management and response reduce the loss of personnel and capabilities due to accidents, health threats, and natural disasters. **As the JFC's mission requires,** the protection function also extends beyond force protection to encompass protection of US noncombatants; the forces, systems, and civil infrastructure of friendly nations; and interorganizational partners. Protection capabilities apply domestically in the context of HD, CS, and emergency preparedness.

b. The **protection function** encompasses a number of tasks, including:

Chapter III

(1) Providing air, space, and missile defense.

(2) Protecting US civilians.

(3) Providing physical security for forces and means.

(4) Conducting defensive countermeasure operations, including counterdeception and counterpropaganda operations and operations to counter-improvised explosive devices (C-IEDs).

(5) Providing chemical, biological, radiological, and nuclear (CBRN) defense.

(6) Conducting OPSEC, CND, information assurance (IA), defensive EA, and electronic protection activities.

(7) Securing and protecting forces, bases, JSAs, and LOCs.

(8) Conducting personnel recovery (PR) operations.

(9) Mitigating the effects of CBRN threats and hazards through WMD consequence management.

(10) Establishing antiterrorism programs.

(11) Establishing capabilities and measures to prevent fratricide.

(12) Providing emergency management and response capabilities and services.

c. Protection considerations affect planning in every joint operation. **Campaigns and major operations** involve large-scale combat against a capable enemy. These operations typically will require the full range of protection tasks, thereby complicating both planning and execution. Although the operational area and joint force may be smaller for a **crisis response or limited contingency operation,** the mission can still be complex and dangerous, thus requiring a variety of protection considerations. Permissive environments associated with **military engagement, security cooperation, and deterrence** still require that commanders and their staffs consider protection measures commensurate with potential risks. These risks may include a wide range of threats such as terrorism, criminal enterprises, environmental threats/hazards, and CNAs. Thus continuous research and access to accurate, detailed information about the operational environment along with realistic training can enhance protection activities.

d. **Force protection** includes preventive measures taken to prevent or mitigate hostile actions **against DOD** personnel (to include family members), resources, facilities, and critical information. These actions preserve the force's fighting potential so it can be applied at the decisive time and place and incorporate integrated and synchronized offensive and defensive measures that enable the effective employment of the joint force while degrading opportunities for the adversary. Force protection does not include actions to defeat the enemy or protect against accidents, weather, or disease. Force health protection (FHP) complements force protection efforts by promoting, improving, preserving, or restoring the mental or physical well being of Service members. Force protection is achieved through the tailored selection and application of multilayered active and passive measures commensurate with the level of risk. Intelligence sources provide information regarding an adversary's capabilities against personnel and resources, as well as information regarding force protection considerations. Foreign and domestic law enforcement agencies can contribute to force protection through the prevention, detection, response, and investigation of crime, and by sharing information on criminal and terrorist organizations.

e. **Key Considerations**

(1) **Security of forces and means** enhances force protection by identifying and reducing friendly vulnerability to hostile acts, influence, or surprise. Security operations protect forces, bases, JSAs, and LOCs. Physical security includes physical measures designed to safeguard personnel; to prevent unauthorized access to equipment, installations, material, and documents; and to safeguard them against espionage, sabotage, damage, and theft. The physical security process includes determining vulnerabilities to known threats; applying appropriate deterrent, control, and denial safeguarding techniques and measures; and responding to changing conditions. Functions in physical security include facility security, law enforcement, guard and patrol operations, special land and maritime security areas, and other physical security operations like military working dog operations or emergency and disaster response support. Measures include fencing and perimeter stand-off areas, land or maritime force patrols, lighting and sensors, vehicle barriers, blast protection, intrusion detection systems and electronic surveillance, and access control devices and systems. Physical security measures, like any defense, should be overlapping and deployed in depth.

For additional guidance on physical security measures, refer to JP 3-10, Joint Security Operations in Theater.

(2) **Defensive Counterair.** DCA encompasses active and passive measures for air and missile defense that contribute to force protection by detecting, identifying, intercepting, and destroying or negating enemy forces attempting to penetrate or attack through friendly airspace to include WMD delivery systems.

(a) **Active air and missile defense** includes all direct defensive actions taken to destroy, nullify, or reduce the effectiveness of hostile air and missile threats against friendly forces and assets. It includes the use of aircraft, air and missile defense weapons, EW, and other available weapons. Ideally, integration of systems will allow for a defense in depth, with potential for multiple engagements that increase the probability for success. Active air and missile defense recognizes both air defense and missile defense as unique and separate capabilities that are closely integrated. The JSA coordinator coordinates with the AADC to ensure that air and missile defense requirements for the JSA are integrated into air defense plans.

(b) **Passive air and missile defense** includes all measures, other than active air and missile defense, taken to minimize the effectiveness of hostile air and missile threats

Chapter III

against friendly forces and assets. These measures include camouflage, concealment, deception, dispersion, reconstitution, redundancy, detection and warning systems, and the use of protective construction.

For additional guidance on countering theater air and missile threats, refer to JP 3-01, Countering Air and Missile Threats.

(3) **Defensive use of IO** ensures timely, accurate, and relevant information access while denying adversaries opportunities to exploit friendly information and information systems for their own purposes.

(a) **OPSEC** is a process that identifies critical information to determine if friendly actions can be observed by enemy intelligence systems, denies critical information to the enemy, determines if information obtained by the enemy could be useful to them, and then executes selected measures that eliminate or reduce enemy exploitation of friendly critical information. Unlike security programs that seek to protect classified information, OPSEC measures identify, control, and protect generally unclassified evidence that is associated with sensitive operations and activities.

For additional guidance on OPSEC, refer to JP 3-13.3, Operations Security.

(b) **CND** includes actions taken to protect, monitor, analyze, detect, and respond to unauthorized activity within DOD information systems and computer networks.

(c) **IA** encompasses measures that protect and defend information and information systems by ensuring their availability, integrity, authentication, confidentiality, and nonrepudiation. IA incorporates protection, detection, response, restoration, and reaction capabilities and processes to shield and preserve information and information systems. IA for DOD information and information systems requires a defense-in-depth that integrates the capabilities of people, operations, and technology to establish multilayer and multidimensional protection to ensure survivability and mission accomplishment. IA must account for the possibility that access to DOD's information and information systems can be gained from outside of DOD's control.

(d) **Electronic protection** is that division of EW involving action taken to protect personnel, facilities, and equipment from any effects of friendly or enemy use of the EMS that degrade, neutralize, or destroy friendly combat capability.

(e) **Defensive EA** activities use the EMS to protect personnel, facilities, capabilities, and equipment. Examples include self-protection and force protection measures such as use of expendables (e.g., chaff and active decoys), jammers, towed decoys, directed energy infrared countermeasure systems, and counter radio-controlled improvised explosive device (IED) systems.

(4) **Personnel Recovery.** PR missions use military, diplomatic, and civil efforts to recover and reintegrate isolated personnel. There are five PR tasks (report, locate, support, recover, and reintegrate) necessary to achieve a complete and coordinated recovery of US military personnel, DOD civilians, DOD contractors, and others designated by the President

or SecDef. JFCs should consider all individual, component, joint, and interorganizational partner capabilities available when planning and executing PR missions.

For further guidance on PR, refer to JP 3-50, Personnel Recovery.

(5) **CBRN Defense.** Preparation for potential enemy use of CBRN weapons is integral to any planning effort. Even when an adversary does not possess traditional CBRN materiel or weapons regarded as WMD, easy access to materials such as radiation sources and toxic industrial chemicals represents a significant planning consideration. The result of a CBRN attack may not be to achieve traditional military objectives, but instead have strategic, operational, psychological, economic, and political impacts. CBRN defense focuses on avoiding CBRN hazards (contamination), protecting individuals and units from CBRN hazards, and decontamination in order to restore operational capability. Effective CBRN defense may also deter enemy WMD use by contributing to the survivability of US forces.

For additional guidance on CBRN defense, refer to JP 3-11, Operations in Chemical, Biological, Radiological, and Nuclear (CBRN) Environments, *and JP 3-40,* Combating Weapons of Mass Destruction.

(6) **Antiterrorism** programs support force protection by establishing defensive measures that reduce the vulnerability of individuals and property to terrorist acts, to include limited response and containment by local military and civilian forces. These programs also include personal security and defensive measures to protect Service members, high-risk personnel, civilian employees, family members, DOD facilities, information, and equipment. Personal security measures consist of commonsense rules for the on- and off-duty conduct of every Service member. They also include employment of dedicated guard forces and use of individual protective equipment (IPE), hardened vehicles, hardened facilities, and duress alarms. Security of high-risk personnel safeguards designated individuals who, by virtue of their rank, assignment, symbolic value, location, or specific threat, are at a greater risk than the general population. Terrorist activity may be discouraged by varying the installation force protection posture through the use of a random antiterrorism measures program, which may include varying patrol routes; staffing guard posts and towers at irregular intervals; and conducting vehicle and vessel inspections, personnel searches, and identification checks on a set but unpredictable pattern. To be effective, these measures should be highly visible to any hostile elements conducting surveillance.

For additional guidance on antiterrorism, refer to JP 3-07.2, Antiterrorism.

(7) The intent of **combat identification (CID)** is to accurately distinguish enemy objects and forces in the operational environment from others to support engagement decisions. Effective CID supports force protection and enhances operations by providing confidence throughout the force in the accuracy of CID characterizations. Effective CID procedures help minimize fratricide and collateral damage.

(a) Depending on operational requirements, CID characterization may be limited to, "friend," "enemy/hostile," "neutral," or "unknown." In some situations, additional characterizations may be required including, but not limited to, class, type,

Chapter III

nationality, and mission configuration. CID characterizations, when applied with ROE, enable engagement decisions concerning use or prohibition of lethal weapons and nonlethal capabilities.

(b) The staff should develop CID procedures early during planning. These procedures must be consistent with ROE and should not interfere with the ability of a unit or individual to engage enemy forces. When developing the JFC's CID procedures, important considerations include the missions, capabilities, and limitations of all participants including interorganizational partners.

For additional guidance on CID, refer to JP 3-09, Joint Fire Support.

(8) **Force Health Protection.** FHP complements force protection efforts, and includes all measures taken by the JFC and the Military Health System to promote, improve, and preserve the well-being of Service members. FHP measures focus on the prevention of illness and injury. The JFC must ensure adequate capabilities are available to identify health threats and implement appropriate FHP measures. **Health threats** are a composite of ongoing or potential enemy actions; occupational, environmental, geographical, and meteorological conditions; endemic diseases; and the employment of chemical, biological, radiological, nuclear, and high-yield explosives (CBRNE) that can reduce the effectiveness of military forces. Therefore, a robust **health surveillance system** is essential to FHP measures. *Health surveillance* includes identifying the population at risk; identifying and assessing hazardous exposures; employing specific countermeasures to eliminate or mitigate exposures; and monitoring and reporting battle injury, disease, and non-battle injury trends and other health outcomes. Occupational and environmental health surveillance enhances the joint force's ability to limit all categories of injuries including combat and operational stress exposure to CBRNE hazards.

For further guidance on FHP, refer to JP 4-02, Health Service Support.

(9) **Critical infrastructure protection** programs support the identification and mitigation of vulnerabilities to defense critical infrastructure, which includes DOD and non-DOD domestic and foreign infrastructures essential to plan, mobilize, deploy, execute, and sustain US military operations on a global basis. Coordination between DOD entities and other USG departments and agencies, state and local governments, the private sector, and equivalent foreign entities, is key in effective protection of critical assets controlled both by DOD and private entities. Vulnerabilities found in defense critical infrastructure shall be remediated and/or mitigated based on risk management decisions made by responsible authorities. These vulnerability mitigation decisions should be made using all available program areas, including antiterrorism, MILDEC, OPSEC, and force protection.

(10) **Counter-Improvised Explosive Device Operations.** C-IED operations are the collective efforts at all levels to neutralize the IED threat to friendly forces and civilians. They are conducted as an integral part of the broader joint operation and include measures taken to neutralize the infrastructure supporting the production and employment of IEDs; technical exploitation of the device to obtain information to support targeting and improve

Joint Functions

friendly force protection measures; and the development of tactics, techniques, and procedures to counter the IED threat at the tactical level.

For further guidance on C-IED, refer to JP 3-15.1, Counter-Improvised Explosive Device Operations.

7. Sustainment

a. **Sustainment** is the provision of logistics and personnel services necessary to maintain and prolong operations through mission accomplishment and redeployment of the force. Sustainment provides the JFC with the means to enable freedom of action and endurance and the ability to extend operational reach. Effective sustainment determines the depth to which the joint force can conduct decisive operations, allowing the JFC to seize, retain, and exploit the initiative. The ultimate goal is for logistics planners to develop a feasible, supportable, and efficient concept of logistic support and to be able to identify risks to the execution of the CONOPS. Prior to the development of contingency plans, CCMDs develop logistic planning products that are part of the CCMD's TCP.

(1) **Logistics** is planning and executing the movement and support of forces. It includes those aspects of military operations that deal with:

(a) The design and development, acquisition, storage, movement, distribution, maintenance, evacuation, and disposition of material.

(b) Movement, evacuation, and hospitalization of personnel.

(c) Acquisition or construction, maintenance, operation, and disposition of facilities.

(d) Acquisition or furnishing of services.

(2) Logistics concerns the integration of strategic, operational, and tactical support efforts within the theater, while scheduling the mobilization and movement of forces and materiel to support the JFC's CONOPS. The relative combat power that military forces can generate against an adversary is constrained by a nation's capability to plan for, gain access to, and deliver forces and materiel to required points of application. **Logistics covers the following core capabilities:** supply, maintenance operations, deployment and distribution, health service support (HSS), logistic services, engineering, and operational contract support.

(3) **Personnel services** are those sustainment functions provided to personnel rather than to systems and equipment. Personnel services complement logistics by planning for and coordinating efforts that provide and sustain personnel during joint operations. These services include the following:

(a) Human resources support.

(b) Religious ministry support.

(c) Financial management.

(d) Legal support.

b. JFCs should identify sustainment capabilities early in planning for an operation. Sustainment should be a priority consideration when the timed-phased force and deployment data list is built. Sustainment provides JFCs with flexibility to develop any required branches and sequels and to refocus joint force efforts as required.

c. The **sustainment function** encompasses a number of tasks including:

(1) Coordinating the supply of food, fuel, arms, munitions, and equipment.

(2) Providing for maintenance of equipment.

(3) Coordinating and providing support for forces, including field services, personnel services support, HSS, mortuary affairs, religious ministry support, postal support, morale, welfare and recreational support, financial support, and legal services.

(4) Building and maintaining sustainment bases.

(5) Assessing, repairing, and maintaining infrastructure.

(6) Acquiring, managing, and distributing funds.

(7) Providing common-user logistics support to OGAs, IGOs, NGOs, and other nations.

(8) Establishing and coordinating movement services.

(9) Establishing large-scale detention compounds and sustaining enduring detainee operations.

For further guidance on logistic support, refer to JP 4-0, Joint Logistics. *For further guidance on personnel services, refer to JP 1-0,* Joint Personnel Support. *For further guidance on legal support, refer to JP 1-04,* Legal Support to Military Operations. *For further guidance on religious affairs, refer to JP 1-05,* Religious Affairs in Joint Operations. *For further guidance on financial management support, refer to JP 1-06,* Financial Management Support in Joint Operations.

d. **Key Considerations**

(1) **Employment of Logistic Forces.** For some operations, logistic forces may be employed in quantities disproportionate to their normal military roles, and in nonstandard tasks. Further, logistic forces may precede other military forces or may be the only forces deployed. Logistic forces also may continue to support interorganizational partners after the departure of combat forces. In such cases, they must be familiar with and adhere to applicable status-of-forces agreements and acquisition and cross-servicing agreements to

Joint Functions

which the United States is a party. Given the potential complexity of operational environments, logistic forces must be familiar with and adhere to legal, regulatory, and political restraints governing US involvement because of the specialized nature and unique authorities in operations such as disaster relief and humanitarian assistance. Logistic forces, like all other forces, must be capable of self-defense, particularly if they deploy alone or in advance of other military forces.

(2) **Facilities.** JFCs need to plan for the early acquisition (leasing) of real estate and facilities for force and logistic bases where temporary occupancy is planned and/or the HN provides inadequate or no property. Early negotiation for facilities can be critical to the successful flow of forces.

(3) **Environmental Considerations.** Environmental considerations are broader than just protection of the environment and environmental stewardship. They also include continuously integrating the FHP, CMO, and other more operationally focused environmental considerations that affect US military forces and objectives. Military operations do not generally focus on environmental compliance and environmental protection, but JFCs are responsible for protecting the environment in which US military forces operate to the greatest extent possible consistent with operational requirements. Commanders comply with the command guidance on environmental considerations specified in the OPLAN or OPORD and included in unit SOPs. Environmental considerations link directly to risk management and the safety and health of Service members. All significant risks must be clearly and accurately communicated to deploying DOD personnel and the chain of command. Environmental considerations, risk management, and health risk communications are enabling elements for the commander and are an essential part of military planning, training, and operations. While complete protection of the environment during military operations may not always be possible, careful planning should address environmental considerations in joint operations, to include legal aspects.

For additional guidance on environmental considerations, refer to JP 3-34, Joint Engineer Operations.

(4) **Health Service Support.** HSS provides services to promote, improve, preserve, or restore the behavioral or physical well-being of personnel. HSS includes, but is not limited to, the management of health services resources, such as manpower, monies, and facilities; preventive and curative health measures; evacuation of the sick, wounded, or injured; selection of the medically fit and disposition of the medically unfit; blood management; medical supply, equipment, and maintenance thereof; combat and operational stress control; and medical, dental, veterinary, laboratory, optometric, nutrition therapy, and medical intelligence services. CCDRs are responsible for HSS of forces assigned or attached to their command and should establish HSS policies and programs accordingly.

(a) **Actions to obtain health threat information** begin prior to deployment and are continually updated as forces are deployed. Disease and injury occurrences can quickly affect combat effectiveness and may adversely affect the success of a mission and can have a greater impact on operations when the forces employed are small independent units.

(b) The **early introduction of preventive medicine personnel** or units into theater helps protect US forces from diseases and injuries. It also permits a thorough assessment of the health threat to and operational requirements of the mission. Preventive medicine support includes education and training on personal hygiene and field sanitation, personal protective measures, epidemiological investigations, pest management, and inspection of water sources and supplies. For maximum effectiveness, preventive medicine needs to be provided to as many as possible within the operational area. In addition to US forces, as much as possible, include multinational forces, HN civilians, and dislocated civilians. JFCs and joint force surgeons must be aware of any legal constraints unique to the operational environment and intended recipient of services. Issues such as eligibility of beneficiaries, reimbursement for supplies used and manpower expended, and provisions of legal agreements and other laws applicable to the theater must be reviewed.

(c) **Medical and rehabilitative care** provides essential care in the operational area and rapid evacuation to definitive care facilities without sacrificing quality of care. It encompasses care provided from the point of illness or injury through rehabilitative care.

For further guidance on HSS, refer to JP 4-02, Health Service Support. For further guidance on procedures for deployment health activities, refer to DOD Instruction 6490.03, Deployment Health.

(5) **Host-Nation Support (HNS).** HNS requires interaction with the HN government to establish procedures for requesting support and negotiating support terms. Logistic planners should analyze the capability of the HN economy to supplement the logistic support that US or multinational forces require and exercise care to limit adverse effects on the HN economy. Accordingly, early mission analysis must consider distribution requirements. This should be a collaborative analysis with all HN providers, which will support a systems analysis for designated focus areas when they are established. The assessment must include airfields, seaports, rail and road networks, particularly those in underdeveloped countries where their status is questionable. Delay in completing the assessment directly affects the flow of strategic lift assets into the region. Additional support forces may be required to build or improve the supporting infrastructure to facilitate follow-on force closure as well as the delivery of humanitarian cargo.

(6) **Operational Contract Support.** Logistic support requirements are often met through contracts with commercial entities inside and outside the operational area. Most joint operations will require a level of contracted support, and certain contracted items or services could be essential to deploying, sustaining, and redeploying joint forces effectively. Operational contract support generally covers three types of contracts: theater support, external support, and system support. *Theater support contracts* are those with local vendors, and processed through in-theater Service or joint contingency contracting offices. *External support contracts* include the Services' civil augmentation programs such as the Army's Logistics Civil Augmentation Program, the Air Force Contract Augmentation Program, and the Navy's Global Contingency Construction Contract program as well as other logistic and combat support contracts processed through authorities outside the theater. *System support contracts* are those awarded by program management offices that provide technical support to newly fielded systems or, in some cases, life-cycle systems support. In

all operations, contracted support must be properly planned, integrated, coordinated, and managed to ensure accurate, timely, and effective support to the deployed joint force.

For more detailed information and guidance on contracting, refer to JP 4-10, Operational Contract Support.

(7) **Disposal Operations.** Disposal is an important link in the logistic chain. Disposal is a consideration throughout planning and execution, and until forces redeploy. Inadequate understanding of disposal operations may cause violations of public and international law, confusion over roles and requirements, increased costs, inefficient operations, and negative health implications. Defense Logistics Agency support to the CCDR's component commands includes the capability to receive and dispose of materiel in a theater. The Defense Reutilization and Marketing Service element in theater establishes theater-specific procedures for the reuse, demilitarization, or disposal of facilities, equipment, and supplies, to include hazardous materiel and waste.

(8) **Legal Support.** Legal support is important across all joint functions. Many decisions and actions have potential legal implications. The JFC's staff judge advocate (SJA) provides the full spectrum of legal support through direct and reachback capability. A key member of the JFC's personal staff, the SJA provides legal advice on the laws, regulations, policies, treaties, and agreements that affect joint operations. Legal advisors actively participate in the planning process from mission analysis to execution, an essential function given the complexity of the operational environment. Legal advisors provide support on fiscal activities, operational limitations, international law, and many other factors that can affect operations. Further, the JFC should integrate HN legal personnel into the command legal staff as soon as practical to provide guidance on unique HN domestic legal practices and customs.

For more detailed information and guidance on legal support, refer to JP 1-04, Legal Support to Military Operations.

(9) **Financial management** encompasses the two core processes of resource management and finance support. The joint force comptroller is the officer responsible for providing the elements of finance operations. The resource management process normally consists of costing functions and the effort to leverage appropriate fund sources. Finance operations provide the necessary funds to conduct contracting and limited pay support. The joint force comptroller's management of these elements provides the JFC with many necessary capabilities, from contracting and banking support to cost capturing and fund control. Financial management support for contracting, subsistence, billeting, transportation, communications, labor, and a myriad of other supplies and services, particularly in distant, austere environments, can be necessary for successful mission accomplishment.

For more detailed information and guidance on financial management support, refer to JP 1-06, Financial Management Support in Joint Operations.

Intentionally Blank

CHAPTER IV
ORGANIZING FOR JOINT OPERATIONS

> *"US military power today is unsurpassed on the land and sea and in the air, space, and cyberspace. The individual Services have evolved capabilities and competencies to maximize their effectiveness in their respective domains. Even more important, the ability to integrate these diverse capabilities into a joint whole that is greater than the sum of the Service parts is an unassailable American strategic advantage."*
>
> **Admiral M.G. Mullen**
> **Chairman of the Joint Chiefs of Staff**
> **Capstone Concept for Joint Operations, January 2009**

1. Introduction

Organizing for joint operations involves many considerations. Most can be associated in three primary groups related to *organizing the joint force, organizing the joint force headquarters*, and *organizing operational areas* to help control operations. Understanding the operational environment helps the JFC understand factors that may affect decisions in each of these areas.

2. Understanding the Operational Environment

a. **General.** Factors that affect joint operations extend far beyond the boundaries of the JFC's assigned operational area. The JFC's *operational environment* is the composite of the conditions, circumstances, and influences that affect employment of capabilities and bear on the decisions of the commander (see Figure IV-2). It encompasses physical areas and factors (of the air, land, maritime, and space domains) and the information environment (which includes cyberspace). **Included within these are enemy, friendly, and neutral systems that are relevant to a specific joint operation.** The nature and interaction of these systems will affect how the commander plans, organizes for, and conducts joint operations.

b. **Physical Areas and Factors**

(1) **Physical Areas.** The pertinent physical areas in the operational environment include the assigned *operational area* and the associated *area of influence* and *area of interest*. Designation of the areas of influence and interest help orient commanders and staffs to relevant physical locations during both planning and execution.

(a) An *operational area* is an overarching term encompassing more descriptive terms for geographic areas in which military operations are conducted. Operational areas include, but are not limited to, such descriptors as AOR, theater of war, theater of operations, JOA, AOA, joint special operations area (JSOA), and AO.

(b) An **area of influence** is a geographical area wherein a commander is directly capable of influencing operations by maneuver or fire support systems normally under the commander's command or control. The area of influence normally surrounds and includes the assigned operational area. The extent of a subordinate command's area of influence is one factor the higher commander considers when defining the subordinate's operational area. Understanding the command's area of influence helps the commander and staff plan branches to the current operation that could require the force to employ capabilities outside the assigned operational area. The commander can describe the area of influence graphically, but the resulting graphic does not represent a boundary for operations or other control measure for maneuver or fire support.

(c) An **area of interest** is that area of concern to the commander, including the area of influence, areas adjacent thereto, and extending into enemy territory to the objectives of current or planned operations if those objectives are not currently within the assigned operational area. This area also includes areas occupied by forces or other factors that could jeopardize the accomplishment of the mission. An area of interest serves to focus ISR support for monitoring enemy, adversary, or other activities outside the operational area that may affect current and future operations. The commander can describe this area graphically, but the resulting graphic does not represent a boundary for operations or other control measure for maneuver or fire support.

(2) **Physical Factors.** The JFC and staff must consider many factors associated with operations in the air, land, maritime, and space domains, and the information environment (which includes cyberspace). These factors include terrain (including urban settings), weather, topography, hydrology, EMS, and other environmental conditions in the operational area; distances associated with the deployment to the operational area and employment of joint capabilities; the location of bases, ports, and other supporting infrastructure; and both friendly and enemy forces and other capabilities. Combinations of these factors greatly affect operations and sustainment.

c. **Information Environment.** The information environment is a global environment composed of all individuals, organizations, and systems that collect, process, disseminate, or act on information.

(1) The information environment is where humans and automated systems observe, orient, decide, and act upon information, and is therefore the principal environment of decision making. This environment is pervasive to all activities worldwide and to the air, land, maritime, and space domains of the JFC's operational environment. The actors in the information environment include military and civilian leaders, decision makers, individuals, and organizations. Resources include the information itself and the materials and systems employed to process, store, display, disseminate, and protect information and produce information-related products.

(2) *Cyberspace* is a global domain within the information environment. It consists of the interdependent network of information technology infrastructures, including the Internet, telecommunications networks, computer systems, and embedded processors and controllers.

Organizing for Joint Operations

(3) *Cyberspace operations* employ cyberspace capabilities primarily to achieve objectives in or through cyberspace. Such operations include computer NETOPS and activities to operate and defend DOD information networks.

For more information on the information environment, refer to JP 3-13, Information Operations.

d. **Visualizing the Operational Environment**

(1) Figure IV-1 illustrates a notional operational environment for a joint force that is conducting operations within a GCC's AOR. Planners have depicted an area of influence. It is not a boundary, but it represents the reach of the joint force's capabilities. Figure IV-1 also shows the area of interest, which includes an enemy mechanized force that is located outside the theater of operations, but close enough to influence the JFC's operations at some point in time.

(2) The purpose of Figure IV-1 is to help visualize the scope of an operation environment, although it normally would not be depicted in graphic form. Within this notional operations environment is a forward base the GCC established outside the JOA. There also is a CONUS installation, which could represent any of the myriad supporting

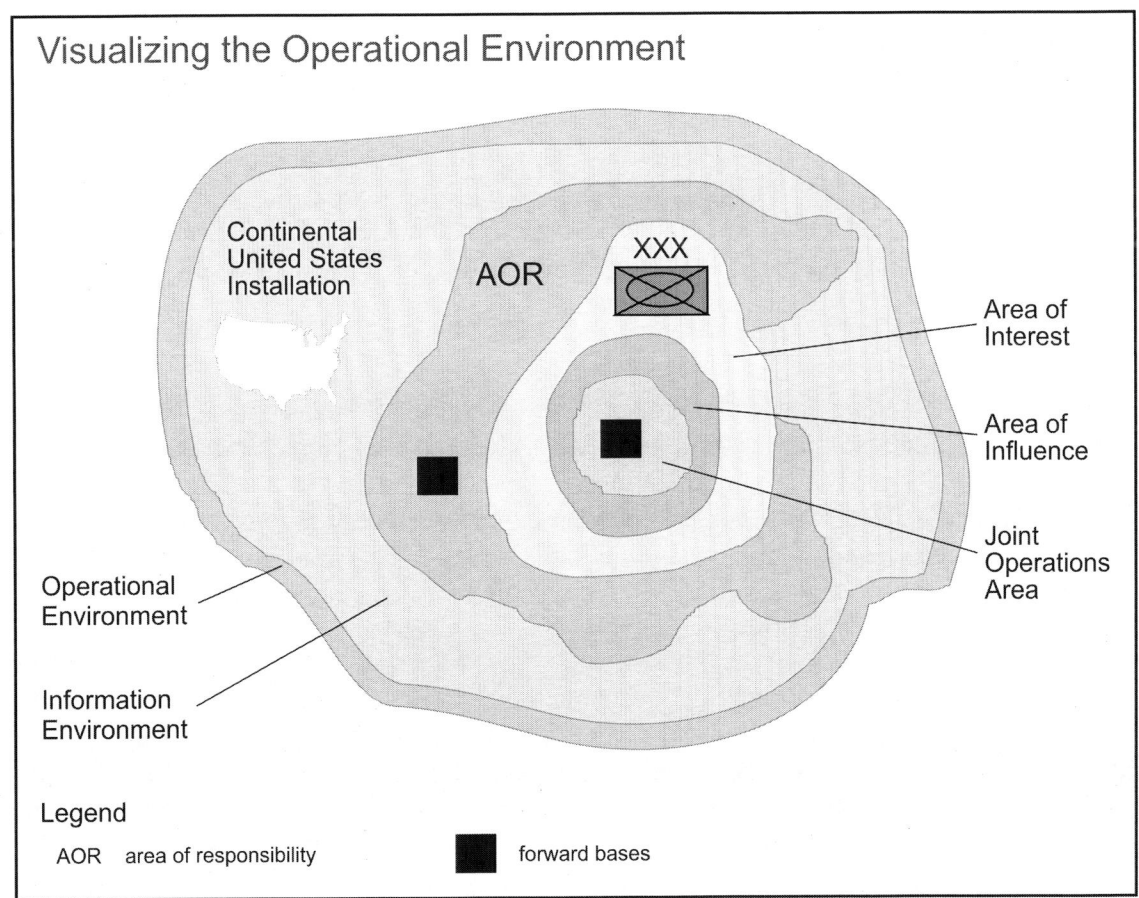

Figure IV-1. Visualizing the Operational Environment

Chapter IV

capabilities outside the AOR that are crucial to successful joint operations. These capabilities typically reside at USG facilities such as military reservations, installations, bases, posts, camps, stations, arsenals, vessels/ships, or laboratories, which support joint functions such as C2, intelligence, and sustainment. Although DOD installations normally lie outside the designated operational area and area of influence, they are part of the JFC's operational environment. For example, the JFC requires force visibility throughout deployment to the completion of reception, staging, onward movement, integration, and redeployment. DOD installations provide support to deployed forces until they return. The ability to receive support from DOD installations can reduce the size of the forward deployed force. To a significant degree, events occurring at DOD installations affect the morale and performance of deployed forces. Thus, the JFC's operational environment encompasses all "home station" installation functions, including family programs. Although not depicted in Figure IV-1, the operational environment also includes a wide variety of intangible factors such as the culture, perceptions, beliefs, and values of enemy, adversary, neutral, or friendly political and social systems.

e. **A Systems Perspective**

(1) A **system** is a functionally, physically, and/or behaviorally related group of regularly interacting or interdependent elements forming a unified whole. One way to think of the operational environment is as a set of complex and constantly interacting political, military, economic, social, information, and infrastructure (PMESII), and other systems as Figure IV-2 depicts. The nature and interaction of these systems will affect how the commander plans, organizes for, and conducts joint operations. The JFC's interorganizational partners routinely focus on systems other than military (political, economic, etc.), so the JFC and staff must understand these systems and how military operations affect them. Equally important is understanding how elements in other PMESII systems can help or hinder the JFC's mission. A commonly shared understanding among partners in the operation can help influence actions beyond the JFC's directive authority and promote a unified, comprehensive approach to achieve objectives.

(2) A systems understanding of the operational environment typically will require cross-functional participation by other joint force staff elements and collaboration with various intelligence organizations, USG departments and agencies, and nongovernmental centers that possess relevant expertise. The JFC must consider the best way to manage or support this cross-functional effort. The J-2 is the staff lead for this effort as part of JIPOE. A variety of factors, including planning time available, will affect the fidelity of a systems perspective.

(3) Understanding PMESII systems, their interaction with each other, and how system relationships will change over time will increase the JFC's knowledge of how actions within a system can affect other system components. Among other benefits, this perspective helps intelligence analysts identify potential sources from which to gain indications and warning, and facilitates understanding the continuous and complex interaction of friendly, adversary, and neutral systems. A systems understanding also supports operational design by enhancing elements such as COGs, LOOs, and decisive

Organizing for Joint Operations

points. For example, Figure IV-2 depicts notional operational and strategic COGs (there could be more). It shows each as a sub-system composed of related nodes and clarifies that the two COGs are related by a common node. This helps commanders and their staffs visualize and design a broad approach to mission accomplishment early in the planning process, which makes detailed planning more efficient.

For further guidance on developing a systems perspective as part of JIPOE, refer to JP 2-01.3, Joint Intelligence Preparation of the Operational Environment. *For further guidance on the use of a systems perspective in operational design and joint operation planning, refer to JP 5-0,* Joint Operation Planning.

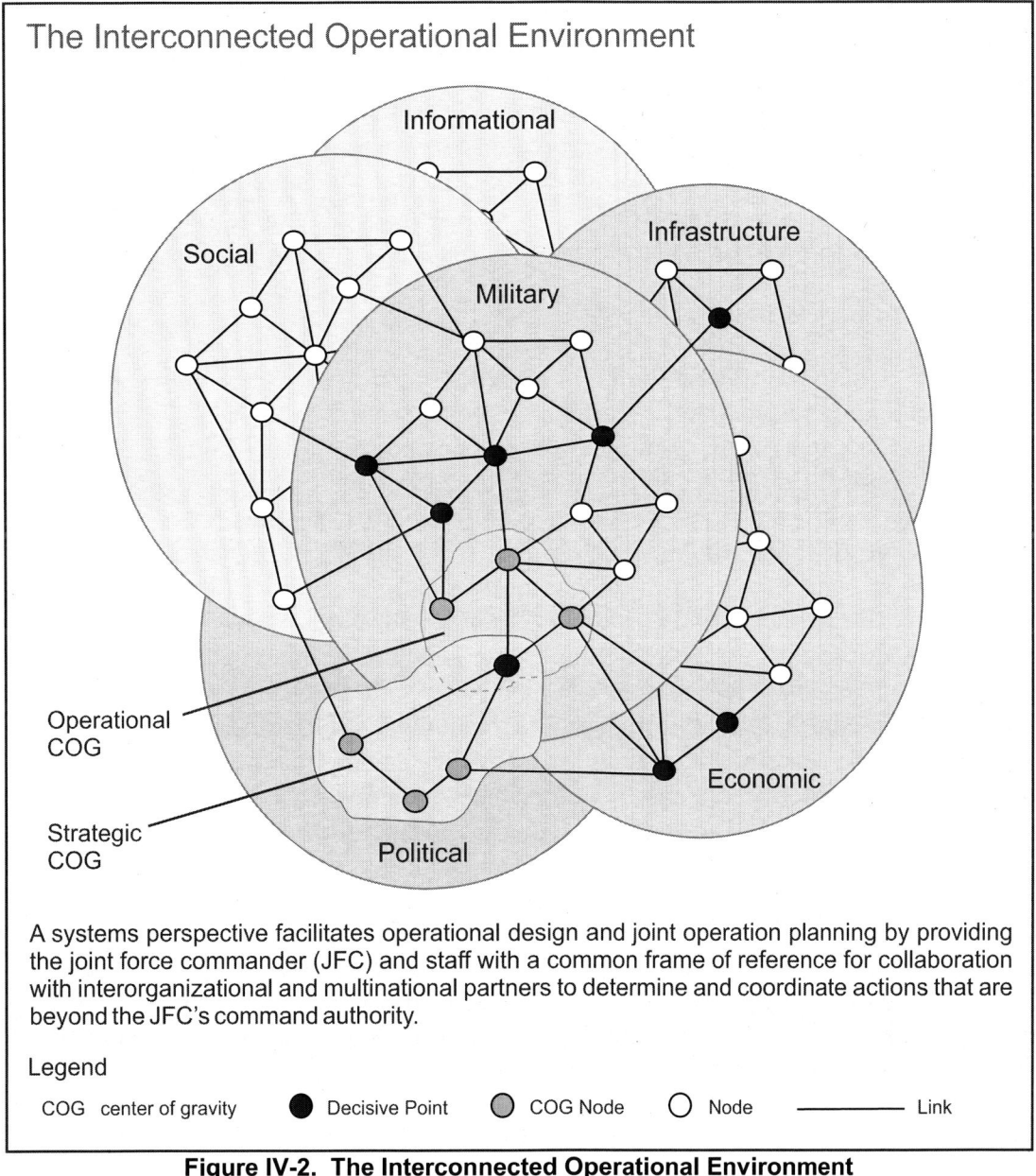

Figure IV-2. The Interconnected Operational Environment

IV-5

Chapter IV

3. Organizing the Joint Force

a. **General.** How JFCs organize their assigned or attached forces directly affects the responsiveness and versatility of joint operations. **The first principle in joint force organization is that JFCs organize forces to accomplish the mission based on their intent and CONOPS.** Unity of command, centralized planning and direction, and decentralized execution are key considerations. Joint forces can be established on a **geographic or functional basis.** JFCs may elect to centralize selected functions within the joint force, but should avoid reducing the versatility, responsiveness, and initiative of subordinate forces. JFCs should allow Service and SOF tactical and operational forces, organizations, and capabilities to function generally as they were designed. All Service components contribute their distinct capabilities to joint operations; however, their interdependence is essential to overall joint effectiveness. Joint interdependence is the purposeful reliance by one Service on another Service's capabilities to maximize the complementary and reinforcing effects of both; the degree of interdependence varies with specific circumstances. When JFCs organize their forces, they should also consider interoperability with multinational forces and interaction with other potential interorganizational partners. Complex or unclear command relationships and organizations are counterproductive to synergy among multinational forces. Simplicity and clarity of expression are essential.

b. **Joint Force Options**

(1) **Combatant Commands.** A CCMD is a unified or specified command with a broad continuing mission under a single commander established and so designated by the President, through SecDef, and with the advice and assistance of the CJCS. **Unified commands** typically are established when a broad continuing mission exists requiring execution by significant forces of two or more Military Departments and necessitating single strategic direction and/or other criteria found in JP 1, *Doctrine for the Armed Forces of the United States*. **Specified commands** normally are composed of forces from one Military Department, but may include units and staff representation from other Military Departments. The UCP defines geographic AORs that are assigned to GCCs that include all associated land, water, and airspace. Other CCDRs (e.g., FCCs) execute assigned functional responsibilities such as deploying trained and ready joint forces, conducting global distribution operations, providing combat-ready SOF, or conducting space and cyberspace operations. Functionally oriented CCDRs operate across all geographical regions and normally provide supporting forces and capabilities to the GCCs. They also may conduct operations as a supported commander when directed by SecDef or the President.

(2) **Subordinate Unified Commands.** When authorized by SecDef through the CJCS, commanders of unified (not specified) commands may establish subordinate unified commands (also called subunified commands) to conduct operations on a continuing basis in accordance with the criteria set forth for unified commands. A subordinate unified command may be established on a geographic area or functional basis. Commanders of subordinate unified commands have functions and responsibilities similar to those of the commanders of unified commands and exercise OPCON of

assigned commands and forces and normally of attached forces within the assigned operational or functional area.

(3) **Joint Task Forces (JTFs).** A JTF is a joint force that is constituted and so designated by SecDef, a CCDR, a subordinate unified command commander, or an existing commander, joint task force (CJTF) to accomplish missions with specific, limited objectives and which do not require centralized control of logistics. However, there may be situations where a CJTF may require directive authority for common support capabilities delegated by the CCDR. JTFs may be established on a geographical area or functional basis. JTFs normally are established to achieve operational objectives. When direct participation by departments other than DOD is significant, the TF establishing authority may designate it as *a joint interagency task force*. This might typically occur when the other interagency partners have primacy and legal authority and the JFC provides supporting capabilities, such as disaster relief and humanitarian assistance. The proper authority dissolves a JTF when the JTF achieves the purpose for which it was created or is no longer required. There are several ways to form a JTF HQ. Normally, the CCMD's Service component HQ or the Service component's existing subordinate HQ (e.g., Army corps, numbered air force, numbered fleet and Marine expeditionary force) to convert themselves to JTF HQ. Also, the theater SO command or a subordinate SOF HQ with the requisite C2 capability can form the basis for a JTF HQ staff. CCDRs are responsible for verifying the readiness of assigned Service HQ staffs to establish, organize, and operate as a JTF-capable HQ. JTF HQ basing depends on the JTF mission, operational environment, and available capabilities and support. JTF HQ can be land- or sea-based with transitions between both basing options. JTFs are normally assigned a JOA.

COMMON OPERATING PRECEPT

Maintain operational and organizational flexibility.

---

(4) Forming the joint force HQ and task organizing the joint force prior to operations can be challenging, particularly in crisis action situations. During operations, the ability to quickly adjust both operations and organization in response to planned operational transitions or unexpected situational transitions is essential. For example, achieving combat-related objectives in the dominate phase of an operation much earlier than anticipated could require the JFC to shift emphasis and organization quickly to stability operations commonly associated with the stabilize (Phase IV), and enable civil authority (Phase V) phases.

For further guidance on the formation and employment of a JTF HQ to command and control a joint operation, refer to JP 3-33, Joint Task Force Headquarters.

c. **Component Options.** Regardless of the organizational and command arrangements within joint commands, **Service component commanders retain responsibility for certain Service-specific functions** and other matters affecting their

Chapter IV

forces, including internal administration, personnel support, training, logistics, and Service intelligence operations. Further, **functional and Service components of the joint force conduct supported, subordinate, and supporting operations, not independent campaigns.**

(1) **Service Components.** CCDRs and subordinate unified commanders conduct either single-Service or joint operations to accomplish a mission. All JFCs may conduct operations through their Service component commanders, lower-echelon Service force commanders, and/or functional component commanders. **Conducting joint operations through Service components has certain advantages, which include clear and uncomplicated command lines.** This arrangement is appropriate when stability, continuity, economy, ease of long-range planning, and scope of operations dictate organizational integrity of Service components. While sustainment remains a Service responsibility, there are exceptions such as arrangements described in Service support agreements, CCDR-directed common-user logistics lead Service, or DOD agency responsibilities.

(2) **Functional Components.** The JFC can establish functional component commands to conduct operations when forces from two or more Services must operate in the same physical domain or accomplish a distinct aspect of the assigned mission. These conditions apply when the scope of operations requires that the similar capabilities and functions of forces from more than one Service be directed toward closely related objectives and unity of command is a primary consideration. For example, functionally oriented components are useful when the scope of operations is large and the JFC's attention must be divided between major operations or phases of operations that are functionally dominated. Functional component commands are subordinate components of a joint force. Except for the JFSOCC/commander, joint special operations task force (JSOTF), functional components do not constitute a "joint force" with a JFC's authorities and responsibilities, even when composed of forces from two or more Military Departments.

(a) JFCs may conduct operations through functional components or employ them primarily to coordinate selected functions. The JFC will normally designate the Service component commander who has the preponderance of forces and the ability to command and control them as the functional component commander. However, the JFC will always consider the mission, nature and duration of the operation, force capabilities, and C2 capabilities when selecting a commander. The establishment of a functional component commander must not affect the command relationship between Service component commanders and the JFC.

(b) The functional component commander's staff composition should reflect the command's composition so that the staff has the required expertise to help the commander effectively employ the component's forces. Functional component staffs require advanced planning, appropriate training, and frequent exercises for efficient operations. Liaison elements from and to other components facilitate coordination and support. Staff billets and individuals to fill them should be identified and used when the commander forms the functional component staff for exercises and actual operations.

Organizing for Joint Operations

The number of staff personnel should be appropriate for the mission and nature of the operation. The staff structure should be flexible enough to add or delete personnel and capabilities in changing conditions without losing effectiveness.

(c) The JFC designates forces and/or military capabilities that will be made available for tasking by the functional component commander and the appropriate command relationship(s). JFCs also may establish a support relationship between components to facilitate operations. Regardless, the establishing JFC defines the authority and responsibilities of functional component commanders based on the CONOPS, and the JFC may alter their authority and responsibilities during the course of an operation.

(3) **Combination.** Joint forces often are organized with a combination of Service and functional components. For example, joint forces organized with Service components normally have SOF organized under a JFSOCC, while the conventional air forces will normally have a JFACC designated, whose authorities and responsibilities are defined by the establishing JFC based on the JFC's CONOPS.

d. **SOF Employment Options**

(1) Used independently with conventional force enable support or integrated with conventional forces, SOF provide additional and unique capabilities to achieve objectives that otherwise may not be attainable. SOF are most effective when SO are fully integrated into the overall plan, and the execution of SO is through proper SOF C2 elements employed intact.

(2) Commander, United States Special Operations Command (CDRUSSOCOM) is responsible for synchronizing planning for global operations against terrorist networks, and will do so in coordination with other CCMDs. When directed to execute global operations, CDRUSSOCOM can establish and employ JSOTFs as a supported commander.

(3) SOF in CONUS are under the COCOM of the CDRUSSOCOM. When directed, CDRUSSOCOM provides CONUS-based SOF to a GCC. The GCC normally exercises COCOM of assigned SOF and OPCON of attached SOF through a theater special operations command commander (a subunified commander). The GCC will define command relationships between the JSOTF commanders and JTF/TF commanders.

For more information on SO, refer to JP 3-05, Special Operations.

e. **Joint HQ Augmentation Options.** There are various options available to augment a joint HQ that is forming for joint operations.

For more information, see JP 3-33, Joint Task Force Headquarters.

IV-9

Chapter IV

4. Organizing the Joint Force Headquarters

a. Joint force HQ include those for unified, subunified, and specified commands and JTFs. While each HQ organizes to accommodate the nature of the JFC's operational area, mission, tasks, and preferences, all generally follow a traditional functional staff alignment (i.e., personnel, intelligence, operations, logistics, plans, and communications) depicted in Figure IV-3. The primary staff functional areas also are generally consistent with those at Service component HQ, which facilitates higher, lower, and lateral cross-command staff coordination and collaboration. Some HQ may combine functions under a staff principal, while other HQ may add staff principals.

b. Figure IV-3 also shows boards, centers, working groups, and other semipermanent and temporary organizations. These facilitate cross-functional coordination, synchronization, planning, and information sharing between principal staff directorates. Although these organizations are cross-functional in their membership, they typically fall under the oversight of a principal staff directorate. For example, the joint operations center aligns under the J-3, the joint intelligence support element under the J-2, and the joint media operations center under PA.

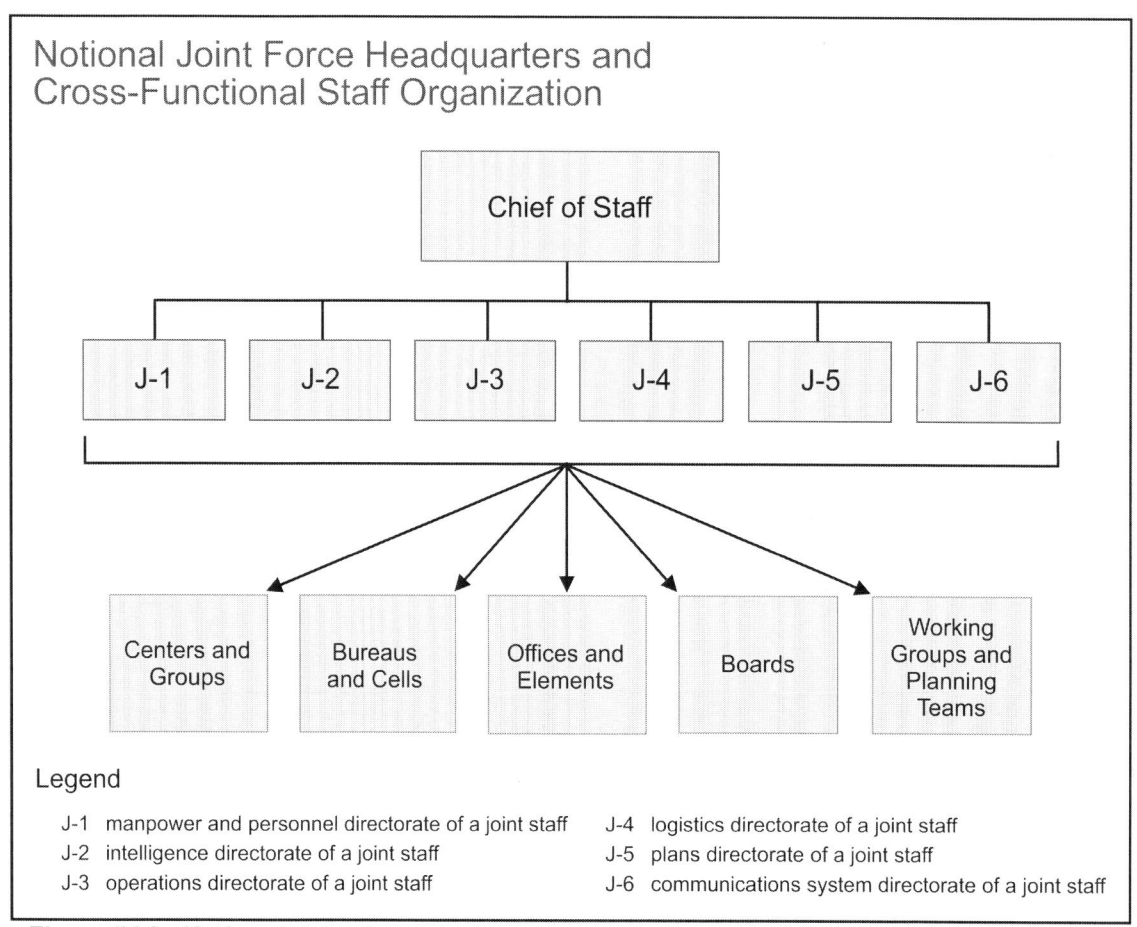

Figure IV-3. Notional Joint Force Headquarters and Cross-Functional Staff Organization

c. HQ also have personal and special staff sections or elements, which perform specialized duties as prescribed by JFC and handle special matters over which the JFC wishes to exercise personal control. Examples include the SJA, provost marshal, and inspector general.

For detailed guidance on the organization of a joint force HQ, refer to JP 3-33, Joint Task Force Headquarters.

5. Organizing Operational Areas

a. **General.** Except for AORs, which are assigned in the UCP, GCCs and other JFCs designate smaller operational areas (e.g., JOA and AO) on a temporary basis. Operational areas have physical dimensions comprised of some combination of air, land, maritime, and space domains. JFCs define these areas with geographical boundaries, which help commanders and staffs coordinate, integrate, and deconflict joint operations among joint force components and supporting commands. The size of these operational areas and the types of forces employed within them depend on the scope and nature of the mission and the projected duration of operations.

> **OPERATIONAL AREAS FOR OPERATION RESTORE HOPE**
>
> **During Operation RESTORE HOPE in Somalia, the joint forces rear area was centered around the separate sites of the embassy compound, port, and airfield in the city of Mogadishu, while its operational area was widely scattered around the towns and villages of the interior. The area of interest included the rest of the country and particularly those population and relief centers not under the joint force commander's supervision.**
>
> **Various Sources**

b. **Combatant Command-Level Areas.** GCCs conduct operations in their assigned AORs. When warranted, the President, SecDef, or GCCs may designate a theater of war and/or theater of operations for each operation (see Figure IV-4). GCCs can elect to control operations directly in these operational areas, or may establish subordinate joint forces for that purpose, while remaining focused on the broader AOR.

(1) **Area of Responsibility.** An AOR is an area established by the UCP that defines geographic responsibilities for a GCC. A GCC has authority to plan for operations within the AOR and conduct those operations approved by the President or SecDef. CCDRs may operate forces wherever required to accomplish approved missions. **All cross-AOR operations must be coordinated between the affected GCCs.**

(2) **Theater of War.** A theater of war is a geographical area established by the President, SecDef, or GCC for the conduct of major operations and campaigns involving combat. A theater of war is established primarily when there is a formal declaration of war or it is necessary to encompass more than one theater of operations (or a JOA and a

Chapter IV

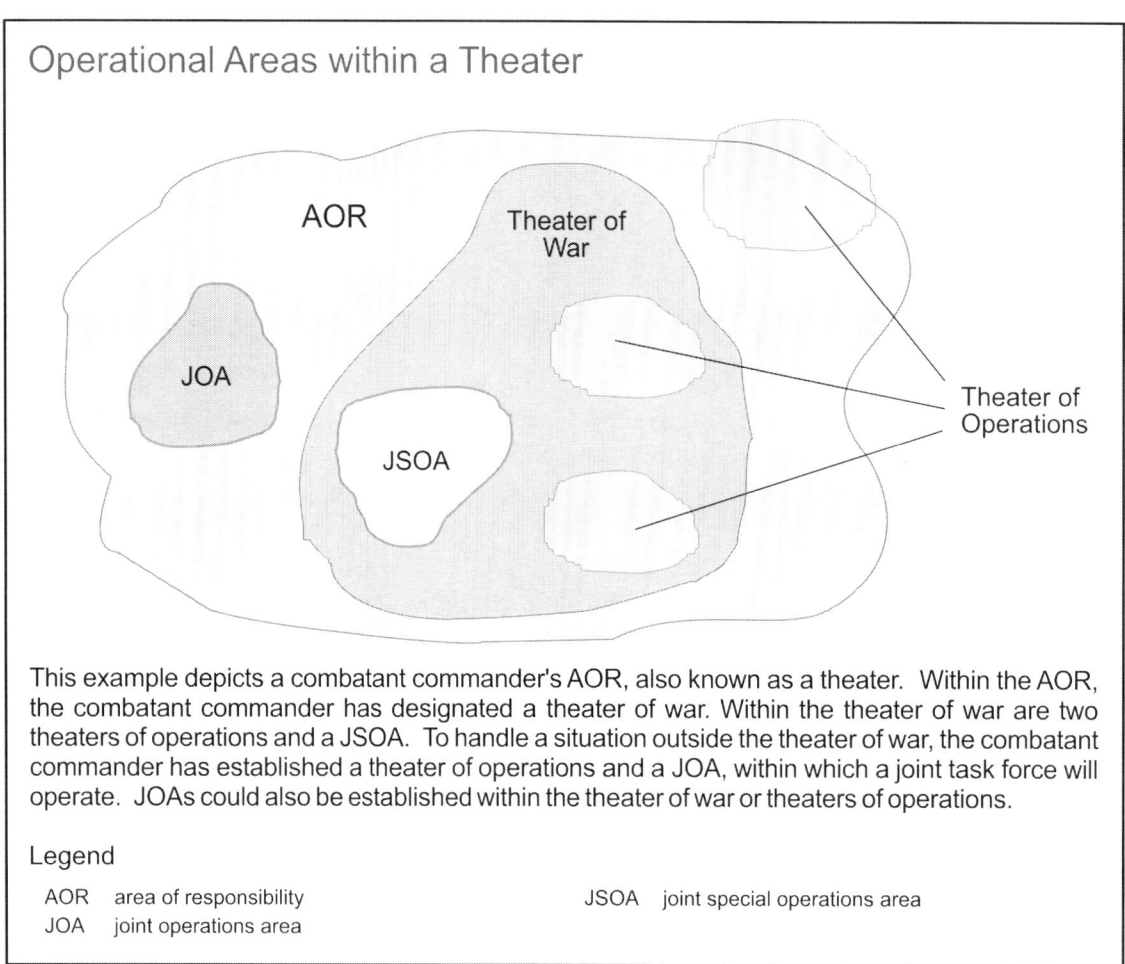

Figure IV-4. Operational Areas within a Theater

separate theater of operations) within a single boundary for the purposes of C2, sustainment, protection, or mutual support. A theater of war does not normally encompass a GCC's entire AOR, but may cross the boundaries of two or more AORs.

(3) **Theater of Operations.** A theater of operations is an operational area defined by the GCC for the conduct or support of specific military operations. A theater of operations is established primarily when the scope of the operation in time, space, purpose, and/or employed forces exceeds what a JOA can normally accommodate. More than one joint force HQ can exist in a theater of operations. A GCC may establish one or more theaters of operations. Different theaters will normally be focused on different missions. A theater of operations typically is smaller than a theater of war, but is large enough to allow for operations in depth and over extended periods of time. Theaters of operations are normally associated with major operations and campaigns and may cross the boundary of two AORs.

c. **Operational- and Tactical-Level Areas.** For operations somewhat limited in scope and duration, the commander can establish the following operational areas.

Organizing for Joint Operations

(1) **Joint Operations Area.** A JOA is an area of land, sea, and airspace, defined by a GCC or subordinate unified commander, in which a JFC (normally a CJTF) conducts military operations to accomplish a specific mission. JOAs are particularly useful when operations are limited in scope and geographic area or when operations are to be conducted on the boundaries between theaters.

(2) **Joint Special Operations Area.** A JSOA is an area of land, sea, and airspace assigned by a JFC to the commander of SOF to conduct SO activities. It may be limited in size to accommodate a discreet direct action mission or may be extensive enough to allow a continuing broad range of unconventional warfare operations. A JSOA is defined by a JFC who has geographic responsibilities. JFCs may use a JSOA to delineate and facilitate simultaneous conventional and SO. The JFSOCC is the supported commander within the JSOA.

For additional guidance on JSOAs, refer to JP 3-05, Special Operations.

(3) **Joint Security Area.** A JSA is a specific surface area, designated by the JFC as critical, that facilitates protection of joint bases and supports various aspects of joint operations such as LOCs, force projection, movement control, sustainment, C2, airbases/airfields, seaports, and other activities. JSAs are not necessarily contiguous with areas actively engaged in combat (see Figure IV-5). JSAs may include intermediate support bases and other support facilities intermixed with combat elements. JSAs may be used in both linear and nonlinear situations.

For additional guidance on JSAs, refer to JP 3-10, Joint Security Operations in Theater.

(4) **Amphibious Objective Area.** The AOA is a geographic area within which is located the objective(s) to be secured by the amphibious force. This area must be of sufficient size to ensure accomplishment of the amphibious force's mission and must provide sufficient area for conducting necessary sea, air, and land operations.

For additional guidance on AOAs, refer to JP 3-02, Amphibious Operations.

(5) **Area of Operations.** JFCs may define AOs for land and maritime forces. AOs typically do not encompass the entire operational area of the JFC, but should be large enough for component commanders to accomplish their missions and protect their forces. Component commanders with AOs typically designate subordinate AOs within which their subordinate forces operate. These commanders employ the full range of joint and Service control measures and graphics as coordinated with other component commanders and their representatives to delineate responsibilities, deconflict operations, and achieve unity of effort.

d. **Contiguous and Noncontiguous Operational Areas**

(1) Operational areas may be contiguous or noncontiguous (see Figure IV-5). When they are contiguous, a boundary separates them. When operational areas are noncontiguous, subordinate commands do not share a boundary. The higher HQ retains responsibility for the unassigned portion of its operational area.

Chapter IV

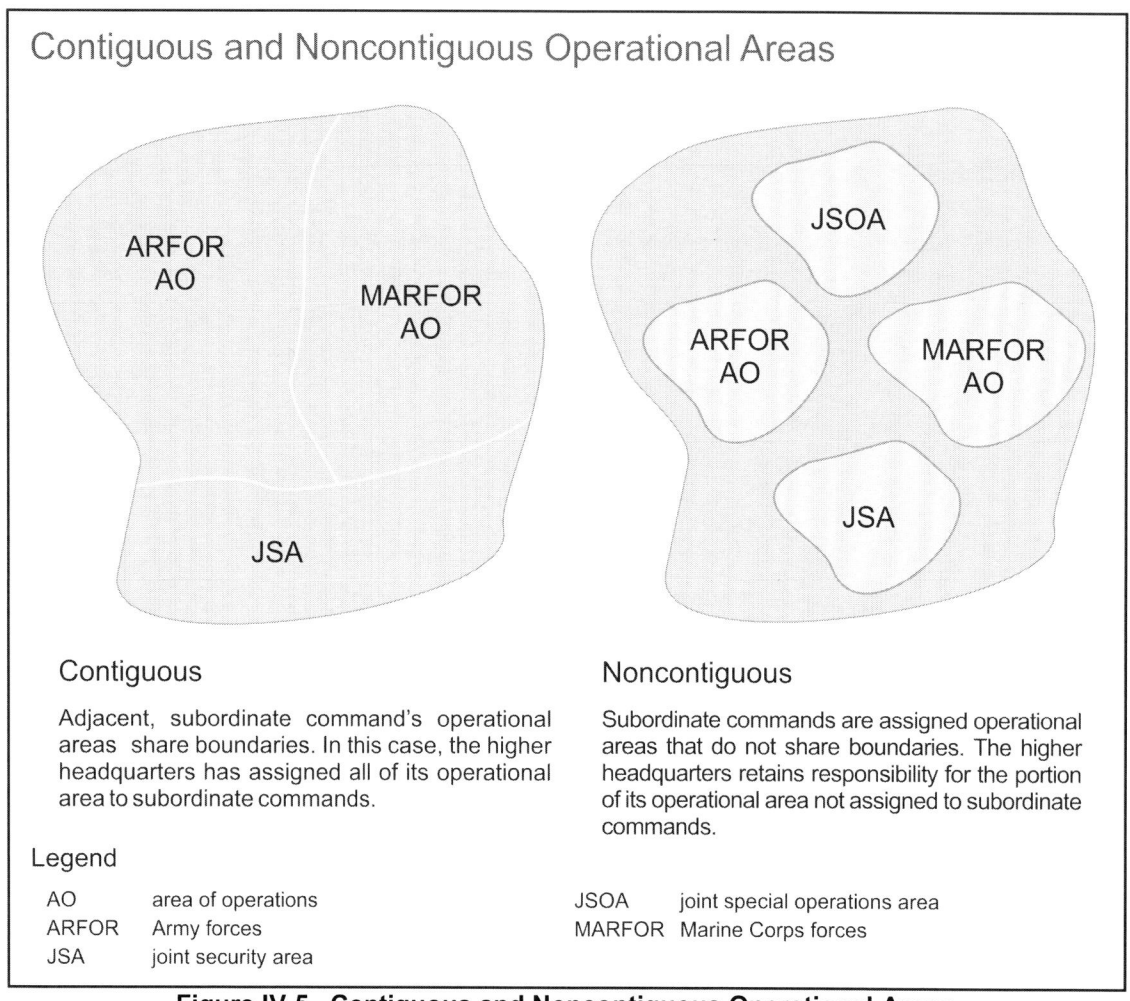

Figure IV-5. Contiguous and Noncontiguous Operational Areas

(2) In some operations, a Service or functional component (typically the ground component) could have such a large operational area that the component's subordinate units operate in a noncontiguous manner, widely distributed and beyond mutually supporting range of each other. In these cases, the JFC should consider options whereby joint capabilities can be pushed to lower levels and placed under control of units that can use them effectively.

e. **Considerations When Assuming Responsibility for an Operational Area.** The establishing commander should activate an assigned operational area at a specified date and time based on mission and situation considerations addressed during COA analysis and wargaming. Among others, common considerations include C2, the information environment, intelligence requirements, communications support, protection, security, LOCs, terrain management, movement control, airspace control, surveillance, reconnaissance, air and missile defense, PR, targeting and fires, interorganizational interactions, and environmental issues.

For specific guidance on assuming responsibility for an operational area, refer to JP 3-33, Joint Task Force Headquarters.

CHAPTER V
JOINT OPERATIONS ACROSS THE RANGE OF MILITARY OPERATIONS

> *"Today's US Armed Forces are, I believe, the most capable in our Nation's history, and these capabilities provide important strategic advantages with respect to nearly any situation or potential adversary. US forces can conduct operations on a scale that very few others can approach. Their ability to project and sustain military power over global distances is unmatched. US joint intelligence capabilities, a key factor in the success of practically any kind of military operation, are the best in the world."*
>
> **Admiral M. G. Mullen**
> Chairman of the Joint Chiefs of Staff
> Capstone Concept for Joint Operations, January 2009

1. Introduction

a. The range of military operations is another fundamental construct that provides context. Military operations vary in scope, purpose, and conflict intensity across a range that extends from military engagement, security cooperation, and deterrence activities to crisis response and limited contingency operations and, if necessary, to major operations and campaigns (Figure V-1). Use of joint capabilities in military engagement, security cooperation, and deterrence activities helps shape the operational environment and keep the day-to-day tensions between nations or groups below the threshold of armed conflict while maintaining US global influence. Many of the missions associated with crisis response and limited contingencies, such as CS and foreign humanitarian assistance (FHA), may not require combat. But others, as evidenced by Operation RESTORE

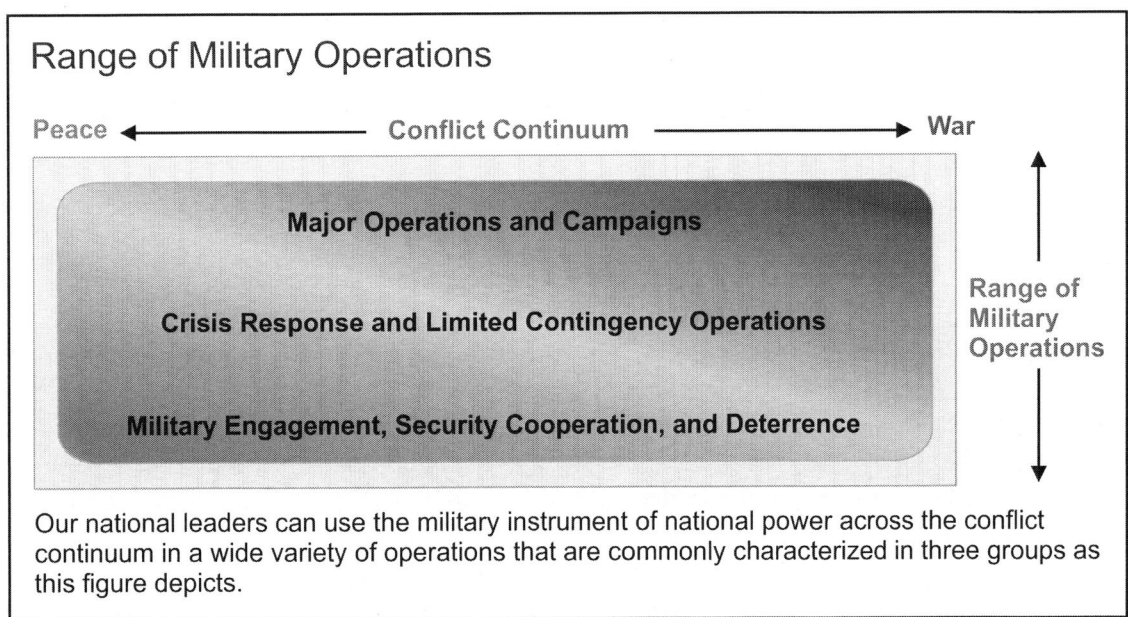

Figure V-1. Range of Military Operations

HOPE in Somalia, can be extremely dangerous and may require combat operations to protect US forces while accomplishing the mission. Individual major operations and campaigns often contribute to a larger, long-term effort (e.g., OEF). The nature of the strategic security environment may require US forces to engage in several types of joint operations simultaneously across the range of military operations. For these missions, commanders combine and sequence offensive, defensive, and stability operations and activities to achieve objectives. The commander for a particular operation determines the emphasis to be placed on each type of mission or activity. Although this publication discusses specific types of operations under the various categories in the range of military operations, each type is not doctrinally fixed and could shift within that range. For instance, a counterinsurgency operation could escalate from a security cooperation activity into a major operation or campaign.

(1) **Military Engagement, Security Cooperation, and Deterrence.** These ongoing activities establish, shape, maintain, and refine relations with other nations and domestic civil authorities (e.g., state governors or local law enforcement). The general strategic and operational objective is to **protect** US interests at home and abroad. See Section C, "Military Engagement, Security Cooperation, and Deterrence."

(2) **Crisis Response and Limited Contingency Operations.** A crisis response or limited contingency operation can be a single small-scale, limited-duration operation or a significant part of a major operation of extended duration involving combat. The associated general strategic and operational objectives are to **protect** US interests and/or **prevent** surprise attack or further conflict. See Section D, "Crisis Response and Limited Contingency Operations."

(3) **Major Operations and Campaigns.** When required to achieve national strategic objectives or protect national interests, the US national leadership may decide to conduct a major operation or campaign normally involving large-scale combat. During major operations, joint force actions are conducted simultaneously or sequentially in accordance with a common plan and are controlled by a single commander. A *campaign* is a series of related major operations aimed at achieving strategic and operational objectives within a given time and space. See Section E, "Major Operations and Campaigns."

b. **Simultaneous Nature of Theater Operations**

(1) **CCDR's can simultaneously conduct joint operations with different military end states within an AOR.** JFCs might initiate major operations and campaigns while security cooperation activities are ongoing in the same or another part of the theater (such as OEF during the enforcement of UN sanctions on Iraq). Further, a crisis response or limited contingency operation could occur separately or as part of a campaign or major operation (such as the 1991 noncombatant evacuation operation [NEO] in Somalia during Operation DESERT SHIELD). In the extreme, major operations or a theater campaign may occur within a theater concurrently with a separate or related global campaign (such as OEF and OIF). **CCDRs should pay particular attention to synchronizing and integrating the activities of assigned, attached, and**

supporting forces through subordinate and supporting JFCs to achieve national, theater, and/or multinational strategic objectives. Due to the transnational nature of various enemies or adversaries (e.g., insurgents, terrorists, drug cartels, pirates), coordination and synchronization requirements may also extend to adjacent GCCs. Additionally, **CCDRs and subordinate JFCs must work with US chiefs of mission, Department of State (DOS), and other departments and agencies** to best integrate military actions with the diplomatic, economic, and informational instruments of national power in unified action.

(2) **Some military operations may be conducted for one purpose.** FHA operations, for example, are military operations with a humanitarian purpose. A strike may be conducted for the specific purpose of compelling action or deterrence (such as Operation EL DORADO CANYON, the 1986 operation to coerce Libya to conform with international laws against terrorism). Often, however, **military operations will have multiple purposes and be influenced by a fluid and changing situation.** Branch and sequel events may require additional tasks by the joint force, challenging the command with multiple missions (e.g., Operations PROVIDE COMFORT and RESTORE HOPE were peace enforcement operations [PEO] that evolved from FHA efforts). Joint forces must strive to meet such challenges with clearly defined objectives addressing diverse purposes.

SECTION A. TYPES OF MILITARY OPERATIONS

2. Military Operations and Related Missions, Tasks, and Actions

a. In general, a military operation is a set of actions intended to accomplish a task or mission. Although the US military is organized, trained, and equipped for sustained, large-scale combat anywhere in the world, the capabilities to conduct these operations also enable a wide variety of other operations as well. No two military operations are exactly alike. Characterizing the employment of military capabilities (people, organizations, and equipment) as one or another type of military operations has several benefits. For example, publications can be developed that describe the nature, tasks, and tactics associated with specific types of diverse operations, such as noncombatant evacuation and counterinsurgency. These publications provide the bases for related joint training and joint professional military education that help joint forces conduct military operations as effectively and efficiently as possible even in difficult and dangerous circumstances. Characterizations also help military and civilian leaders explain US military involvement in various situations to the US and international public and news media in order to minimize misinterpretation of purpose. Likewise, such characterizations, supplemented by operational experience, can clarify the need for specific capabilities that enhance certain operations. For example, facial recognition software associated with biometric capabilities helps military and law enforcement personnel identify terrorists and piece together their human networks as part of combating terrorism (see JP 3-07.2, *Antiterrorism*). The titles of many operations (such as NEO) listed as "types" in the following paragraph describe the operation's focused task or mission. In some cases (such as *stability operations*), the title covers a variety of missions, tasks, and activities.

Chapter V

b. Following is a brief summary of examples of military operations. (See Figure V-2).

Examples of Military Operations

- Stability operations
- Civil support
- Foreign humanitarian assistance
- Recovery
- Noncombatant evacuation
- Peace operations
- Combating weapons of mass destruction
- Chemical, biological, radiological, and nuclear consequence management
- Foreign internal defense
- Counterdrug operations
- Combating terrorism
- Counterinsurgency
- Homeland defense

Figure V-2. Examples of Military Operations

(1) **Stability Operations.** Stability operations is an umbrella term for various military missions, tasks, and activities conducted outside the United States in coordination with other instruments of national power to maintain or reestablish a safe and secure environment and to provide essential governmental services, emergency infrastructure reconstruction, and humanitarian relief. (See JP 3-07, *Stability Operations*)

(2) **Civil Support.** DOD support to US civil authorities for domestic emergencies and for designated law enforcement and other activities. (See JP 3-28, *Civil Support*)

(3) **Foreign Humanitarian Assistance.** DOD activities, normally in support of the United States Agency for International Development or DOS, conducted outside the United States, its territories, and possessions to relieve or reduce human suffering, disease, hunger, or privation. (See JP 3-29, *Foreign Humanitarian Assistance*)

(4) **Recovery.** An operation to search for, locate, identify, recover, and return isolated personnel, human remains, sensitive equipment, or items critical to national security. (See JP 3-50, *Personnel Recovery*)

(5) **Noncombatant Evacuation.** An operation to evacuate noncombatants and civilians from foreign countries to safe havens or to the United States when their lives are endangered by war, civil unrest, or natural disaster. (See JP 3-68, *Noncombatant Evacuation Operations*)

(6) **Peace Operations (PO).** A category that encompasses operations to contain conflict, redress the peace, and shape the environment to support reconciliation and rebuilding and facilitate the transition to legitimate governance. PO include

peacekeeping operations (PKO), peace enforcement, peacemaking (PM), peace building (PB), and conflict prevention efforts. (See JP 3-07.3, *Peace Operations*)

(7) **Combating Weapons of Mass Destruction.** Activities within eight military mission areas that include WMD-related security cooperation and partner activities, offensive operations against WMD, defensive operations, and managing the consequences of WMD attacks. (See JP 3-40, *Combating Weapons of Mass Destruction*)

(8) **CBRN Consequence Management.** DOD support to USG actions that plan for, prepare for, respond to, and recover from the effects of domestic and foreign chemical, biological, radiological, and nuclear incidents. (See JP 3-41, *Chemical, Biological, Radiological, and Nuclear Consequence Management*)

(9) **Foreign Internal Defense (FID).** Participation by civilian and military agencies of a government in any of the action programs taken by another government or other designated organization to free and protect its society from subversion, lawlessness, insurgency, terrorism, and other threats to its security. FID is an example of nation assistance. (See JP 3-22, *Foreign Internal Defense*)

(10) **Counterdrug Operations.** Support provided by the DOD to law enforcement agencies to detect, monitor, and counter the production, trafficking, and use of illegal drugs. (See JP 3-07.4, *Joint Counterdrug Operations*)

(11) **Combating Terrorism.** Actions, including antiterrorism (defensive measures taken to reduce vulnerability to terrorist acts) and CT (actions taken directly against terrorist networks) to oppose terrorism. (See JP 3-07.2, *Antiterrorism*, and JP 3-26, *Counterterrorism*)

(12) **Counterinsurgency.** This is an operation that encompasses comprehensive civilian and military efforts taken to defeat an insurgency and to address any core grievances. (See JP 3-24, *Counterinsurgency Operations*)

(13) **Homeland Defense.** The protection of United States sovereignty, territory, domestic population, and critical defense infrastructure against external threats and aggression or other threats as directed by the President. (See JP 3-27, *Homeland Defense*)

SECTION B. A PHASING CONSTRUCT

3. Phasing a Joint Operation

a. **Purpose.** A phase is a definitive stage of an operation or campaign during which a large portion of the forces and capabilities are involved in similar or mutually supporting activities for a common purpose. Phasing, which can be used in any operation regardless of size, helps the JFC organize large operations by integrating and synchronizing subordinate operations. Phasing helps JFCs and staffs visualize, design, and plan the entire operation or campaign and define requirements in terms of forces, resources, time, space, and purpose. It helps them systematically achieve military

Chapter V

objectives that cannot be attained all at once by arranging smaller, related operations in a logical sequence. Phasing also helps commanders mitigate risk in the more dangerous or difficult portions of an operation.

b. **Application.** The JFC's vision of how the operation should unfold drives subsequent decisions regarding phasing. In turn, phasing helps the commander and staff synchronize the CONOPS and organize tasks assigned to subordinate commanders. By arranging operations and activities into phases, the JFC can better integrate and synchronize subordinate operations in time, space, and purpose. Each phase should represent a natural subdivision of the campaign/operation's intermediate objectives.

c. **Sequence, Level of Effort, and Overlap.** Figure V-3 shows OPLAN phases and the notional level of effort for each as the operation progresses. Working within this generic phasing construct, the actual phases will vary (e.g., compressed, expanded, or omitted entirely) according to the nature of the operation and the JFC's decisions. During planning, the JFC establishes conditions, objectives, or events for transitioning

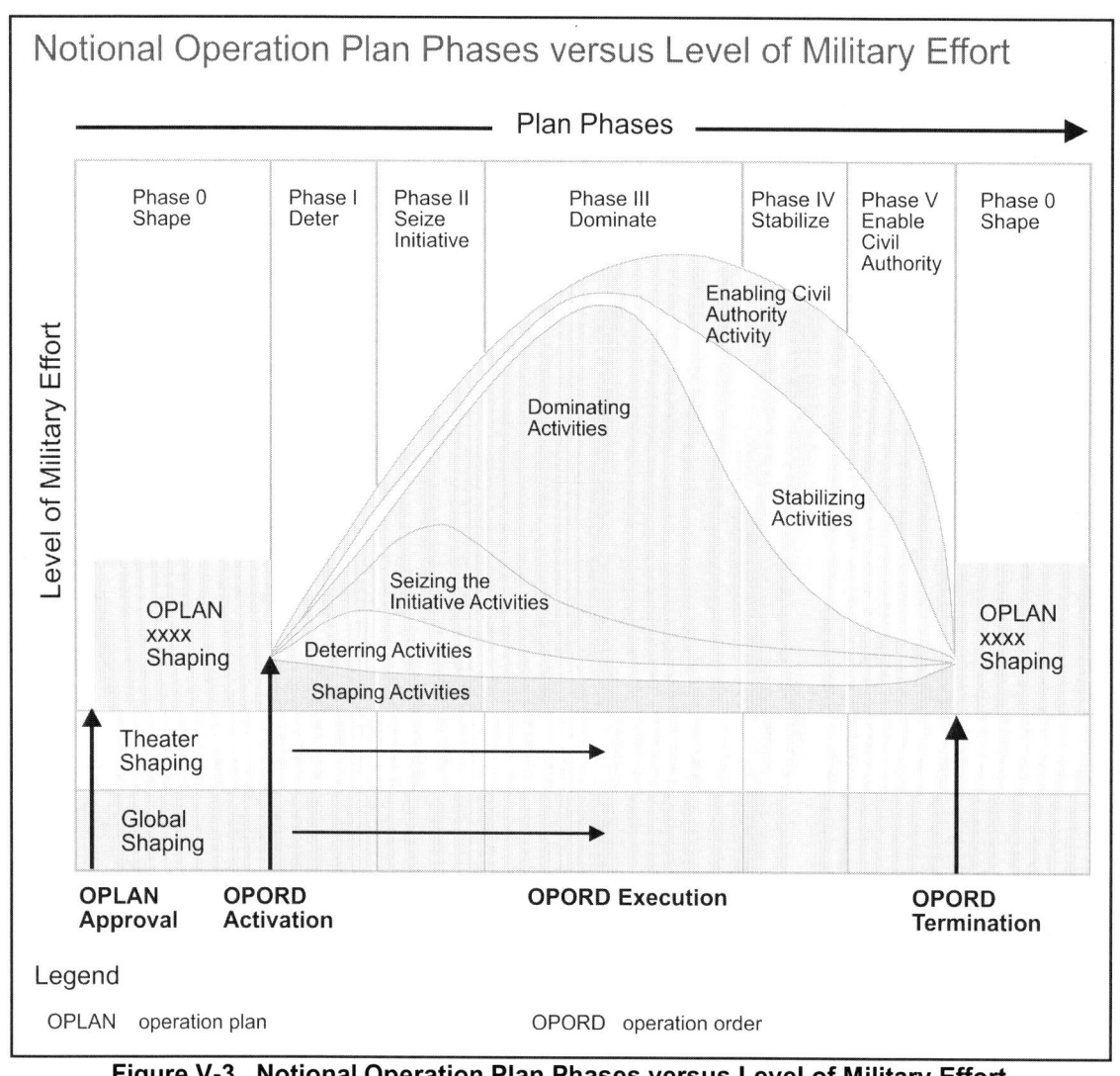

Figure V-3. Notional Operation Plan Phases versus Level of Military Effort

from one phase to another and plans sequels and branches for potential contingencies. Phases are designed to be conducted sequentially, but some activities from a phase may begin in a previous phase and continue into subsequent phases. The JFC adjusts the phases to exploit opportunities presented by the adversary and operational situation or to react to unforeseen conditions.

   d. **Transitions**

      (1) A *transition* marks a change of focus between phases or between the ongoing operations and execution of a branch or sequel. Transitions between phases are designed to be distinct shifts in focus of operations by the joint force, often accompanied by changes in command or support relationships and priorities of effort. They require planning and preparation well before their execution. The activities that predominate during a given phase, however, rarely align with neatly definable breakpoints. The need to move into another phase normally is identified by assessing that a set of objectives has been achieved or that the enemy has acted in a manner that requires a major change in focus for the joint force. Thus, the transition to a new phase is usually driven by events rather than time. An example is the shift of focus from sustained combat operations in the *dominate* phase to a preponderance of stability operations in the *stabilize* and *enable civil authority* phases. Through continuous assessment, the staff measures progress toward planned transitions so that the force prepares for and executes them.

      (2) Sometimes, however, the situation facing the JFC will undergo an unexpected change in conditions that is not necessarily associated with a planned transition, yet may require the JFC to direct an abrupt shift in operations. Such a change in conditions will rarely be uniform in time and space across an operational area, but can represent a critical period in the course of operations. The JFC must be able to recognize this fundamental transformation in the situation, and transition quickly and smoothly in response. Failure to do so can cause the joint force to lose momentum, miss an important opportunity, experience a significant setback, or even fail to accomplish the mission. Conversely, successful transition can allow the joint force to seize the initiative in a situation and garner disproportionately favorable results. The JFC must seek to anticipate potential situational transformations as well as planned shifts during the course of operations.

COMMON OPERATING PRECEPT

Plan for and manage operational transitions over time and space.

   e. **Phasing Model.** Although the commander determines the number and actual phases for the operation, the phases shown in Figure V-3 and described below comprise a flexible model to arrange combat and stability operations. **Within the context of these phases established by a higher-level JFC, subordinate JFCs and component commanders may establish additional phases that fit their CONOPS.** OPLANs for contingencies that support the CCDR's TCP generally do not include security

Chapter V

cooperation activities that are addressed in other approved documents. CCDRs generally use the phasing model in Figure V-3 to link security cooperation activities in the TCP to pertinent OPLANs. Following is a discussion of each phase in the phasing model.

For more information on the phasing model and details on the individual phases, refer to JP 5-0, Joint Operation Planning.

(1) **Shape.** *Shape* phase missions, task, and actions are those that are designed to dissuade or deter adversaries and assure friends, as well as set conditions for the contingency plan and are generally conducted through security cooperation activities. Joint and multinational operations and various interagency activities occur routinely during the *shape* phase. *Shape* activities are executed continuously with the intent to enhance international legitimacy and gain multinational cooperation by shaping perceptions and influencing adversaries' and allies' behavior; developing allied and friendly military capabilities for self-defense and multinational operations; improving information exchange and intelligence sharing; providing US forces with peacetime and contingency access; and mitigating conditions that could lead to a crisis.

(2) **Deter.** The intent of this phase is to deter an adversary from undesirable actions because of friendly capabilities and the will to use them. *Deter* is generally weighted toward security activities that are characterized by preparatory actions to protect friendly forces and indicate the intent to execute subsequent phases of the planned operation. A number of flexible deterrent options (FDOs) could be implemented during this phase. Once the crisis is defined, these actions may include mobilization, tailoring of forces, and other predeployment activities; initial deployment into a theater; employment of ISR assets; and development of mission-tailored C2, intelligence, force protection, and logistic requirements to support the JFC's CONOPS. CCDRs continue to engage multinational partners, thereby providing the basis for further crisis response. Many actions in the *deter* phase build on activities from the previous phase, and are conducted as part of security cooperation activities. They can also be part of stand-alone operations.

(3) **Seize Initiative.** JFCs seek to seize the initiative in all situations through decisive use of joint force capabilities. In combat, this involves both defensive and offensive operations at the earliest possible time, forcing the enemy to culminate offensively and setting the conditions for decisive operations. Rapid application of joint combat power may be required to delay, impede, or halt the enemy's initial aggression and to deny the enemy its initial objectives. Operations to gain access to theater infrastructure and expand friendly freedom of action continue during this phase, while the JFC seeks to degrade enemy capabilities with the intent of resolving the crisis at the earliest opportunity.

(4) **Dominate.** This phase focuses on breaking the enemy's will to resist or, in noncombat situations, to control the operational environment. Success in the *dominate* phase depends on overmatching enemy capabilities at the critical time and place. Operations can range from large-scale combat to various stability operations depending on the nature of the enemy. *Dominate* phase activities may establish the conditions to

achieve strategic objectives early or may set the conditions for transition to the next phase of the operation.

(5) **Stabilize.** The *stabilize* phase is typically characterized by a shift in focus from sustained combat operations to stability operations. These operations help reestablish a safe and secure environment and provide essential government services, emergency infrastructure reconstruction, and humanitarian relief. The intent in this phase is to help restore local political, economic, and infrastructure stability. Civilian officials may lead operations during part or all of this phase, but the JFC typically will provide significant supporting capabilities and activities. The joint force may be required to perform limited local governance, and integrate the efforts of other supporting interorganizational partners until legitimate local entities are functioning. The JFC continuously assesses the impact of operations in this phase on the ability to transfer authority for remaining requirements to a legitimate civil entity, which marks the end of the phase.

(6) **Enable Civil Authority.** This phase is predominantly characterized by joint force support to legitimate civil governance. The commander provides this support by agreement with the appropriate civil authority. In some cases, and especially for operations within the United States, the commander provides this support under direction of the civil authority. The purpose is to help the civil authority regain its ability to govern and administer to the services and other needs of the population. The military end state is achieved during this phase, signaling the end of the joint operation. CCMD involvement with other nations and OGAs, beyond the termination of the joint operation, may be required to achieve the national strategic end state.

For more information on stability operations, refer to JP 3-07, Stability Operations.

SECTION C. MILITARY ENGAGEMENT, SECURITY COOPERATION, AND DETERRENCE

4. Military Engagement, Security Cooperation, and Deterrence

a. **Scope.** Military engagement, security cooperation, and deterrence missions, tasks, and actions encompass a wide range of actions where the military instrument of national power is tasked to support OGAs and cooperate with IGOs (e.g., UN, NATO) and other countries to protect and enhance national security interests, deter conflict, and set conditions for future contingency operations. These activities generally occur continuously in all GCCs' AORs regardless of other ongoing contingencies, major operations, or campaigns. They usually involve a combination of military forces and capabilities separate from but integrated with the efforts of interorganizational partners. Because DOS is frequently the major player in these activities, JFCs should maintain a working relationship with the chiefs of the US diplomatic missions in their area. Commanders and their staffs should establish and maintain dialogue with pertinent interorganizational partners to share information and facilitate future operations.

Chapter V

b. **Engagement.** Military engagement is the routine contact and interaction between individuals or elements of the Armed Forces of the United States and those of another nation's armed forces, or foreign and domestic civilian authorities or agencies to build trust and confidence, share information, coordinate mutual activities, and maintain influence. Military engagement occurs as part of security cooperation, but also extends to interaction with domestic civilian authorities. Support to military engagement may include specific mission areas such as religious affairs and medical support.

c. **Security Cooperation.** Security cooperation involves all DOD interactions with foreign defense and security establishments to build defense relationships that promote specific US security interests, develop allied and friendly military and security capabilities for internal and external defense for and multinational operations, and provide US forces with peacetime and contingency access to the HN. Developmental actions enhance a host government's willingness and ability to care for its people. Security cooperation is a key element of global and theater shaping operations. GCCs shape their AORs through security cooperation activities by continually employing military forces to complement and reinforce other instruments of national power. The GCC's security cooperation strategy provides a framework within which CCMDs engage regional partners in cooperative military activities and development. Ideally, security cooperation activities lessen the causes of a potential crisis before a situation deteriorates and requires coercive US military intervention.

d. **Deterrence**

(1) Deterrence prevents adversary action through the presentation of a credible threat of counteraction. In both peace and war, the Armed Forces of the United States help to deter adversaries from using violence to reach their aims. Deterrence stems from an adversary's belief that a credible threat of retaliation exists, the contemplated action cannot succeed, or the costs outweigh the perceived benefits of acting. Thus, a potential aggressor chooses not to act for fear of failure, cost, or consequences. Ideally, deterrent forces should be able to conduct decisive operations immediately. However, if committed forces lack the combat power to conduct decisive operations, they conduct defensive operations while additional forces deploy. Effective deterrence requires a security cooperation plan that emphasizes the willingness of the US to employ forces in defense of its interests. Various joint operations (such as show of force and enforcement of sanctions) support deterrence by demonstrating national resolve and willingness to use force when necessary. Others (such as nation assistance and FHA) support deterrence by enhancing a climate of peaceful cooperation, thus promoting stability. Joint actions such as nation assistance, antiterrorism, DOD support to counterdrug (CD) operations, show of force operations, and arms control are applied to meet military engagement, security cooperation, and deterrence objectives.

(2) Sustained presence contributes to deterrence and promotes a secure environment in which diplomatic, economic, and informational programs designed to reduce the causes of instability can perform as designed. Presence can take the form of forward basing, forward deploying, or pre-positioning assets. Forward presence activities demonstrate our commitment, lend credibility to our alliances, enhance regional stability,

and provide a crisis response capability while promoting US influence and access. Joint force presence often keeps unstable situations from escalating into larger conflicts. The sustained presence of strong, capable forces is the most visible sign of US commitment to allies and adversaries alike. However, if sustained forward presence fails to deter an adversary, committed forces must be agile enough to transition rapidly to combat operations. In addition to forces stationed overseas and afloat, forward presence involves periodic rotational deployments and redeployments, access and storage agreements, multinational exercises, port visits, foreign military training, foreign community support, and both military-to-military and military-to-civilian contacts. Given their location and knowledge of the region, forward presence forces could be the first that a CCDR commits when responding to a crisis.

5. Typical Operations

a. Even when the US is not conducting limited contingency operations, major operations, or campaigns, numerous routine missions (such as security cooperation) and continuing operations or tasks (such as ensuring freedom of navigation) are occurring under the general heading of *engagement*. In some cases, what begins as an engagement activity (such as limited support to a counterinsurgency through a security assistance program) can expand to a limited contingency operation or even a major operation when the President commits US forces. Engagement activities generally are governed by various directives and agreements and do not require a joint OPLAN or OPORD for execution.

b. **Emergency Preparedness.** Emergency preparedness consists of measures taken in advance of an emergency to reduce the loss of life and property and to protect a nation's institutions from all types of hazards through a comprehensive emergency management program of preparedness, mitigation, response, and recovery. At the strategic level, emergency preparedness encompasses those planning activities, such as *continuity of operations* and *continuity of government*, undertaken to ensure DOD processes, procedures, and resources are in place to support the President and SecDef in a designated national security emergency.

(1) *Continuity of operations* ensures the degree or state of being continuous in the conduct of functions, tasks, or duties necessary to accomplish a military action or mission in carrying out the national military strategy. Continuity of operations includes the functions and duties of the commander, as well as the supporting functions and duties performed by the staff and others under the authority and direction of the commander. If the President directs, DOD may be tasked with additional missions relating to emergency preparedness.

(2) *Continuity of government* involves a coordinated effort within each USG branch (executive, legislative, and judicial) to ensure the capability to continue minimum essential functions and responsibilities during a catastrophic emergency.

c. **Arms control, nonproliferation, and disarmament** involves the necessary steps to establish an effective system of international control, or to create and strengthen

Chapter V

international organizations for the maintenance of peace. **Although it may be viewed as a diplomatic mission, the military can play an important role.** For example, US military personnel may be involved in verifying an arms control treaty; seizing WMD; escorting authorized deliveries of weapons and other materials (i.e., enriched uranium) to preclude loss or unauthorized use of these assets; conducting and hosting site inspections; participating in military data exchanges; implementing armament reductions; or dismantling, destroying, or disposing of weapons and hazardous material.

    d. **Combating Terrorism.** Combating terrorism involves actions taken to oppose terrorism from wherever the threat exists. It encompasses antiterrorism—defensive measures taken to reduce vulnerability to terrorist acts—and CT—offensive measures taken to prevent, deter, preempt, and respond to terrorism.

        (1) **Antiterrorism** involves defensive measures used to reduce the vulnerability of individuals and property to terrorist acts, to include limited response and containment by local military forces and civilians. Antiterrorism programs form the foundation for effectively combating terrorism. The USG may provide antiterrorism assistance to foreign countries under the provisions of Title 22, USC (under Antiterrorism Assistance).

For further guidance on antiterrorism, refer to JP 3-07.2, Antiterrorism.

        (2) **Counterterrorism.** CT is primarily a SO core task and consists of actions taken directly against terrorist networks and indirectly to influence and render global and regional environments inhospitable to terrorist networks. Normally, CT operations require specially trained personnel capable of mounting swift and effective action. **CT is often associated with IW.** However, terrorism can also occur in conjunction with large-scale traditional combat and require commanders to integrate CT with these operations. An enemy using irregular methods often will use terrorist tactics to wage protracted operations in an attempt to break the will of their opponent and influence relevant populations. At the same time, terrorists and insurgents also seek to bolster their own legitimacy and credibility with those same populations. Therefore, CT efforts should include all instruments of national power to undermine an adversary's power, will, and its credibility and legitimacy, as well as its ability to influence the relevant population.

For further details concerning CT and SO, refer to JP 3-05, Special Operations, *and JP 3-26,* Counterterrorism. *For US policy on CT, refer to the* National Strategy for Combating Terrorism.

    e. **DOD Support to CD Operations.** DOD supports federal, state, and local law enforcement agencies in their effort to **disrupt the transport and/or transfer of illegal drugs into the United States.** Specific DOD CD authorities are contained in the National Defense Authorization Act of 1991; Public Law Number 101-510, Section 1004, as amended; as well as Title 10, USC, Sections 124 and 371-382.

> **JOINT TASK FORCE-NORTH**
>
> An example of Department of Defense support to counterdrug operations was the establishment of joint task force (JTF)-6 in 1989. Its mission originally focused exclusively along the Southwest border of the United States. A succession of National Defense Authorization Acts expanded the JTF-6 charter by adding specific mission tasks for the organization. In 1995, the JTF-6 area of responsibility expanded to include the continental United States. In June 2004, JTF-6 was officially renamed JTF-North and its mission was expanded to include providing support to federal law enforcement agencies in countering transnational threats.
>
> Mission: JTF-North provides military support to civil law enforcement agencies, conducts theater security cooperation as directed, and facilitates interagency synchronization within the US Northern Command area of responsibility in order to anticipate, detect, deter, prevent, and defeat transnational threats to the homeland.
>
> *Various Sources*

For additional guidance on CD operations, refer to JP 3-07.4, Joint Counterdrug Operations.

f. **Enforcement of sanctions** is an operation that employs coercive measures to interdict the movement of certain types of designated items into or out of a nation or specified area. **Maritime interception operations** are a form of maritime interdiction that may include seaborne coercive enforcement measures. These operations are military in nature and serve both political and military purposes. The **political objective** is to compel a country or group to conform to the objectives of the initiating body, while the military objective focuses on establishing a barrier that is selective, allowing only authorized goods to enter or exit. Depending on the geography, **sanction enforcement normally involves some combination of air and surface forces.** Assigned forces should be capable of **complementary mutual support** and **full communications interoperability.**

g. **Enforcing Exclusion Zones.** A sanctioning body establishes an exclusion zone to **prohibit specified activities in a specific geographic area.** Exclusion zones usually are imposed due to **breaches of** international standards of human rights or flagrant violations of international law regarding the conduct of states. Situations that may warrant such action include the persecution of the civil population by a government and efforts to deter an attempt by a hostile nation to acquire territory by force. Exclusion zones can be established in the air (no-fly zones), sea (maritime), or on land (no-drive zones). An exclusion zone's purpose may be to persuade nations or groups to modify their behavior to meet the desires of the sanctioning body or face continued imposition of sanctions or threat or use of force. **Such measures usually are imposed by the UN or another international body** of which the United States is a member, although they may be imposed unilaterally by the United States (e.g., Operation SOUTHERN WATCH in

Iraq, initiated in August 1992, and Operation DENY FLIGHT in Bosnia, from March 1993 to December 1995).

h. **Ensuring Freedom of Navigation and Overflight.** These operations are conducted to protect US navigation, overflight, and related interests on, under, and over the seas against excessive maritime claims. Freedom of navigation is a sovereign right accorded by international law.

> **ENSURING OVERFLIGHT AND FREEDOM OF NAVIGATION OPERATIONS**
>
> **The Berlin air corridors, established between 1948 and 1990, which allowed air access to West Berlin, were taken to maintain international airspace to an "air-locked" geographical area. The ATTAIN DOCUMENT series of operations against Libya in 1986 were freedom of navigation operations, both air and sea, in the Gulf of Sidra.**
>
> **Various Sources**

(1) International law has long recognized that a coastal state may exercise jurisdiction and control within its territorial sea in the same manner that it can exercise sovereignty over its own land territory. International law accords the right of "innocent" passage to ships of other nations through a state's territorial waters. Passage is "innocent" as long as it is not prejudicial to the peace, good order, or security of the coastal state. The high seas are free for reasonable use of all states.

(2) Freedom of navigation by aircraft through international airspace is a well-established principle of international law. Aircraft threatened by nations or groups through the extension of airspace control zones outside the established international norms will result in a measured legal response, appropriate to the situation. The **International Civil Aviation Organization,** a specialized agency of the UN, codifies the principles and techniques of international air navigation and fosters the planning and development of international air transport to ensure safe and orderly use of international airspace.

i. **Nation assistance is civil or military assistance** (other than FHA) **rendered to a nation by US forces** within that nation's territory during peacetime, crises or emergencies, or war, based on agreements mutually concluded between the United States and that nation (such as Operation PROMOTE LIBERTY, in 1990, following Operation JUST CAUSE in Panama). Nation assistance operations support the HN by promoting sustainable development and growth of responsive institutions. **The goal is to promote long-term regional stability.** Nation assistance programs include, but are not limited to, security assistance, FID, and other Title 10, USC, programs. Collaborative planning between the JFC and interorganizational and HN authorities can greatly enhance the effectiveness of nation assistance. The JIACG can help facilitate this coordination. All nation assistance actions are integrated into the US ambassador's country plan.

(1) *Security assistance* refers to a group of programs by which the United States provides defense articles, military training, and other defense-related services to foreign nations by grant, loan, credit, or cash sales in furtherance of national policies and objectives. Some **examples of US security assistance programs** are the Foreign Military Sales Program, the Foreign Military Financing Program, the International Military Education and Training Program, the Economic Support Fund, and commercial sales licensed under the Arms Export Control Act. **Security assistance surges accelerate release of equipment, supplies, or services** when an allied or friendly nation faces an imminent military threat. Security assistance surges are **military in nature** and are focused on providing additional combat systems (e.g., weapons and equipment) or supplies, but may include the full range of security assistance, to include financial and training support.

(2) **Foreign internal defense** programs encompass the diplomatic, economic, informational, and military support provided to another nation to assist its fight against subversion, lawlessness, insurgency, terrorism, and other threats to their security. US military support to FID should focus on the operational assistance to HN personnel and collaborative planning with interorganizational and HN authorities to anticipate, preclude, and counter these threats. FID supports HN internal defense and development programs. US military involvement in FID has traditionally been focused on helping a nation defeat an organized movement attempting to overthrow its lawful government. US FID programs may address other threats to the internal stability of an HN, such as civil disorder, illicit drug trafficking, and terrorism. While FID is a legislatively-mandated core task of SOF, conventional forces also contain and employ organic capabilities to conduct these activities.

For further guidance on FID, refer to JP 3-22, Foreign Internal Defense. *For further guidance on SOF involvement in FID, refer to JP 3-05,* Special Operations, *and JP 3-05.1,* Joint Special Operations Task Force Operations.

(3) **Security Force Assistance (SFA).** SFA is DOD's contribution to a unified action effort to support and augment the development of the capacity and capability of foreign security forces (FSF) and their supporting institutions to facilitate the achievement of specific objectives shared by the USG. The US military engages in activities to enhance the capabilities and capacities of a partner nation (or regional security organization) by providing training, equipment, advice, and assistance to those FSF organized in national ministry of defense (or equivalent regional military or paramilitary forces), while other USG departments and agencies focus on those forces assigned to other ministries (or their equivalents) such as interior, justice, or intelligence services.

For further guidance on SFA, refer to JP 3-22, Foreign Internal Defense.

(4) **Humanitarian and civic assistance** programs are governed by Title 10, USC, Section 401. This assistance may be provided in conjunction with military operations and exercises and must fulfill unit training requirements that incidentally create humanitarian benefit to the local populace. In contrast to emergency relief

Chapter V

conducted under FHA operations, humanitarian and civic assistance programs generally encompass planned activities in the following categories:

(a) **Medical, dental, and veterinary care** provided in rural or underserved areas of a country.

(b) Construction and repair of basic **surface transportation systems.**

(c) **Well drilling** and construction of basic **sanitation facilities.**

(d) Rudimentary construction and repair of **public facilities** such as schools, health and welfare clinics, and other nongovernmental buildings.

j. **Protection of Shipping.** When necessary, **US forces provide protection** of US flag vessels, US citizens (whether embarked in US or foreign vessels), and US property **against unlawful violence in and over international waters** (such as Operation EARNEST WILL, in which Kuwaiti ships were reflagged under the US flag in 1987). This protection may be extended to foreign flag vessels under international law and with the consent of the flag state. Actions to protect shipping include **coastal sea control, harbor defense, port security, countermine operations,** and **environmental defense,** in addition to operations on the high seas. Protection of shipping, which is a critical element in the fight against piracy, requires the coordinated employment of surface, air, space, and subsurface units, sensors, and weapons, as well as a command structure both ashore and afloat and a logistic base. Protection of shipping may require a combination of operations to be successful. These actions can include area operations, escort duties, mine countermeasures, and environmental defense missions.

k. **Show of force operations** are designed to demonstrate US resolve. They involve the **appearance of a credible military force** in an attempt to defuse a situation that, if allowed to continue, may be detrimental to US interests. These operations also underscore US commitment to our multinational partners.

(1) The US deploys forces abroad to **lend credibility** to its promises and commitments, **increase its regional influence,** and **demonstrate its resolve to use military force** if necessary. In addition, SecDef orders a show of force to bolster and reassure friends and allies. Show of force operations are military in nature but often serve both diplomatic and military purposes. These operations may influence other governments or politico-military organizations to refrain from belligerent acts.

SHOW OF FORCE IN THE PHILIPPINES

Operation Joint Task Force-PHILIPPINES was conducted by US forces in 1989 in support of President Aquino during a coup attempt against the Philippine government. During this operation, a large special operations force was formed, fighter aircraft patrolled above rebel air bases, and two aircraft carriers were positioned off the coastline of the Philippines.

Various Sources

(2) **Political concerns dominate a show of force operation,** and as such, military forces often are under significant legal and political constraints and restraints. The military force coordinates its operations with the country teams affected. A show of force can involve a wide range of military forces including joint US or multinational forces. Often, bilateral or multinational training and exercises are scheduled (time and location) with the intent of demonstrating strength and resolve. Forces conducting a show of force operation are also capable of FDOs and transitioning to crisis response or limited contingency activities.

l. **Support to Insurgency.** An insurgency is defined as the organized use of subversion and violence by a group or movement that seeks to overthrow or force change of a governing authority. Insurgency can also refer to the group itself. It uses a mixture of political, economic, informational, and combat actions to achieve its political aims. It is a protracted politico-military struggle designed to weaken the control and legitimacy of an established government, an interim governing body, or a peace process while increasing insurgent control and legitimacy—the central issues in an insurgency. The US may support selected insurgencies that oppose oppressive regimes. The US coordinates this support with its friends and allies. Because support for an insurgency is often covert, many of the operations connected with it are special activities. Due to their extensive unconventional warfare training, Special Forces are well suited to provide this support. Conventional forces may assist when the situation requires their functional specialties. US forces may provide logistic and training support as it did for the Mujahadin resistance in Afghanistan during the Soviet occupation in the 1980s. In certain circumstances the US can provide direct combat support, such as support to the French Resistance in World War II, the Afghanistan Northern Alliance to remove the Taliban in 2001-2002, or for NATO's liberation of Kosovo in 1999.

m. **Counterinsurgency** operations include support provided to a government in the military, paramilitary, political, economic, psychological, and civic actions it undertakes to defeat insurgency. Insurgents will increasingly resort to irregular forms of warfare as effective ways to undermine their adversaries' legitimacy and credibility and to isolate their adversaries from the relevant populations and their external supporters, physically as well as psychologically. At the same time, they also seek to bolster their own legitimacy and credibility to exercise authority over that same population. COIN operations often include security assistance programs such as foreign military sales, foreign military financing, and international military education and training. Such support also may include FID and SFA. In some cases, US COIN operations can be much more extensive and involve joint force limited contingency or major operations.

For further guidance on support to COIN, refer to JP 3-24, Counterinsurgency Operations, *and JP 3-22*, Foreign Internal Defense.

6. Other Considerations

> *"Instead of thinking about warfighting agencies like command and control, you create a political committee, a civil-military operations center to interface with volunteer organizations. These become the heart of your operations, as opposed to a combat or fire-support operations center."*
>
> **Lieutenant General A. C. Zinni, US Marine Corps**
> **Commanding General, I Marine Expeditionary Force**
> **1994-1996**

a. **Interagency, Intergovernmental, and Nongovernmental Organizations and Host Nation Coordination.** There is an increased need for the military to work with interorganizational and HN authorities to plan and conduct military engagement, security cooperation, and deterrence operations and activities. Liaison organizations such as a JIACG can help promote interaction and cooperation among diverse agencies. Consensus building is a primary task and can be aided by understanding each agency's capabilities and limitations as well as any constraints that may preclude the use of a capability. The goal—to develop and promote the unity of effort needed to accomplish a specific mission—can be achieved by establishing an atmosphere of trust and cooperation.

For further discussion on interorganizational coordination, refer to JP 3-08, Interorganizational Coordination During Joint Operations.

b. **Information Sharing.** NGOs and IGOs, by the very nature of what they do, become familiar with the infrastructure in a region and the culture, language, sensitivities, and status of the populace. This information is very valuable to commanders and staffs who may have neither access nor current information. NGOs and IGOs also may need information from commanders and staffs concerning security issues. However, these organizations hold *neutrality* as a fundamental principle. They will resist being used as sources of intelligence, and they may be hesitant to associate with the military. Careful coordination is necessary to maintain their neutrality. Consequently, the JFC should establish mechanisms like a CMOC or a similar organization to coordinate activities and facilitate information sharing. IGOs and NGOs will likely participate if they perceive that mutual sharing of information aids their work and is not a threat to their neutrality.

c. **Cultural Awareness.** The social, economic, and political environments in which security cooperation activities occur require a great degree of cultural understanding. Military support and operations that are intended to support a friendly HN require an in-depth understanding of the HN's cultural and political realities because of the increased likelihood that military elements will be required to work with and among the HN population. A fundamental requirement for military success is a sound understanding of the operational environment. This requires a careful study of the geography, population, and culture. The JFC may augment Service-provided language and cultural awareness training and tailor these to the JOA and mission. This also requires intelligence and engagement strategies and actions that provide a continuously updated picture of relevant information. The beliefs, perceptions, lifestyles, and economic underpinnings of the society, among other considerations, influence the operational environment and will affect planning and execution.

(1) Security cooperation efforts likely will impact countries throughout a region. Traditional rivalries among neighboring states and hostility toward the United States may be factors. For example, US assistance to a nation with long-standing enemies in the area may be perceived by these enemies as upsetting the regional balance of power. These same nations or others may see US intervention in the area simply as US imperialism. While such factors will not dictate US policy, they will require careful evaluation and consideration when conducting military operations under those conditions.

(2) The emergence of non-state regional actors and an increase in multinational efforts to enhance stability and foster development, have increased cultural and language challenges faced by joint forces and increased interpreter and translator requirements to support multinational operations.

SECTION D. CRISIS RESPONSE AND LIMITED CONTINGENCY OPERATIONS

7. Crisis Response and Limited Contingency Operations

a. A limited contingency operation in response to a crisis includes all of those operations for which a JFC must develop an OPLAN or OPORD. The level of complexity, duration, and resources depends on the circumstances. Included are operations to ensure the safety of American citizens and US interests while maintaining and improving US ability to operate with multinational partners to deter the hostile ambitions of potential aggressors (such as **JTF SHINING HOPE** in the spring of 1999 to support refugee humanitarian relief for hundreds of thousands of Albanians fleeing their homes in Kosovo). Many of these operations involve a combination of military forces and capabilities in close cooperation with interorganizational partners.

b. **Initial Response.** When crises develop and the President directs, CCDRs respond. If the crisis revolves around external threats to a regional partner, CCDRs employ joint forces to deter aggression and signal US commitment (such as deploying joint forces to train in Kuwait). If the crisis is caused by an internal conflict that threatens regional stability, US forces may intervene to restore or guarantee stability (such as Operation RESTORE DEMOCRACY, the 1994 intervention in Haiti). If the crisis is within US territory (e.g., natural or man-made disaster, deliberate attack), US joint forces will conduct CS and HD operations as directed by the President and SecDef. Prompt deployment of sufficient forces in the initial phase of a crisis can preclude the need to deploy larger forces later. Effective early intervention also can deny an adversary time to set conditions in their favor or achieve destabilizing objectives; or mitigate the effects of a natural or man-made disaster. Deploying a credible force rapidly is one step in deterring or blocking aggression. However, deployment alone will not guarantee success. Achieving successful deterrence involves convincing the adversary that the deployed

Chapter V

force is able to conduct decisive operations and the national leadership is willing to employ that force and to deploy more forces if necessary.

c. **Scope.** Crisis response and limited contingency operations are typically limited in scope and scale and conducted to achieve a very specific strategic or operational objective in an operational area. They may be conducted as stand-alone operations in response to a crisis (such as a NEO) or executed as an element of a larger, more complex campaign or major operation. Crisis response and limited contingency operations may be conducted to achieve operational and, sometimes, strategic objectives.

d. **Political Aspects.** Two important factors about political primacy in crisis response and foreign limited contingency operations stand out. **First, understanding the political objective helps avoid actions that may have adverse effects.** It is not uncommon in some operations, such as peacekeeping, for junior leaders to make decisions that have significant political implications. **Second, commanders should remain aware of changes not only in the operational situation, but also in political objectives that may warrant a change in military operations.** These changes may not always be obvious. Therefore, commanders must strive to detect subtle changes, which may eventually lead to disconnects between political objectives and military operations. Failure to recognize changes in political objectives early may lead to ineffective or counterproductive military operations.

e. **Economy of Force.** The strategic environment requires the United States to maintain and prepare joint forces for crisis response and limited contingency operations simultaneously with other operations, preferably in concert with allies and/or coalition partners when appropriate. This approach recognizes that these operations will vary in duration, frequency, intensity, and the number of personnel required. The burden of many crisis response and limited contingency operations may lend themselves to using small elements like SOF in coordination with allied HNs. Initially, SOF may take the lead of these operations as an economy of force measure to enable major operations and campaigns with conventional focus to progress more effectively.

8. Typical Operations

a. **NEOs** are operations directed by the DOS or other appropriate authority, in conjunction with DOD, whereby noncombatants and civilians are evacuated from locations within foreign countries to safe havens when their lives are endangered by, or in anticipation of, war, civil unrest, or natural disaster. Although principally conducted to evacuate US citizens, NEOs also may include citizens from the HN as well as citizens from other countries. Pursuant to Executive Order 12656, *Assignment of Emergency Preparedness Responsibilities,* DOS is responsible for the protection and evacuation of American citizens abroad and for safeguarding their property. This order also directs DOD to advise and assist DOS in preparing and implementing plans for the evacuation of US citizens. The US ambassador, or chief of the diplomatic mission, is responsible for preparation of emergency action plans that address the military evacuation of US citizens and designated foreign nationals from a foreign country. The conduct of military operations to assist in the implementation of emergency action plans is the responsibility of the GCC, as directed by SecDef.

(1) **NEOs are often characterized by uncertainty.** They may be directed without warning because of sudden changes in a country's government, reoriented diplomatic or military relations with the United States, a sudden hostile threat to US

OPERATION EASTERN EXIT

On 2 January 1991, the United States Ambassador to Somalia requested military assistance to evacuate the Embassy. Americans and other foreign nationals had sought shelter in the Embassy compound that day as the reign of Somali dictator Siad Barre disintegrated into a confused battle for control of Mogadishu.

The next day, Operation EASTERN EXIT was initiated. Despite the priorities of the Gulf War, special operations forces helicopters were put on alert, Air Force C-130 transport aircraft were deployed to Kenya, and two Navy amphibious ships with elements of a Marine expeditionary brigade embarked were sent south from the North Arabian Sea toward Somalia. Initial plans called for evacuation of the endangered Americans through Mogadishu's international airport, utilizing Air Force aircraft staged in Kenya. The situation in Mogadishu rapidly worsened and aircraft, even those of the United States Air Force, could not land safely at the airport. It seemed unlikely in any case that those sheltered at the Embassy could travel safely through the embattled city to the airport.

By 4 January, it had become apparent that the Embassy's only hope lay with the two ships still steaming south at flank speed. At 0247, two CH-53E helicopters with Marines and Navy SEALs departed the USS Guam for the 466-mile flight to Mogadishu. After two in-flight refuelings from KC-130 aircraft, the helicopters arrived over the Embassy at dawn. About 100 armed Somali stood with ladders by one wall. As the CH-53Es flew into the compound, the Somalis scattered. Shortly after the helicopters touched down, a special operations AC-130 gunship arrived overhead to provide fire support, if needed. The CH-53Es unloaded the security force, embarked 61 evacuees, and took off for the 350-mile return flight.

The ships continued to steam at full speed toward Somalia throughout the day. The final evacuation of the Embassy started at midnight, after the ships had arrived off the coast. The remaining 220 evacuees and the security force were extracted during the night.

Operation EASTERN EXIT, which resulted in the rescue of 281 people—from 30 different countries—from a bloody civil war, was the result of the synergistic employment of widely dispersed joint forces that rapidly planned and conducted a noncombatant evacuation operation in the midst of the Gulf War.

Various Sources

citizens from elements within or external to a foreign country, or in response to a natural disaster.

(2) NEO methods and timing are significantly influenced by diplomatic considerations. Under ideal circumstances there may be little or no opposition; however, commanders should anticipate opposition and plan the operation like any combat operation.

(3) NEOs, conducted in an uncertain or hostile operational environment, are similar to a raid in that the operation involves swift insertion of a force, temporary occupation of physical objectives, and ends with a planned withdrawal. It differs from a raid in that if force is used, it is normally limited to that required to protect the evacuees and the evacuation force. Forces employed within foreign territory should be kept to the minimum consistent with mission accomplishment.

For additional guidance on NEOs, refer to JP 3-68, Noncombatant Evacuation Operations.

> *"Peacekeeping is a job not suited to soldiers, but a job only soldiers can do."*
>
> **Dag Hammarskjold**
> **UN Secretary-General, 1953-1961**

b. **Peace Operations.** PO are multiagency and multinational operations involving all instruments of national power—including international humanitarian and reconstruction efforts and military missions—to contain conflict, redress the peace, and shape the environment to support reconciliation and rebuilding and facilitate the transition to legitimate governance. For the Armed Forces of the United States, PO encompass PKO, predominantly military PEO, predominantly diplomatic PB actions, PM processes, and conflict prevention. PO are conducted in conjunction with the various diplomatic activities and humanitarian efforts necessary to secure a negotiated truce and resolve the conflict. PO are tailored to each situation and may be conducted in support of diplomatic activities before, during, or after conflict. PO support national/multinational strategic objectives. Military support improves the chances for success in the peace process by lending credibility to diplomatic actions and demonstrating resolve to achieve viable political settlements.

(1) **PKO are military operations** undertaken with the consent of all major parties to a dispute, **designed to monitor and facilitate implementation of an agreement** (cease fire, truce, or other such agreements) and support diplomatic efforts to reach a long-term political settlement. Such actions are often taken under the authority of Chapter VI, Pacific Settlement of Disputes, of the UN Charter. An example of PKO is the US commitment to the Multinational Force Observers in the Sinai since 1982.

Joint Operations Across the Range of Military Operations

US joint forces are often deployed with military forces from other nations to carry out operations and exercises focused on United Nations-mandated ground level peacekeeping tasks.

(2) **PEO** are the application of military force or threat of its use, normally pursuant to international authorization, to compel compliance with resolutions or sanctions designed to maintain or restore peace and order. **PEO may include the enforcement of sanctions and exclusion zones, protection of FHA, restoration of order, and forcible separation of belligerent parties or parties to a dispute.** Unlike PKO, such operations do not require the consent of the states involved or of other parties to the conflict (e.g., Operations JOINT ENDEAVOR, JOINT GUARD, and JOINT FORGE, 1995-2001 in Bosnia and JOINT GUARDIAN, 1999-2001 in Kosovo).

(3) **Peace Building.** This consists of stability actions (predominantly diplomatic, economic, and security related) that strengthen and rebuild governmental infrastructure and institutions, build confidence, and support economic reconstruction to prevent a return to conflict. **Military support to PB may include rebuilding roads, reestablishing or creating government entities, or training defense forces.**

(4) **Peacemaking.** This is the process of diplomacy, mediation, negotiation, or other forms of peaceful settlement that **arranges an end to a dispute or resolves issues** that led to conflict. It can be an ongoing process, supported by military, economic, diplomatic, and informational instruments of national power. The purpose is to instill in the parties an understanding that reconciliation is a better alternative to fighting. The military can assist in establishing incentives, disincentives, and mechanisms that promote reconciliation. Military activities that support PM include military-to-military exchanges and security assistance.

> **OPERATION JOINT ENDEAVOR**
>
> Beginning in December 1995, US and allied nations deployed peace operations forces to Bosnia in support of Operation JOINT ENDEAVOR. Task Force EAGLE, comprised of 20,000 American soldiers (primarily from the 1st Armored Division), implemented the military elements of the Dayton Peace Accords. This operation marked the first commitment of forces in the North Atlantic Treaty Organization's (NATO's) history as well as the first time since World War II that American and Russian soldiers have shared a common mission. Today, thousands of people are alive in Bosnia because of these soldiers' service.
>
> During Operation JOINT ENDEAVOR, deployed intelligence personnel provided aircrews and staffs at several locations with critical threat information and airfield data. Taking advantage of the Combat Intelligence System (CIS) capabilities and an emerging global connectivity to military networks and databases, intelligence personnel provided the best and most timely support ever to air mobility forces. This improvement was particularly evident during the Mission Report (MISREP) process, when intelligence analysts used CIS to provide MISREP data very quickly to aircrews and staffs, ensuring the people in need of this intelligence received it while the data were still useful.
>
> The European Command's Amphibious Ready Group/Marine Expeditionary Unit (Special Operations Capable) was assigned as theater reserve for NATO forces, while Naval Mobile Construction Battalions 133 and 40 constructed base camps for implementation force personnel. In addition, from June to October a Marine Corps unmanned aerial vehicle (UAV) squadron, VMU-1, supported the operation with Pioneer UAV imagery both to US and multinational units. VMU-2 continues to provide similar support.
>
> **Various Sources**

(5) **Conflict prevention** consists of diplomatic and other actions taken in advance of a predictable crisis to prevent or limit violence, deter parties, and reach an agreement before armed hostilities. These actions are normally conducted under Chapter VI, Pacific Settlement of Disputes, of the UN Charter. However, military deployments designed to deter and coerce parties will need to be credible, and this may require a combat posture and an enforcement mandate under the principles of Chapter VII, Action with Respect to Threats to the Peace, Breaches of the Peace, and Acts of Aggression, of the UN Charter. Conflict prevention activities include diplomatic initiatives, efforts designed to reform a country's security sector and make it more accountable to democratic control, and deployment of forces designed to prevent a dispute or contain it from escalating to hostilities. Other conflict prevention activities may include military fact-finding missions, consultations, warnings, inspections, and monitoring. Military forces used for conflict prevention should be focused on support to political and developmental efforts to ameliorate the causes of tension and unrest. Military activities will be tailored to meet political and development demands.

For additional guidance on PO, refer to JP 3-07.3, Peace Operations.

c. **Foreign Humanitarian Assistance.** FHA operations relieve or reduce the impact of natural or man-made disasters or other endemic conditions such as human pain, disease, hunger, or privation in countries or regions outside the United States. These operations are different from nation assistance primarily because they occur on short notice to provide aid in specific crises or similar events rather than as more deliberate programs to promote long-term regional stability. FHA provided by US forces is generally limited in scope and duration; it is intended to supplement or complement efforts of HN civil authorities or agencies with the primary responsibility for providing assistance. DOD provides assistance when the need for relief is gravely urgent and when the humanitarian emergency dwarfs the ability of normal relief agencies to effectively respond.

(1) The US military is capable of rapidly responding to emergencies or disasters and restoring relative order in austere locations. US forces may provide logistics, planning, and communications resources required to initiate and sustain FHA operations.

(2) FHA operations may be directed by the President or SecDef when a serious international situation threatens the political or military stability of a region considered of interest to the United States, or when SecDef deems the humanitarian situation itself sufficient and appropriate for employment of US forces. **DOS or the US Ambassador in country is responsible for declaring a foreign disaster or situation that requires**

US Navy Sailors and members of Joint Task Force-Bravo working with Project Handclasp, a San Diego-based organization, unload humanitarian supplies in Honduras in 2007. US forces can effectively assist civilian humanitarian organizations such as Project Handclasp by accepting and transporting educational, humanitarian, and goodwill material overseas on a space-available basis aboard military ships and aircraft.

Chapter V

FHA. Within DOD, the Undersecretary of Defense for Policy has the overall responsibility for developing the military policy for international FHA operations.

(3) **FHA operations** include a broad range of tasks, including establishing a secure environment for humanitarian relief efforts. US military forces participate in **three basic types of FHA operations**—those coordinated by the UN, those where the United States acts in concert with other multinational forces, or those where the United States responds unilaterally.

For further guidance on FHA operations, refer to JP 3-29, Foreign Humanitarian Assistance.

d. **Recovery operations** may be conducted to search for, locate, identify, recover, and return isolated personnel, sensitive equipment, items critical to national security, or human remains (such as **JTF—Full Accounting,** which had the mission to achieve the fullest possible accounting of Americans still unaccounted for as a result of the war in Southeast Asia). Regardless of the recovery purpose, each type of recovery operation is generally a sophisticated activity requiring detailed planning in order to execute. Recovery operations may be clandestine, covert, or overt depending on whether the operational environment is hostile, uncertain, or permissive.

OPERATION ATLAS RESPONSE

In the early part of February 2000, Cyclone Connie drenched the Southern Africa region with over 40 inches of rain causing many rivers in the region to overflow and flood populated areas. US European Command sent a humanitarian assistance survey team (HAST) to get "eyes on the ground." Just as the effects of Connie were lessening and the HAST was preparing to head home, Cyclone Eline hit Madagascar. The storm pushed further inland and rain fell in Zimbabwe, adding to reservoirs that were already full. This forced the release of water from reservoirs, causing even more flooding. Mozambique (MZ) was the country with the greatest needs in the region. Consequently, between 18 February and 1 April 2000, Joint Task Force (JTF)-ATLAS RESPONSE, under the command of Major General Joseph H. Wehrle, Jr., US Air Force, was sent to aid the people of Mozambique, South Africa, Botswana, Zimbabwe, and Zambia.

The joint force commander established a small, main headquarters in Maputo, MZ to be near the US Ambassador. The majority of forces and staff resided at Air Force Base Hoedspriut, South Africa. Eventually, a small contingent of forces would deploy to Beira, MZ to work at a supply distribution hub. The primary predeployment tasks of the JTF: 1) Search and rescue (SAR), 2) Coordination and synchronization of relief efforts, and 3) Relief supply distribution changed during the operation. Upon arrival, the JTF discovered SAR efforts were essentially complete and a fourth key task became the ability to conduct aerial assessment of the lines of communications. This fourth task was important because it was also a key indicator in the exit strategy.

> **During the brief time of the operation, the JTF's aircraft carried a total of 714.3 short tons of intergovernmental organization (IGO)/nongovernmental organization (NGO) cargo, most of it for direct support of the local population. Helicopters and C-130s also moved 511 non-US passengers. The majority were medics or aid workers carried on special operations forces HH-60s bringing immediate relief to populations cut off from the rest of the world.**
>
> **Important lessons were learned during this operation. First, the best course of action may not be bringing enough manpower and resources to dominate the running of a foreign humanitarian assistance operation. In this case, supporting the essentially civil-run operation and providing effective counsel worked far better than trying to control the operation as a supported commander. Political feathers were not ruffled and future operations with these nations or aid agencies likely will be that much easier. Second, the civil-military operations center (CMOC) was key to working with the participating IGOs and NGOs. CMOC personnel were able to set up information nodes that moved information among aid agencies that were sometimes in competition with each other. Because of CMOC's low key approach, it was able to steer each organization it touched to greater organization and efficiency. Finally, early development of an exit strategy provided decision points with tangible measures. All parties must have buy-in to execute it together and there must be "top cover" from the civilian side to ensure national objectives are met.**
>
> **Operation ATLAS RESPONSE was a political and military success. Not only was humanitarian aid provided to the people of Mozambique, but good relations with South African military and many IGOs and NGOs were forged.**
>
> **SOURCE: Derived from Dr. Robert Sly's, "ATLAS RESPONSE Study," Third Air Force History Office, 2000**

e. **Strikes and Raids**

(1) *Strikes* are attacks conducted to damage or destroy an objective or a capability. Strikes may be used to punish offending nations or groups, uphold international law, or prevent those nations or groups from launching their own attacks (e.g., Operation EL DORADO CANYON conducted against Libya in 1986, in response to the terrorist bombing of US Service members in Berlin). Although often tactical in nature with respect to the ways and means used and duration of the operation, strikes can achieve strategic objectives as did the strike against Libya.

(2) Raids are operations to temporarily seize an area, usually through forcible entry, in order to secure information, confuse an adversary, capture personnel or equipment, or destroy an objective or capability (e.g., Operation URGENT FURY,

Chapter V

> **OPERATION EL DORADO CANYON**
>
> The strike was designed to hit directly at the heart of Gaddafi's ability to export terrorism with the belief that such a preemptive strike would provide him "incentives and reasons to alter his criminal behavior." The final targets were selected at the National Security Council level "within the circle of the President's advisors." Ultimately, five targets were selected. All except one of the targets were chosen because of their direct connection to terrorist activity. The single exception was the Benina military airfield which based Libyan fighter aircraft. This target was hit to preempt Libyan interceptors from taking off and attacking the incoming US bombers.
>
> The actual combat commenced at 0200 (local Libyan time), lasted less than 12 minutes, and dropped 60 tons of munitions. Navy A-6 Intruders were assigned the two targets in the Benghazi area, and the Air Force F-111s hit the other three targets in the vicinity of Tripoli. Resistance outside the immediate area of attack was nonexistent, and Libyan air defense aircraft never launched. One F-111 strike aircraft was lost during the strike.
>
> **Various Sources**

Grenada 1983, to protect US citizens and restore the lawful government). Raids end with a planned withdrawal upon completion of the assigned mission.

f. **Homeland Defense and Defense Support of Civil Authorities.** Security and defense of the US homeland is the USG's top responsibility and is conducted as a continuous cooperative effort among all federal agencies as well as state, tribal, and local government. Military operations inside the United States and its territories, though limited in many respects, are conducted to accomplish two missions—HD and DSCA. HD is the protection of US sovereignty, territory, domestic population, and critical defense infrastructure against external threats and aggression **or other threats as directed by the President.** DSCA consists of DOD support to US civil authorities for domestic emergencies and for designated law enforcement and other activities. Requests for federal assistance of this nature must be submitted to the DOD Executive Secretary.

(1) **Homeland Defense.** The purpose of HD is to protect against and mitigate the impact of incursions or attacks on sovereign territory, the domestic population, and critical defense infrastructure. **DOD is the federal agency with lead responsibility, supported by other agencies, in defending against external threats/aggression.** However, against internal threats DOD may be in support of an OGA. **When ordered to conduct HD operations within US territory, DOD will coordinate closely with OGAs.** Consistent with laws and policy, the Services will provide capabilities to support CCDR requirements against a variety of threats to national security. These include invasion, CNA, and air and missile attacks.

(2) **Defense Support of Civil Authorities.** Support provided by US federal military forces, DOD civilians, contract personnel, component assets, and National Guard forces (when SecDef, in coordination with the Governors of the affected states, elects and requests to use those forces in Title 32, USC status) in response to requests for assistance from civil authorities for domestic emergencies, law enforcement support, and other domestic activities, or from qualifying entities for special events. For DSCA operations, DOD supports and does not supplant civil authorities. Within a state, that state's governor is the key decision maker.

(a) The majority of DSCA operations are conducted in accordance with the NRF. The NRF establishes a comprehensive, national, all-hazards approach to domestic incident response. The NRF identifies the key response principles, as well as the roles and structures that organize national response. It describes how communities, states, the USG and private-sector and nongovernmental partners apply these principles for a coordinated, effective national response. In addition, it describes special circumstances where the USG exercises a larger role, including incidents where federal interests are involved and catastrophic incidents where a state would require significant support. It lays the groundwork for first responders, decision makers, and supporting entities to provide a unified national response. DOD provides this support with the stipulation that it does not conflict with DOD's mission or its ability to respond to military contingencies.

(b) Other DSCA operations can include CD activities, incident awareness and assessment or investigative support, or other support to civilian law enforcement in accordance with specific DOD policies and US law.

(3) **Global Perspective.** Commander, US Northern Command, and Commander, US Pacific Command, have specific responsibilities for HD and DSCA. These responsibilities include conducting operations to deter, prevent, and defeat threats and aggression aimed at the United States, its territories, and interests within their assigned AORs, as directed by the President or SecDef. However, DOD support to HD is global in nature and is often conducted by all CCDRs beginning at the source of the threat. In the forward regions outside US territories, the objective is to detect and deter threats to the homeland before they arise and to defeat these threats as early as possible when so directed.

For detailed guidance on CS, see JP 3-28, Civil Support, *and for more detailed guidance on DSCA, see DODD 3025.18,* Defense Support of Civil Authorities.

For detailed guidance on HD, see JP 3-27, Homeland Defense.

9. Other Considerations

a. **Duration and End State.** Crisis response and limited contingency operations may last for a relatively short period of time (e.g., NEO, strike, raid) or for an extended period of time to attain the national strategic end state (such as US participation with ten other nations in the independent [non-UN] peacekeeping operation, *Multinational Force and Observers*, in the Sinai Peninsula since 1982). Short duration operations are not always possible, particularly in situations where destabilizing conditions have existed for years or where conditions are such that a long-term commitment is required to achieve national strategic objectives. Nevertheless, it is imperative to have a clear national strategic end state for all types of contingencies.

b. **Intelligence Collection.** As soon as practical, JFCs and their staffs determine intelligence requirements to support the anticipated operation. Intelligence planners also consider the capability for a unit to receive external intelligence support, the capability to store intelligence data, the timeliness of collection systems, the availability of intelligence publications, and the possibility of using other agencies and organizations as intelligence sources. In some contingencies (such as PKO), the term *information collection* is used rather than the term *intelligence* because of the operation's sensitivity.

(1) **HUMINT** often may provide the most useful source of information and is essential to determining foreign intent. If a HUMINT infrastructure is not in place when US forces arrive, it needs to be established as quickly as possible. HUMINT also complements other intelligence sources with information not available through technical means. For example, while overhead imagery may graphically depict the number of people gathered in a town square, it cannot gauge the motivations or enthusiasm of the crowd. Additionally, in underdeveloped areas, belligerent forces may not rely heavily on radio communication, thereby denying US forces intelligence derived through signal intercept.

(2) Where there is little USG or US military presence, open-source intelligence (OSINT) may be the best immediately available information to prepare US forces to operate in a foreign country. OSINT from radio broadcasts, newspapers, and periodicals often provide tip-offs for HUMINT and other intelligence and information collection methods.

(3) Intelligence collection requires a focus on adversary system factors that affect the situation. This requires a depth of expertise in, and a mental and psychological integration with, all aspects of the operational environment's peoples and their cultures, politics, religion, economics, and related factors; and any variances within affected groups of people. In addition, intelligence collection must focus quickly on transportation infrastructure in the operational area, to include capabilities and limitations of major seaports, airfields, and surface LOCs.

(4) Intelligence organizations (principally at the JTF HQ level) should include **foreign area officers**. They add valuable cultural awareness to the production of useable intelligence.

c. **Constraints and Restraints.** A JFC tasked with conducting or supporting a crisis response or limited contingency operation may face numerous constraints and restraints. For example, international acceptance of each operation may be extremely important, not only because military forces may be used to support international sanctions, but also because of the probability of involvement by IGOs. As a consequence, legal and fiscal constraints unique to the operation should be addressed in detail by the CCDR's staff. Also, operational limitations imposed on any agency or organization involved in the operation should be clarified for other agencies and organizations to facilitate coordination.

d. **Force Protection.** Limited contingency operations may involve a requirement to protect nonmilitary personnel. In the absence of the rule of law, the JFC must address when, how, and to what extent he will extend force protection to civilians and what that protection means.

e. **Training.** Participation in or around the operational environment of certain types of smaller-scale contingencies may preclude normal mission-related training. For example, infantry units or fighter squadrons conducting certain protracted PO may not have the time, facilities, or environment in which to maintain individual or unit proficiency for traditional missions. In these situations, commanders should develop programs that enable their forces to maintain proficiency in their core competencies/mission essential tasks to the greatest extent possible.

SECTION E. MAJOR OPERATIONS AND CAMPAIGNS

10. Major Operations and Campaigns

a. When required to achieve national strategic objectives or protect national interests, the US national leadership may decide to conduct a major operation or campaign involving large-scale combat, placing the United States in a wartime state. In such cases, the general goal is to prevail against the enemy as quickly as possible, conclude hostilities, and establish conditions favorable to the HN, the United States, and its multinational partners. Establishing these conditions often requires joint forces to conduct stability operations to restore security, provide essential services and humanitarian relief, and conduct emergency reconstruction.

b. Major operations and campaigns typically include multiple phases (such as the 1990-1991 Operations DESERT SHIELD and DESERT STORM and 2003 OIF). Some specific crisis-response or limited contingency operations may not involve large-scale combat, but could be considered major operations or campaigns depending on their scale and duration (such as Tsunami relief efforts in Indonesia or Hurricane Katrina relief efforts in the US, both in 2005).

c. A *major operation* is a series of tactical actions, such as battles, engagements, and strikes, and is the primary building block of a campaign. Within a campaign, combat forces of a single or several Services, coordinated in time and place, conduct major operations to achieve strategic or operational objectives in an operational area. Forces conduct these actions simultaneously or sequentially in accordance with a common plan and are controlled by a single Service commander or the JFC. A noncombat operation, such as FHA, can be a *major operation* if the combination of size, scope, and duration requires the commander to phase the operation as a set of tasks, activities, and missions over time.

d. **A campaign is a series of related military operations aimed at accomplishing a military strategic or operational objective within a given time and space.** Planning for a campaign is appropriate when the contemplated military operations exceed the scope of a single major operation. Thus, campaigns are often the most extensive joint operations in terms of time and other resources. Campaign planning has its greatest application in the conduct of large-scale combat operations, but can be used across the range of military operations. While intended primarily to guide the use of military power, campaign plans consider all instruments of national power and how their integrated efforts work to attain national strategic objectives.

e. Campaigns are joint in nature—functional and Service components conduct supporting operations, not independent campaigns. A campaign plan is not a unique type of joint OPLAN. JFCs normally prepare a campaign plan in OPLAN format in accordance with the Joint Operation Planning and Execution System under APEX. However, the size, complexity, and anticipated duration of operations typically magnify the planning challenges. There are three categories of campaigns, which differ generally in scope.

(1) **Global Campaign.** A *global campaign* is one that requires the accomplishment of military strategic objectives within multiple theaters that extend beyond the AOR of a single GCC.

(2) **Theater Campaign.** A *theater campaign* encompasses the activities of a supported GCC, and accomplishes military strategic or operational objectives within a theater of war or theater of operations that is primarily within the supported commander's AOR. OIF has shown that adjacent GCCs can, at the direction of SecDef, conduct supporting operations within the AOR of the supported commander, or within their own AORs, under the overall direction of the supported GCC.

(3) **Subordinate Campaign.** A subordinate JFC may conduct a *subordinate campaign* to accomplish (or contribute to) military strategic or operational objectives in support of a global or theater campaign. Subordinate JFCs develop subordinate campaign plans if their assigned missions require military operations of substantial size, complexity, and duration and cannot be accomplished within the framework of a single major joint operation. Subordinate campaign plans must be consistent with the strategic and operational guidance and direction provided in the supported JFC's campaign plan.

THE GULF WAR, 1990-1991

On 2 August 1990, Iraq invaded and occupied Kuwait. Much of the rest of the world, including most other Arab nations, united in condemnation of that action. On 7 August, the operation known as DESERT SHIELD began. Its principal objectives were to deter further aggression and to force Iraq to withdraw from Kuwait. The United Nations (UN) Security Council passed a series of resolutions calling for Iraq to leave Kuwait, finally authorizing "all necessary means," including the use of force, to force Iraq to comply with UN resolutions.

The United States led in establishing a political and military coalition to force Iraq from Kuwait and restore stability to the region. The military campaign to accomplish these ends took the form, in retrospect, of a series of major operations. These operations employed the entire capability of the international military coalition and included operations in war and operations other than war throughout.

The campaign—which included Operations DESERT SHIELD and DESERT STORM and the subsequent period of postconflict operations—can be viewed in the following major phases.

- DEPLOYMENT AND FORCE BUILDUP (to include crisis action planning, mobilization, deployment, and deterrence)

- DEFENSE (with deployment and force buildup continuing)

- OFFENSE

- POSTWAR OPERATIONS (to include redeployment)

DEPLOYMENT AND FORCE BUILDUP. While diplomats attempted to resolve the crisis without combat, the coalition's military forces conducted rapid planning, mobilization, and the largest strategic deployment since World War II. One of the earliest military actions was a maritime interdiction of the shipping of items of military potential to Iraq.

The initial entry of air and land forces into the theater was unopposed. The Commander, United States Central Command (CDRUSCENTCOM), balanced the arrival of these forces to provide an early, viable deterrent capability and the logistic capability needed to receive, further deploy, and sustain the rapidly growing force. Planning, mobilization, and deployment continued throughout this phase.

DEFENSE. While even the earliest arriving forces were in a defensive posture, a viable defense was possible only after the buildup of sufficient coalition air, land, and maritime combat capability. Mobilization and deployment of forces continued. Operations security (OPSEC) measures, operational military deception, and operational psychological operations were used to influence Iraqi dispositions, expectations, and combat effectiveness and thus degrade their abilities to resist CDRUSCENTCOM's selected course of action before engaging enemy forces. This phase ended on 17 January 1991, when Operation DESERT STORM began.

OFFENSE. Operation DESERT STORM began with a major airpower effort—from both land and sea—against strategic targets; Iraqi air, land, and naval forces; logistic infrastructure; and command and control (C2). Land and special operations forces supported this air effort by attacking or designating for attack forward-based Iraqi air defense and radar capability. The objectives of this phase were to gain air supremacy, significantly degrade Iraqi C2, deny information to enemy commanders, destroy enemy forces and infrastructure, and deny freedom of movement. This successful air operation would establish the conditions for the attack by coalition land forces.

While airpower attacked Iraqi forces throughout their depth, land forces repositioned from deceptive locations to attack positions using extensive OPSEC measures and simulations to deny knowledge of movements to the enemy. Two Army corps moved a great distance in an extremely short time to positions from which they could attack the more vulnerable western flanks of Iraqi forces. US amphibious forces threatened to attack from eastern seaward approaches, drawing Iraqi attention and defensive effort in that direction.

On 24 February, land forces attacked Iraq and rapidly closed on Iraqi flanks. Under a massive and continuous air component operation, coalition land forces closed with the Republican Guard. Iraqis surrendered in large numbers. To the extent that it could, the Iraqi military retreated. Within 100 hours of the start of the land force attack, the coalition achieved its strategic objectives and a cease-fire was ordered.

POSTWAR OPERATIONS. Coalition forces consolidated their gains and enforced conditions of the cease-fire. The coalition sought to prevent the Iraqi military from taking retribution against its own dissident populace. Task Force Freedom began operations to rebuild Kuwait City.

The end of major combat operations did not bring an end to conflict. The coalition conducted peace enforcement operations, humanitarian relief, security operations, extensive weapons and ordnance disposal, and humanitarian assistance. On 5 April, for example, President Bush announced the beginning of a relief operation in the area of northern Iraq. By 7 April, US aircraft from Europe were dropping relief supplies over the Iraqi border. Several thousand Service personnel who had participated in Operation DESERT STORM eventually redeployed to Turkey and northern Iraq in this joint and multinational relief operation.

This postwar phase also included the major operations associated with the redeployment and demobilization of forces.

Various Sources

11. The Balance of Offense, Defense, and Stability Operations

a. Combat missions and tasks can vary widely depending on context of the operation and the objective. Most combat operations will require the commander to balance offensive, defensive, and stability operations. This is particularly evident in a campaign or operation, where combat occurs during several phases and stability operations may occur throughout the campaign or operation.

b. **Offensive and Defensive Operations.** Major operations and campaigns, whether or not they involve large-scale combat, normally will include some level of both offense and defense (including interdiction, maneuver, forcible entry, fire support, counterair, CND, base defense, etc.). Although defense may be the stronger force posture, it is the offense that is normally decisive in combat. In striving to achieve military strategic objectives quickly and at the least cost, JFCs normally will seek the earliest opportunity to conduct decisive offensive operations. Nevertheless, during sustained offensive operations, selected elements of the joint force may need to pause, defend, resupply, or reconstitute, while other forces continue the attack. Further, force protection includes certain defensive measures that are required throughout each joint operation or campaign phase. Forces at all levels within the joint force must possess the agility to rapidly transition between offense and defense and vice versa. The relationship between offense and defense, then, is a complementary one. Defensive operations enable JFCs to conduct or prepare for decisive offensive operations.

c. **Stability Operations.** These missions, tasks, and activities seek to maintain or reestablish a safe and secure environment and provide essential governmental services, emergency infrastructure reconstruction, or humanitarian relief. Many of these missions and tasks are the essence of CMO. **To achieve the desired military end state and conclude the operations successfully, JFCs must integrate and synchronize stability operations with other operations (offense and defense) within each major operation or campaign phase.** Stability operations support USG stabilization efforts and contribute to USG initiatives to build partnerships. These initiatives set the conditions for interaction with partner, competitor, or adversary leaders, military forces, or relevant populations by developing and presenting information and conducting activities to affect their perceptions, will, behavior, and capabilities. The JFC will likely conduct them in coordination with interorganizational partners and the private sector in support of HN authorities. Since stability operations are conducted outside the United States, DOD provides similar support to US civil authorities through CS operations.

For further guidance on stability operations, refer to JP 3-07, Stability Operations.

d. **Balance and Simultaneity**

(1) Commanders strive to apply the many dimensions of military power simultaneously across the depth, breadth, and height of the operational area. This applies in all combat operations, but is the most extensive in a campaign. Consequently, JFCs normally achieve concentration in some areas or in specific functions and require economy of force in others. However, plans for major operations and campaigns require

Chapter V

an **appropriate balance between offensive and defensive operations and stability operations in all phases.** Therefore, **planning for stability operations should begin when joint operation planning begins.**

(2) Figure V-4 relates to Figure V-3 and the phasing explanation in paragraph 3, "Phasing a Joint Operation." Figure V-4 illustrates the notional balance between offensive, defensive, and stability operations as a major operation or campaign progresses. Since the focus of the *shape* phase is on prevention and preparation, any stability operations in the JFC's proposed operational area might continue, and combat (offense and defense) may be limited or absent. Defensive measures might be limited to providing an increased level of security. A similar balance applies to the *deter* phase,

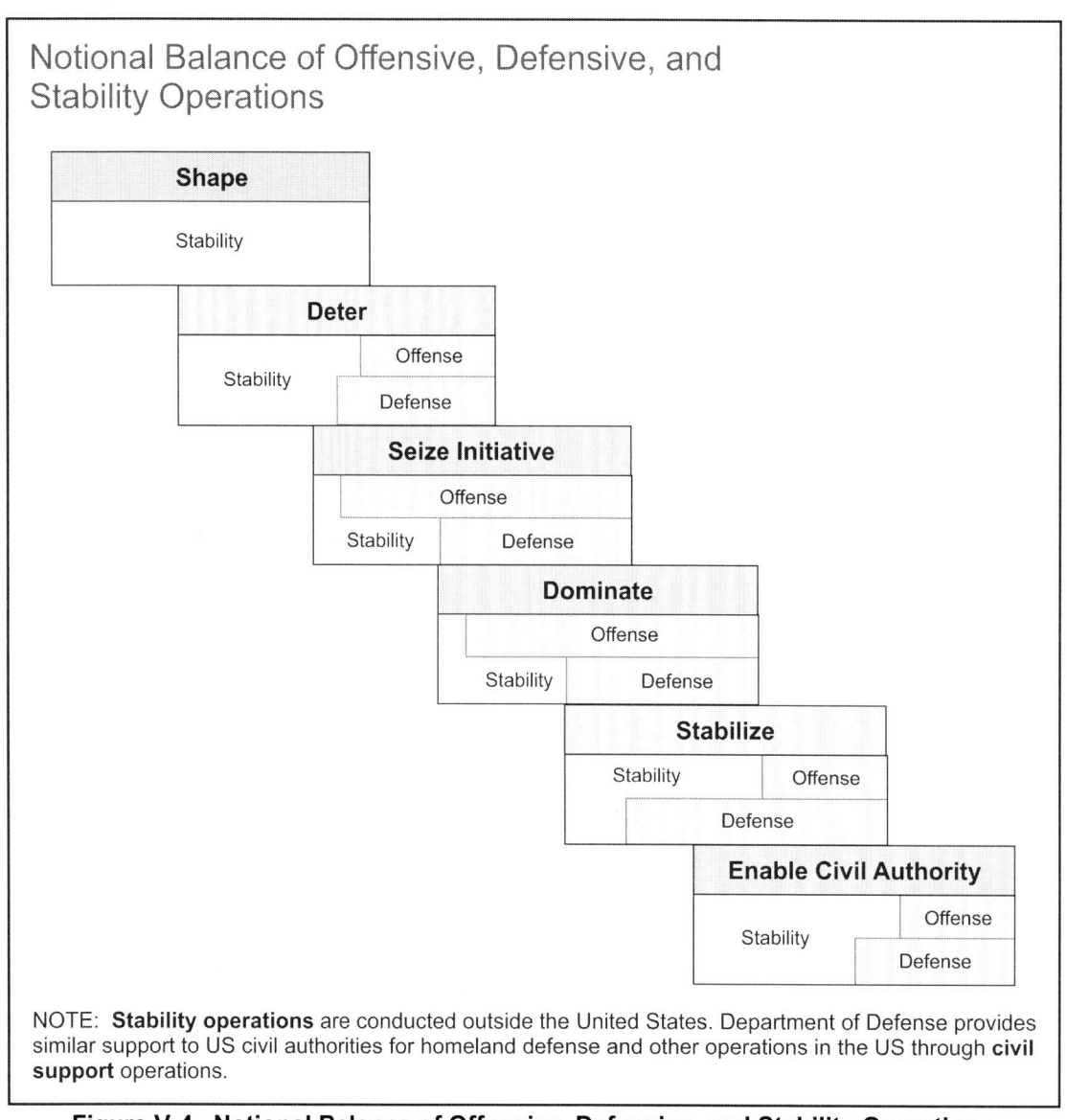

Figure V-4. Notional Balance of Offensive, Defensive, and Stability Operations

since the intent is to limit escalation in the operational area. A JFC might begin to limit stability operations if an adversary's potential combat actions are imminent. In combat operations, *seize the initiative* and *dominate* phases focus on offense and defense. Stability operations are likely restricted to parts of the operational area away from immediate combat, or might not occur at all. As the joint force achieves objectives and combat abates, the focus shifts to actions typical of *stabilize* and *enable civil authority*. Stability operations resume and will usually increase in proportion to the decrease in combat as the situation approaches relative peace.

(3) Planning for the transition from sustained combat operations to the termination of joint operations, and then a complete handover to civil authority, must commence during plan development and be ongoing during all phases of a campaign or major operation. Planning for redeployment should be considered early and continued throughout the operation and is best accomplished in the same time-phased process in which deployment was accomplished. An unnecessarily narrow focus on planning offensive and defensive operations in the *dominate* phase may threaten full development of the *stabilize* and *enable civil authority* phases and negatively affect joint operation momentum. Even while sustained combat operations are ongoing, it is necessary to establish or restore security and control and provide humanitarian relief as succeeding areas are occupied, bypassed, or transitioned to civilian control.

12. Considerations for Shaping

a. **General.** JFCs are able to assist in determining the shape and character of potential future operations before committing forces. In many cases, these actions enhance bonds between potential multinational partners, increase understanding of the region, help ensure access when required, strengthen future multinational operations, and prevent crises from developing.

b. **Organizing and Training Forces.** Organizing and, where possible, training forces to conduct operations throughout the operational area can be a deterrent. JTFs and components that are likely to be employed in theater operations should be exercised regularly during peacetime. Staffs should be identified and trained for planning and controlling joint and multinational operations. The composition of joint force staffs should reflect the composition of the joint force to ensure that those responsible for employing joint forces have thorough knowledge of their capabilities and limitations. When possible, JFCs and their staffs should invite non-DOD agencies to participate in training to facilitate a common understanding and to build a working relationship prior to actual execution. When it is not possible to train forces in the theater of employment, as with US-based forces with multiple taskings, maximum use should be made of regularly scheduled and ad hoc exercise opportunities. The training focus for all forces and the basis for exercise objectives should be the CCDR's joint mission-essential task list.

c. **Rehearsals.** Rehearsal is the process of learning, understanding, and practicing a plan in the time available before actual execution. Rehearsing key combat and logistic actions allows participants to become familiar with the operation and to visualize the plan. This process assists them in orienting joint and multinational forces to their

Chapter V

surroundings and to other units during execution. Rehearsals also provide a forum for subordinate leaders to analyze the plan, but they must exercise caution in adjusting the plan. Changes must be coordinated throughout the chain of command to prevent errors in integration and synchronization. HQ at the tactical level often conduct rehearsals involving participation of maneuver forces positioned on terrain that mirrors the operational environment. HQ at the operational level rehearse key aspects of a plan using command post exercises, typically supported by computer-aided simulations. While the joint force may not be able to rehearse an entire operation, the JFC should identify essential elements for rehearsal.

d. **Maintaining Operational Area Access.** JFCs establish and maintain access to operational areas where they are likely to operate, ensuring forward presence, basing (to include availability of airfields), freedom of navigation, and cooperation with allied and/or coalition nations to enhance operational reach. In part, this effort is national or multinational, involving maintenance of intertheater (between theaters) air and sea LOCs. Supporting CCDRs can greatly enhance this effort.

e. **Space Considerations.** Space operations are a critical enabler that supports all joint operations. When conflict occurs, commanders need to ensure US, allied, and/or multinational forces gain and maintain space superiority, which is achieved through global and theater space control, space force enhancement, space support, and space force application operations. Also, commanders must anticipate hostile actions that may affect friendly space operations. Commanders should anticipate the proliferation and increasing sophistication of commercial space capabilities and products available that the commander can leverage, but which also may be available to the adversary. USSTRATCOM has the responsibility to plan and conduct space operations. **The GCC has the responsibility to conduct theater space operations,** and may request the CDRUSSTRATCOM's assistance in integrating space forces, capabilities, and considerations into each phase of campaign and major OPLANs. Global and theater space operations require robust planning and skilled employment to synchronize and integrate space operations with the joint operation. It is therefore incumbent upon the GCCs to coordinate as required to minimize conflicts. Space capabilities help shape the operational environment in a variety of ways including providing ISR and communications necessary for keeping commanders and leaders informed worldwide. JFCs and their components should request space support early in the planning process to ensure effective and efficient use of space assets.

f. **Stability Operations.** Activities in the *shape* phase primarily will focus on continued planning and preparation for anticipated stability operations in the subsequent phases. These activities should include conducting collaborative interagency planning to synchronize the civil-military effort, confirming the feasibility of pertinent military objectives and the military end state, and providing for adequate intelligence, an appropriate force mix, and other capabilities. Stability operations in this phase may be required to quickly restore security and infrastructure or provide humanitarian relief in select portions of the operational area to dissuade further adversary actions or to help gain and maintain access and future success.

Joint Operations Across the Range of Military Operations

13. Considerations for Deterrence

a. **General.** The *deter* phase is characterized by preparatory actions that indicate the intent to execute subsequent phases of the operation. Deterrence should be based on capability (having the means to influence behavior), credibility (maintaining a level of believability that the proposed actions may actual be employed), and communication (transmitting the intended message to the desired audience) to ensure greater effectiveness. Before hostilities begin, the JFC and staff analyze and assess the adversary's goals and decision-making process to determine how, where, and when these can be affected and what friendly actions (military and others) can influence events and act as a deterrent. Emphasis should be placed on setting the conditions for successful joint operations in the *dominate* and follow-on phases should deterrence fail.

b. **Preparing the Operational Area**

(1) **Special Operations.** SOF play a major role in preparing and shaping the operational area and environment by setting conditions which mitigate risk and facilitate successful follow-on operations. The regional focus, cross-cultural/ethnic insights, language capabilities, and relationships of SOF provide access to and influence in nations where the presence of conventional US forces is unacceptable or inappropriate. SOF contributions can provide operational leverage by gathering critical information, undermining a potential adversary's will or capacity to wage war, and enhancing the capabilities of conventional US, multinational, or indigenous/surrogate forces. CDRUSSOCOM synchronizes planning for global operations against terrorist networks in coordination with other CCMDs, the Services, and, as directed, appropriate USG agencies. In coordination with GCCs and the supported JFC, CDRUSSOCOM plans and executes or synchronizes the execution of activities related to preparing the operational environment and operational area, or provides SOF to other CCMDs.

For further guidance on SO, refer to JP 3-05, Special Operations.

(2) **Stability Operations.** Joint force planning and operations conducted prior to commencement of hostilities should establish a sound foundation for operations in the *stabilize* and *enable civil authority* phases. JFCs should anticipate and address how to fill the power vacuum created when sustained combat operations wind down. Accomplishing this task should ease the transition to operations in the *stabilize* phase and shorten the path to the national strategic end state and handover to another authority. Considerations include:

(a) Limiting the damage to key infrastructure and services.

(b) Establishing the intended disposition of captured leadership and demobilized military and paramilitary forces.

(c) Providing for the availability of cash or other means of financial exchange.

Chapter V

(d) Determining the proper force mix (e.g., combat, military police, CA, engineer, medical, multinational).

(e) Assessing availability of HN law enforcement and HSS resources.

(f) Securing key infrastructure nodes and facilitating HN law enforcement and first responder services.

(g) Developing and disseminating information necessary to suppress potential new enemies and promote new governmental authority.

(3) **CA** units contain a variety of specialty skills that may support the joint operation being planned. CA units can assess the civil infrastructure, assist in the operation of temporary shelters, and serve as liaisons between the military and civil organizations. Establishing and maintaining military-to-civil relations may include interaction among US, allied or multinational, HN forces, as well as OGAs, IGOs, and NGOs. CA forces can provide expertise on factors that directly affect military operations to include culture, social structure, economic systems, language, and HNS capabilities. CA may be able to perform functions for limited durations that normally are the responsibility of local or indigenous governments. Employment of CA forces should be based upon a clear concept of CA mission requirements for the type operation being planned.

For further guidance on CA, refer to JP 3-57, Civil-Military Operations.

(4) **Sustainment.** Thorough planning for logistic and personnel support is critical. For example, the infrastructure required to deploy and support combat operations must be identified, resourced, and emplaced in a timely manner. Planning must include active participation by all deploying and in-theater US and multinational forces.

c. **Isolating the Enemy**

(1) With Presidential and SecDef approval, guidance, and national support, **JFCs strive to isolate enemies by denying them allies and sanctuary.** The intent is to strip away as much enemy support or freedom of action as possible, while limiting the enemy's potential for horizontal or vertical escalation. JFCs also may be tasked by the President and SecDef to support diplomatic, economic, and informational actions.

(2) **The JFC also seeks to isolate the main enemy force from both its strategic leadership and its supporting infrastructure.** Such isolation can be achieved through the use of IO and the interdiction of LOCs or resources affecting the enemy's ability to conduct or sustain military operations. This step serves to deny the enemy both physical and psychological support and may separate the enemy leadership and military from their public support.

d. **Flexible Deterrent Options.** FDOs are preplanned, deterrence-oriented actions carefully tailored to bring an issue to early resolution without armed conflict. Both military and nonmilitary FDOs can be used to dissuade actions before a crisis arises or to deter further aggression during a crisis. FDOs are developed for each instrument of national power, but they are most effective when used in combination.

(1) **Military FDOs** can be initiated before or after unambiguous warning. Deployment timelines, combined with the requirement for a rapid, early response, generally require economy of force; however, military FDOs should not increase risk to the force that exceeds the potential benefit of the desired effect. Military FDOs must be carefully tailored regarding timing, efficiency, and effectiveness. They can rapidly improve the military balance of power in the operational area; especially in terms of early warning, intelligence gathering, logistic infrastructure, air and maritime forces, MISO, and protection without precipitating armed response from the adversary. Care should be taken to avoid undesired effects such as eliciting an armed response should adversary leadership perceive that friendly military FDOs are being used as preparation for a preemptive attack.

(2) **Nonmilitary FDOs** are preplanned, preemptive actions taken by OGAs to dissuade an adversary from initiating hostilities. Nonmilitary FDOs need to be coordinated, integrated, and synchronized with military FDOs to focus all instruments of national power.

For further guidance on planning FDOs, refer to JP 5-0, Joint Operation Planning.

e. **Protection.** JFCs must protect their forces and their freedom of action to accomplish their mission. This dictates that JFCs not only provide force protection, but be aware of and participate as appropriate in the protection of interagency and regional multinational capabilities and activities. JFCs may spend as much time on protection as on direct preparation of their forces for combat.

f. **Space Force Enhancement.** JFCs depend upon and exploit the advantages of space capabilities. During the *deter* phase, space forces are limited to already fielded and immediately deployable assets and established priorities for service. As the situation develops, priorities for space force enhancement may change to aid the JFC in assessing the changing operational environment. Most importantly, the JFC and component commanders need to anticipate "surge" space capabilities needed for future phases due to the long lead times to reprioritize or acquire additional capabilities.

g. **Geospatial Intelligence Support to Operations.** Geospatial products or services—including maps, charts, imagery products, web services, and support data—must be fully coordinated with JFC components as well as with the Joint Staff, Office of SecDef, and the NGA through the JFC's GEOINT cell. Requests for or updates to GEOINT products, including maps or annotated imagery products, should be submitted as early as possible through the JFC's GEOINT cell to the NGA support team at the JFC's HQ. US products should be used whenever possible, since the accuracy, scale, and reliability of foreign maps and charts may vary widely from US products. In any joint or multinational operation, the *World Geodetic System-1984* should be the common system. If US products are to be used in a coalition environment or within a multinational HQ, the release of US mapping materials or imagery products may first require foreign disclosure/release adjudication.

For further guidance on GEOINT, refer to JP 2-03, Geospatial Intelligence Support to Joint Operations.

h. **Physical Environment**

(1) **Weather, terrain, and sea conditions** can significantly affect operations and logistic support of the joint force and should be carefully assessed before sustained combat operations. Mobility of the force, integration and synchronization of operations, and ability to employ precision munitions can be affected by degraded conditions. Climatological and hydrographic planning tools, studies, and forecast products help the JFC determine the most advantageous time and location to conduct operations.

(2) **Urban areas** possess all of the characteristics of the natural landscape, coupled with man-made construction and the associated infrastructure, resulting in a complicated and dynamic environment that influences the conduct of military operations in many ways. **The most distinguishing characteristic of operations in urban areas, however, is not the infrastructure but the density of noncombatants.** Joint urban operations (JUOs) are conducted in large, densely populated areas with problems unique to clearing enemy forces while possibly restoring services and managing major concentrations of people. For example, industrial areas and port facilities often are collocated with highly populated areas creating the opportunity for accidental or deliberate release of toxic industrial materials which could impact JUOs. During JUOs, joint forces may not focus only on destruction of enemy forces but also may be required to take steps necessary to protect and support noncombatants and their infrastructure from which they receive services necessary for survival. As such, ROE during JUOs may be more restrictive than for other types of operations. When planning JUOs, the JFC and staff should consider the impact of military operations on noncombatants to include their culture, values, and infrastructure; thereby viewing the urban area as a dynamic and complex system—not solely as terrain. This implies the joint force should be capable of understanding the specific urban environment; sensing, locating, and isolating the enemy among noncombatants; and applying combat power precisely and discriminately.

For additional guidance on JUOs, refer to JP 3-06, Joint Urban Operations.

(3) **Littoral Areas.** The littoral area contains two parts. First is the seaward area from the open ocean to the shore, which must be controlled to support operations ashore. Second is the landward area inland from the shore that can be supported and defended directly from the sea. Control of the littoral area often is essential to maritime superiority. Maritime operations conducted in the littoral area can project power, fires, and forces to support achieving the JFC's objectives; and facilitate the entry of other elements of the joint force through the seizure of an adversary's port, naval base, or air base to allow entry and movement of other elements of the joint force. Depending on the situation, mine warfare may be critical to control of the littoral areas.

(4) **The electromagnetic spectrum,** which has become increasingly complex, contested, and congested as technology has advanced, can significantly affect joint force operations. Operational experiences demonstrate not only how successful control of the EMS can influence the outcome of the conflict, but highlight US dependence on the EMS in order to successfully operate. When planning operations, the JFC should consider both the impact of military operations on the current EM operational environment as well as its affect on military operations.

14. Considerations for Seizing the Initiative

a. **General.** As operations commence, the JFC needs to exploit friendly advantages and capabilities to shock, demoralize, and disrupt the enemy immediately. The JFC seeks decisive advantage through the use of all available elements of combat power to seize and maintain the initiative, deny the enemy the opportunity to achieve its objectives, and generate in the enemy a sense of inevitable failure and defeat. Additionally, the JFC coordinates with OGAs to facilitate coherent use of all instruments of national power in achieving national strategic objectives.

b. **Force Projection**

(1) The President and SecDef may direct a CCDR to resolve a crisis quickly, employing immediately available forces and appropriate FDOs as discussed above to preclude escalation. When these forces and actions are not sufficient, follow-on strikes and/or the **deployment** of forces from CONUS or another theater and/or the use of multinational forces may be necessary. Consequently, the CCDR must sequence, enable, and protect the deployment of forces to achieve early decisive advantage. The CCDR should not overlook enemy capabilities to affect deployment from bases to ports of embarkation. The CCDR may have to adjust the time-phased force and deployment data to meet a changing operational environment. The deployment of forces may be either opposed or unopposed by an adversary.

(a) **Opposed.** Initial operations may be designed to suppress adversary anti-access capabilities. For example, the ability to generate sufficient combat power through long-range air operations or from the sea can provide for effective force projection in the absence of timely or unencumbered access. Other opposed situations may require a forcible entry capability. In other cases, force projection can be accomplished rapidly by forcible entry operations coordinated with strategic air mobility, sealift, and pre-positioned forces. For example, the seizure and defense of lodgment areas by amphibious forces would then serve as initial entry points for the continuous and uninterrupted flow of pre-positioned forces and materiel into the theater. Both efforts demand a versatile mix of forces that are organized, trained, equipped, and poised to respond quickly.

(b) **Unopposed** deployment operations provide the JFC and subordinate components a more flexible operational environment to efficiently and effectively build combat power, train, rehearse, acclimate, and otherwise establish the conditions for successful combat operations. In unopposed entry, JFCs arrange the flow of forces, to

Chapter V

include significant theater opening logistic forces, that best facilitates the CONOPS. In these situations, logistic forces may be a higher priority for early deployment than combat forces, as determined by the in-theater protection requirements.

(2) Commanders should brief deploying forces on the threat and force protection requirements prior to deployment and upon arrival in the operational area. Also, JFCs and their subordinate commanders evaluate the timing, location, and other factors of force deployment in each COA for the impact of sabotage, criminal activity, and terrorist acts and their impact on joint reception, staging, onward movement, and integration (JRSOI) and the follow-on CONOPS. The threat could involve those not directly supporting or sympathetic to the adversary, but those seeking to take advantage of the situation.

(3) During force projection, US forces and ports of debarkation must be protected. JFCs should introduce forces in a manner that provides security for rapid force buildup. Therefore, early entry forces should deploy with sufficient organic and supporting capabilities to preserve their freedom of action and protect personnel and equipment from potential or likely threats. Early entry forces also should include a deployable joint C2 capability to rapidly assess the situation, make decisions, and conduct initial operations.

(4) JRSOI occurs in the operational area and comprises the essential processes required to transition arriving personnel, equipment, and materiel into forces capable of meeting operational requirements. Forces are vulnerable during JRSOI, so planning must include force protection requirements.

For further information on JRSOI, refer to JP 3-35, Deployment and Redeployment Operations.

c. **Unit Integrity During Deployment**

(1) US Service forces normally train as units, and are best able to accomplish a mission when deployed intact. By deploying as an existing unit, forces are able to continue to operate under established procedures, adapting them to the mission and situation, as required. When personnel and elements are drawn from various commands, effectiveness may be decreased. By deploying without established operating procedures, an ad hoc force takes more time to form and adjust to requirements of the mission. This not only complicates mission accomplishment, but also may have an impact on force protection.

(2) Even if political restraints on an operation dictate that a large force cannot be deployed intact, commanders should select elements for deployment that have established internal procedures and structures, have trained and operated together, and possess appropriate joint force combat capabilities. In order to provide a JFC with needed versatility, it may not be possible to preserve complete unit integrity. In such cases, units must be prepared to send elements that are able to operate independently of parent units. Attachment to a related unit is the usual mode. In this instance, units not

accustomed to having attachments may be required to provide administrative and logistic support to normally unrelated units.

(3) The CCDR, in coordination with Commander, United States Transportation Command, subordinate JFCs, and the Service component commanders, needs to carefully balance the desire to retain unit integrity through the deployment process with the effective use of strategic lift platforms. While maximizing unit integrity may reduce JRSOI requirements and allow combat units to be employed more quickly, doing so will often have a direct negative impact on the efficient use of the limited strategic lift. In some cases, this negative impact on strategic lift may have a negative effect on DOD deployment and sustainment requirements beyond the GCC's AOR. A general rule of thumb is that unit integrity is much more important for early deploying units than for follow-on forces.

d. **Forcible entry** is a joint military operation conducted either as a major operation or a part of a larger campaign to **seize and hold a military lodgment in the face of armed opposition** for the continuous landing of forces. Forcible entry operations can strike directly at the enemy COGs and can open new avenues for other military operations.

(1) Forcible entry operations may include amphibious, airborne, and air assault operations, or any combination thereof. Forcible entry operations can create multiple dilemmas by creating threats that exceed the enemy's capability to respond. The joint forcible entry operation commander will employ distributed, yet coherent, operations to attack the objective area or areas. The net result will be a coordinated attack that overwhelms the adversary before the adversary has time to react. A well-positioned and networked force enables the defeat of any adversary reaction and facilitates follow-on operations, if required.

(2) **Forcible entry normally is complex and risky** and should therefore be kept as simple as possible in concept. These operations require extensive intelligence, detailed coordination, innovation, and flexibility. Schemes of maneuver and coordination between forces need to be clearly understood by all participants. Forces are tailored for the mission and echeloned to permit simultaneous deployment and employment. When airborne, amphibious, and air assault operations are combined, unity of command is vital. Rehearsals are a critical part of preparation for forcible entry. Participating forces need to be prepared to fight immediately upon arrival and require robust communications and intelligence capabilities to move with forward elements.

(3) **The forcible entry force must be prepared to immediately transition to follow-on operations and should plan accordingly.** Joint forcible entry actions occur in both singular and multiple operations. These actions include establishing forward presence, preparing the operational area, opening entry points, establishing and sustaining access, receiving follow-on forces, conducting follow-on operations, sustaining the operations, and conducting decisive operations.

> **OPERATION JUST CAUSE**
>
> In the early morning hours of 20 December 1989, the Commander, US Southern Command, Joint Task Force (JTF) Panama, conducted multiple, simultaneous forcible entry operations to begin Operation JUST CAUSE. By parachute assault, forces seized key lodgments at Torrijos-Tucumen Military Airfield and International Airport and at the Panamanian Defense Force (PDF) base at Rio Hato. The JTF used these lodgments for force buildup and to launch immediate assaults against the PDF.
>
> The JTF commander synchronized the forcible entry operations with numerous other operations involving virtually all capabilities of the joint force. The parachute assault forces strategically deployed at staggered times from bases in the continental United States, some in C-141 Starlifters, others in slower C-130 transport planes. One large formation experienced delays from a sudden ice storm at the departure airfield—its operations and timing were revised in the air. H-hour was even adjusted for assault operations because of intelligence that indicated a possible compromise. Special operations forces (SOF) reconnaissance and direct action teams provided last-minute information on widely dispersed targets.
>
> At H-hour the parachute assault forces, forward-deployed forces, SOF, and air elements of the joint force simultaneously attacked 27 targets—most of them in the vicinity of the Panama Canal Zone. Illustrating that joint force commanders organize and apply force in a manner that fits the situation, the JTF commander employed land and SOF to attack strategic targets and stealth aircraft to attack tactical and operational-level targets.
>
> The forcible entry operations, combined with simultaneous and follow-on attack against enemy command and control facilities and key units, seized the initiative and paralyzed enemy decision making. Most fighting was concluded within 24 hours. Casualties were minimized. It was a classic coup de main.
>
> **Various Sources**

(4) **Successful OPSEC and MILDEC may confuse the adversary and ease forcible entry operations.** OPSEC helps foster a credible MILDEC. Additionally, the actions, themes, and messages portrayed by all friendly forces must be consistent if MILDEC is to be believable.

(5) **SOF may precede forcible entry forces** to identify, clarify, and modify conditions in the lodgment. SOF may conduct the assaults to seize small, initial lodgments such as airfields or seaports. They may provide or assist in employing fire support and conduct other operations in support of the forcible entry, such as seizing air fields or conducting reconnaissance of landing zones or amphibious landing sites. They may conduct special reconnaissance and direct action well beyond the lodgment to identify, interdict, and destroy forces that threaten the conventional entry force.

(6) **The sustainment requirements and challenges** for forcible entry operations **can be formidable**, but must not be allowed to become such an overriding concern that the forcible entry operation itself is jeopardized. JFCs must carefully balance the introduction of sustainment forces needed to support initial combat with combat forces required to establish, maintain, and protect the lodgment as well as forces required to transition to follow-on operations.

For additional and detailed guidance on forcible entry operations, refer to JP 3-18, Joint Forcible Entry Operations.

e. **Attack of Enemy Centers of Gravity.** As part of achieving decisive advantages early, joint force operations may be directed immediately against enemy COGs using conventional and SO forces and capabilities. These attacks may be decisive or may begin offensive operations throughout the enemy's depth that can create dilemmas causing paralysis and destroying cohesion.

US Marines assigned to a Landing Force participate in a live fire amphibious landing exercise on Binturan Beach, Brunei during Cooperation Afloat Readiness and Training Brunei 2010.

f. **Full-Spectrum Superiority.** The cumulative effect of dominance in the air, land, maritime, and space domains and information environment (which includes cyberspace) that permits the conduct of joint operations without effective opposition or prohibitive interference is essential to joint force mission success. JFCs seek superiority in these domains to prepare the operational area and information environment and to accomplish the mission as rapidly as possible. The JFC may have to initially focus all available joint forces on seizing the initiative. A delay at the outset of combat may damage US

Chapter V

credibility, lessen coalition support, and provide incentives for other adversaries to begin conflicts elsewhere.

(1) **JFCs normally strive to achieve air and maritime superiority early.** Air and maritime superiority allows joint forces to conduct operations without prohibitive interference from opposing air and maritime forces. Control of the air is a critical enabler because it allows joint forces both freedom from attack and freedom to attack. Using both defensive and offensive operations, JFCs employ complementary weapon systems and sensors to achieve air and maritime superiority.

(2) **Land forces** can be moved quickly into an area to deter the enemy from inserting forces, thereby precluding the enemy from gaining an operational advantage. The rapid deployment and employment of land forces with support of other components enable sustained operations more quickly contribute to the enemy's defeat and help restore stability in the operational area.

(3) **Space superiority must be achieved early to support freedom of action.** Space superiority allows the JFC access to communications, weather, navigation, timing, remote sensing, and ISR assets without prohibitive interference by the opposing force. Space control operations are conducted by joint and allied and/or coalition forces to gain and maintain space superiority.

(4) Cyberspace superiority may enable freedom of action throughout the operational area.

(5) Early **superiority in the information environment** also is vital in joint operations. **It degrades the enemy's C2 while allowing the JFC to maximize friendly C2 capabilities.** Superiority in the information environment also allows the JFC to better understand the enemy's intentions, capabilities, and actions and influence foreign attitudes and perceptions of the operation.

(6) Control of the EM environment must be achieved early to support freedom of action. This control is important for superiority across the physical domains and information environment.

g. **C2 in Littoral Areas**

(1) **Controlled littoral areas often offer the best positions from which to begin, sustain, and support joint operations,** especially in operational areas with limited or poor infrastructure for supporting US joint operations ashore. The ability to project fires and employ forces from sea-based assets combined with their C2, ISR, and IO capabilities are formidable tools that JFCs can use to gain and maintain initiative. Maritime forces operating in littoral areas can dominate coastal areas and rapidly generate high intensity offensive power at times and in locations required by JFCs. Maritime forces' relative freedom of action enables JFCs to position these capabilities where they can readily strike opponents. Maritime forces' very presence, if made known, can pose a threat that the enemy cannot ignore.

(2) **JFCs can operate from an HQ platform at sea.** Depending on the nature of the joint operation, a maritime commander can serve as the JFC or function as a JFACC while the operation is primarily maritime, and shift that command ashore if the operation shifts landward in accordance with the JFC's CONOPS. In other cases, a maritime HQ may serve as the base of the joint force HQ, or subordinate JFCs or other component commanders may use the C2 and intelligence facilities aboard ship.

(3) **Transferring C2 from sea to shore** requires detailed planning, active liaison, and coordination throughout the joint force. Such a transition may involve a simple movement of flags and supporting personnel, or it may require a complete change of joint force HQ. The new joint force HQ may use personnel and equipment, especially communications equipment, from the old HQ, or it may require augmentation from different sources. One technique is to transfer C2 in several stages. Another technique is for the JFC to satellite off the capabilities of one of the components ashore until the new HQ is fully prepared. Whichever way the transition is done, staffs should develop detailed checklists to address all of the C2 requirements and the timing of transfer of each. The value of joint training and rehearsals in this transition is evident.

h. **SOF-Conventional Force Integration.** The JFC, using SOF independently or integrated with conventional forces, gains an additional and specialized capability to achieve objectives that might not otherwise be attainable. Integration enables the JFC to take fullest advantage of conventional and SOF core competencies. SOF are most effective when SO are fully integrated into the overall plan and the execution of SO is through proper SOF C2 elements in a supporting or supported relationship with conventional forces. Joint SOF C2 elements are provided to conduct a specific SO or prosecute SO in support of a joint campaign or operation. SO commanders also provide liaison to component commands to integrate, coordinate, and deconflict SOF and conventional force operations. Exchange of SOF and conventional force LNOs is essential to enhance situational awareness and reduce risk of fratricide.

SPECIAL OPERATIONS FORCES AND CONVENTIONAL FORCES INTEGRATION DURING OPERATION ENDURING FREEDOM

Special operations forces (SOF) and conventional forces integration demonstrated powerful air-ground synergies in Operation ENDURING FREEDOM. Army special forces, while performing the classic special operations core task of unconventional warfare, organized and coordinated operations of the Northern Alliance against the Taliban and their al Qaeda allies. Supported by other joint SOF, they frequently directed massive and effective close air support from Air Force, Navy, and Marine Corps assets. The effects of the continuous SOF-directed air strikes so weakened the Taliban and al Qaeda that the Northern Alliance was able to quickly capture the major cities of Afghanistan early in the campaign.

Various Sources

Chapter V

i. **Stability Operations.** Combat in this phase provides an opportunity to begin various stability operations that will help achieve military strategic and operational objectives and create the conditions for the later stability and enable civil authority phases. Operations to neutralize or eliminate potential *stabilize* phase enemies may be initiated. National and local HN authorities may be contacted and offered support. Key infrastructure may be seized or otherwise protected. Civil IM, which is broadly tasked to support the overall intelligence collection on the status of enemy infrastructure, government organizations, and humanitarian needs, should be increased. MISO used to influence the behavior of approved foreign target audiences in support of military strategic and operational objectives can ease the situation encountered when sustained combat is concluded. In coordination with interorganizational partners, the JFC must arrange for necessary financial support of these operations well in advance.

j. **Protection.** JFCs must strive to conserve the fighting potential of the joint/multinational force at the onset of combat operations. Further, HN infrastructure and logistic support key to force projection and sustainment of the force must be protected. JFCs counter the enemy's fires and maneuver by making personnel, systems, and units difficult to locate, strike, and destroy. They protect their force from enemy maneuver and fires, including the effects of WMD. OPSEC and MILDEC are key elements of this effort. Operations to gain air, space, and maritime superiority; defensive use of IO; PR; and protection of airports and seaports, LOCs, and friendly force lodgment also contribute significantly to force protection at the onset of combat operations.

k. **Prevention of Fratricide.** JFCs must make every effort to reduce the potential for the unintentional killing or wounding of friendly personnel by friendly fire. The destructive power and range of modern weapons, coupled with the high intensity and rapid tempo of modern combat, increase the potential for fratricide. Commanders must be aware of those situations that increase the risk of fratricide and institute appropriate preventive measures. The primary mechanisms for reducing fratricide are command emphasis, disciplined operations, close coordination among component commands and multinational partners, SOPs, technology solutions (e.g., identify friend or foe, blue force tracking), rehearsals, effective CID, and enhanced awareness of the operational environment. Commanders should seek to minimize fratricide while not limiting boldness and initiative.

15. **Considerations for Dominance**

a. **General.** JFCs conduct sustained combat operations when a "coup de main" is not possible. During sustained combat operations, JFCs simultaneously employ conventional and SO forces and capabilities throughout the breadth and depth of the operational area. The JFC may designate one component or LOO to be the main effort, with other components providing support and other LOOs as supporting efforts. When conditions or plans change, the main effort might shift. Some missions and operations (i.e., strategic attack, interdiction, and IO) continue throughout to deny the enemy sanctuary, freedom of action, or informational advantage. These missions and operations, when executed concurrently with other operations, degrade enemy morale and physical cohesion and bring the enemy closer to culmination. When prevented from concentrating, opponents can be attacked, isolated at tactical and operational levels, and defeated in detail. At other times, JFCs may cause their opponents to concentrate their forces, facilitating their attack by friendly forces.

   b. **Linear and Nonlinear Operations**

      (1) **In linear operations,** each commander directs and sustains combat power toward enemy forces in concert with adjacent units. Linearity refers primarily to the conduct of operations with identified forward lines of own troops (FLOTs). In linear operations, emphasis is placed on maintaining the position of friendly forces in relation to other friendly forces. From this relative positioning of forces, security is enhanced and massing of forces can be facilitated. Also inherent in linear operations is the security of rear areas, especially LOCs between sustaining bases and fighting forces. Protected LOCs, in turn, increase the endurance of joint forces and ensure freedom of action for extended periods. A linear operational area organization may be best for some operations or certain phases of an operation. Conditions that favor linear operations include those where US forces lack the information needed to conduct nonlinear operations or are severely outnumbered. Linear operations also are appropriate against a deeply arrayed, echeloned enemy force or when the threat to LOCs reduces friendly force freedom of action. In these circumstances, linear operations allow commanders to concentrate and synchronize combat power more easily. Multinational operations also may require a linear design. World Wars I and II offer multiple examples of linear operations.

      (2) **In nonlinear operations,** forces orient on objectives without geographic reference to adjacent forces. Nonlinear operations typically focus on creating specific effects on multiple decisive points. **Nonlinear operations emphasize simultaneous operations along multiple LOOs from selected bases (ashore or afloat).** Simultaneity overwhelms opposing C2 and allows the JFC to retain the initiative. In nonlinear operations, sustaining functions may depend on sustainment assets moving with forces or aerial delivery. Noncombatants and the fluidity of nonlinear operations require careful judgment in clearing fires, both direct and indirect. Situational awareness, coupled with precision fires, frees commanders to act against multiple objectives. Swift maneuver against several decisive points supported by precise, concentrated fire can induce paralysis and shock among enemy troops and commanders. Nonlinear operations were applied during Operation JUST CAUSE. The joint forces oriented more on their assigned objectives (e.g., destroying an enemy force or seizing and controlling critical terrain or population centers) and less on their geographic relationship to other friendly forces. To protect themselves, individual forces relied more on situational awareness, mobility advantages, and freedom of action than on mass. Nonlinear operations place a premium on the communications, intelligence, mobility, and innovative means for sustainment.

         (a) During **nonlinear offensive operations,** attacking forces must focus offensive actions against decisive points, while allocating the minimum essential combat power to defensive operations. Reserves must have a high degree of mobility to respond where needed. JFCs may be required to dedicate combat forces to provide for LOC and base defense. Vulnerability increases as operations extend and attacking forces are

Chapter V

exposed over a larger operational area. Linkup operations, particularly those involving vertical envelopments, require extensive planning and preparation. The potential for fratricide increases due to the fluid nature of the nonlinear operational area and the changing disposition of attacking and defending forces. The presence of noncombatants in the operational area further complicates operations.

(b) During **nonlinear defensive operations,** defenders focus on destroying enemy forces, even if it means losing physical contact with other friendly units. Successful nonlinear defenses require all friendly commanders to understand the JFCs intent and maintain a common operational picture (COP). Noncontiguous defenses are generally mobile defenses; however, some subordinate units may conduct area defenses to hold key terrain or canalize attackers into engagement areas. Nonlinear defenses place a premium on reconnaissance and surveillance to maintain contact with the enemy, produce relevant information, and develop and maintain a COP. The defending force focuses almost exclusively on defeating the enemy force rather than retaining large areas. Although less challenging than in offensive operations, LOC and sustainment security will still be a test and may require allocation of combat forces to protect LOCs and other high risk functions or bases. The JFC must ensure that clear command relationships are established to properly account for the added challenges to base, base cluster, and LOC security.

(3) **Areas of Operations and Linear/Nonlinear Operations**

(a) **General.** JFCs consider incorporating combinations of contiguous and noncontiguous AOs with linear and nonlinear operations as they conduct operational design. They choose the combination that fits the operational environment and the purpose of the operation. Association of contiguous and noncontiguous AOs with linear and nonlinear operations creates the four combinations in Figure V-5.

(b) **Linear Operations in Contiguous AOs.** Linear operations in contiguous AOs (upper left-hand pane in Figure V-5) typify sustained offensive and defensive operations against powerful, echeloned, and symmetrically organized forces. The contiguous areas and continuous FLOT focus combat power and protect sustainment functions.

(c) **Linear Operations in Noncontiguous AOs.** The upper right-hand pane of Figure V-5 depicts a JFC's operational area with subordinate component commanders conducting linear operations in noncontiguous AOs. In this case, the JFC retains responsibility for that portion of the operational area outside the subordinate commanders' AOs.

Joint Operations Across the Range of Military Operations

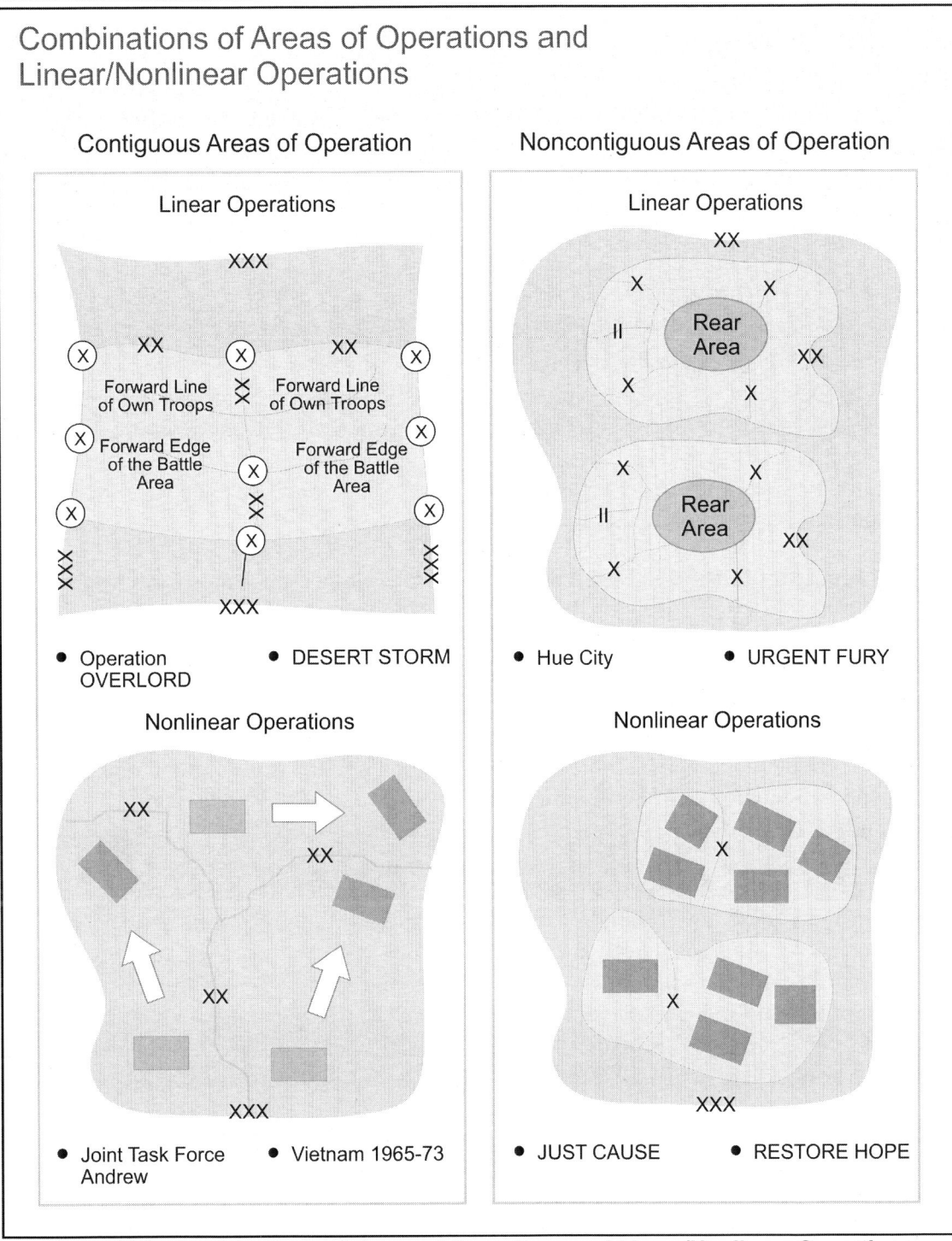

Figure V-5. Combinations of Areas of Operations and Linear/Nonlinear Operations

(d) **Nonlinear Operations in Contiguous AOs.** The lower left-hand pane in Figure V-5 illustrates the JFC's entire assigned operational area divided into subordinate AOs. Subordinate component commanders are conducting nonlinear operations within their AOs. This combination typically is applied in stability operations and CS operations.

Chapter V

(e) **Nonlinear Operations in Noncontiguous AOs.** The lower right-hand pane of Figure V-5 depicts both the JFC and subordinate JFCs conducting nonlinear operations (e.g., during 1992 in Somalia, joint forces conducted nonlinear stability operations in widely separated AOs around Kismayu and Mogadishu). The size of the operational area, composition and distribution of enemy forces, and capabilities of friendly forces are important considerations in deciding whether to use this combination of operational area organization.

(f) Commanders should seek ways to improve tactical effectiveness by making select joint capabilities available at the lowest appropriate level. The control and management of joint capabilities typically resides at a JTF or higher joint command or national agency. But operational circumstances could dictate that low-level tactical units exercise selective or routine control of certain joint assets. Advances in areas such as communications, information sharing, and targeting can increase the JFC's opportunities to push joint capabilities to lower echelons in ways that improve tactical effectiveness while contributing to operational objectives.

c. **Operating in the Littoral Areas.** Even when joint forces are firmly established ashore, littoral operations provide JFCs with excellent opportunities to achieve leverage over the enemy by operational maneuver from the sea. Such operations can introduce significant size forces over relatively great distances in short periods of time into the rear or flanks of the enemy. The mobility and fire support capability of maritime forces at sea, coupled with the ability to rapidly land operationally significant forces, can be key to achieving military operational objectives. These capabilities are further enhanced by operational flexibility and the ability to identify and take advantage of fleeting opportunities.

d. **Attack on Enemy COGs.** Attacks on enemy COGs typically continue during sustained operations. JFCs should time their actions to coincide with actions of other operations of the joint force and vice versa to achieve military strategic and operational objectives. As with all operations of the joint force, direct and indirect attacks of enemy COGs should be designed to achieve the required military strategic and operational objectives per the CONOPS, while limiting potential undesired effects on operations in follow-on phases.

e. **Synchronizing and/or Integrating Maneuver and Interdiction**

(1) Synchronizing and/or integrating air, land, and maritime interdiction and maneuver, enabled by space-based capabilities, provides one of the most dynamic concepts available to the joint force. Interdiction and maneuver usually are not considered separate operations against a common enemy, but rather are complementary

---

COMMON OPERATING PRECEPT

Drive synergy to the lowest echelon at which it can be managed effectively.

operations designed to achieve the military strategic and operational objectives. Moreover, maneuver by air, land, or maritime forces can be conducted to interdict enemy military potential. Potential responses to integrated and synchronized maneuver and interdiction can create a dilemma for the enemy. If the enemy attempts to counter the maneuver, enemy forces may be exposed to unacceptable losses from interdiction. If the enemy employs measures to reduce such interdiction losses, enemy forces may not be able to counter the maneuver. The synergy achieved by integrating and synchronizing interdiction and maneuver assists commanders in optimizing leverage at the operational level.

(2) As a guiding principle, JFCs should exploit the flexibility inherent in joint force command relationships, joint targeting procedures, and other techniques to resolve the issues that can arise from the relationship between interdiction and maneuver. When interdiction and maneuver are employed, JFCs need to carefully balance the needs of surface maneuver forces, area-wide requirements for interdiction, and the undesirability of fragmenting joint force capabilities. The JFC's objectives, intent, and priorities, reflected in mission assignments and coordinating arrangements, enable subordinates to exploit fully the military potential of their forces while minimizing the friction generated by competing requirements. Effective targeting procedures in the joint force also alleviate such friction. As an example, interdiction requirements often will exceed interdiction means, requiring JFCs to prioritize requirements. Land and maritime force commanders responsible for integrating and synchronizing maneuver and interdiction within their AOs should be knowledgeable of JFC priorities and the responsibilities and authority assigned and delegated to commanders designated by the JFC to execute theater- and/or JOA-wide functions. JFCs alleviate this friction through the CONOPS and clear statements of intent for interdiction conducted relatively independent of surface maneuver operations. In doing this, JFCs rely on their vision as to how the major elements of the joint force contribute to achieving military strategic objectives. JFCs then employ a flexible range of techniques to assist in identifying requirements and applying capabilities to meet them. JFCs must define appropriate command relationships, establish effective joint targeting procedures, and make apportionment decisions.

(3) All commanders should consider how their operations can complement interdiction. These operations may include actions such as MILDEC, withdrawals, lateral repositioning, and flanking movements that are likely to cause the enemy to reposition surface forces, making them better targets for interdiction. Likewise, interdiction operations need to conform to and enhance the JFC's scheme of maneuver. This complementary use of maneuver and interdiction places the enemy in the operational dilemma of either defending from disadvantageous positions or exposing forces to interdiction strikes during attempted repositioning.

(4) Within the joint force operational area, all joint force component operations must contribute to achievement of the JFC's objectives. To facilitate these operations, JFCs may establish AOs within their operational area. **Synchronization and/or integration of maneuver and interdiction within land or maritime AOs is of**

particular importance, particularly when JFCs task component commanders to execute theater- and/or JOA-wide functions.

(a) Air, land, and maritime commanders are directly concerned with those enemy forces and capabilities that can affect their current and future operations. Accordingly, that part of interdiction with a near-term effect on air, land, and maritime maneuver normally supports that maneuver. In fact, successful operations may depend on successful interdiction operations; for instance, to isolate the battle or weaken the enemy force before battle is fully joined.

(b) JFCs establish land and maritime AOs to decentralize execution of land and maritime component operations, allow rapid maneuver, and provide the ability to fight at extended ranges. The size, shape, and positioning of land or maritime AOs will be based on the JFC's CONOPS and the land or maritime commanders' requirements to accomplish their missions and protect their forces. **Within these AOs, land and maritime commanders are designated the supported commander for the integration and synchronization of maneuver, fires, and interdiction.** Accordingly, land and maritime commanders designate the target priority, effects, and timing of interdiction operations within their AOs. Further, in coordination with the land or maritime commander, a component commander designated as the supported commander for theater/JOA-wide interdiction has the latitude to plan and execute JFC prioritized missions within a land or maritime AO. If theater/JOA-wide interdiction operations would have adverse effects within a land or maritime AO, then the commander conducting those operations must either readjust the plan, resolve the issue with the appropriate component commander, or consult with the JFC for resolution.

(c) The land or maritime commander should clearly articulate the vision of maneuver operations to other commanders that may employ interdiction forces within the land or maritime AO. The land or maritime commander's intent and CONOPS should clearly state how interdiction will enable or enhance land or maritime force maneuver in the AO and what is to be accomplished with interdiction (as well as those actions to be avoided, such as the destruction of key transportation nodes or the use of certain munitions in a specific area). Once this is understood, other interdiction-capable commanders normally can plan and execute their operations with only that coordination required with the land or maritime commander. However, the land or maritime commander should provide other interdiction-capable commanders as much latitude as possible in the planning and execution of interdiction operations within the AO.

(d) Joint force operations in maritime or littoral operational areas often require additional coordination among the maritime commander and other interdiction-capable commanders because of the highly specialized nature of some maritime operations, such as antisubmarine and mine warfare. This type of coordination requires that the interdiction-capable commanders maintain communication with the maritime commander. As in all operations, lack of close coordination among commanders in maritime operational areas can result in fratricide and failed missions. The same principle applies concerning joint force air component mining operations in land or maritime operational areas.

(5) JFCs need to pay particular attention and give priority to activities impinging on and supporting the maneuver and interdiction needs of all forces. In addition to normal target nomination procedures, JFCs establish procedures through which land or maritime force commanders can specifically identify those interdiction targets they are unable to engage with organic assets within their operational areas that could affect planned or ongoing maneuver. These targets may be identified individually or by category, specified geographically, or tied to a desired effect or time period. Interdiction target priorities within the land or maritime operational areas are considered along with theater and/or JOA-wide interdiction priorities by JFCs and reflected in the air apportionment decision. The JFACC uses these priorities to plan, coordinate, and execute the theater- and/or JOA-wide air interdiction effort. The purpose of these procedures is to afford added visibility to, and allow JFCs to give priority to, targets directly affecting planned maneuver by air, land, or maritime forces.

f. **Operations When WMD are Employed or Located**

(1) **Locating WMD and WMD materials.** Since an enemy's use of WMD can quickly change the character of an operation or campaign, joint forces may be required to locate and control WMD, materials used to develop WMD, or dual-use materials when discovered or located in an operational area. Commanders should consider locating and controlling WMD-related weapons and materials when planning in order to deny their use by a potential adversary. Such a requirement can exist across the conflict continuum. Once located, resources may be required to secure, inventory, destroy, neutralize, dispose of, or transport these materials. Materials that can be used to create a CBRN weapon or device, such as a radiological dispersal device, exist in even the most austere locations. Would-be terrorists can exploit materials that are often present at medical and industrial facilities. For example, cesium-137 is present at many medical facilities and is ideal for the creation of a radiological dispersal device.

(2) **Enemy Employment.** The use or the threatened use of WMD can cause large-scale shifts in strategic and operational objectives, phases, and COAs. Multinational operations become more complicated with the threatened employment of these weapons. An enemy may use WMD against other multinational partners, especially those with little or no defense against these weapons, to disintegrate the alliance or coalition.

(a) Intelligence and other joint staff members advise JFCs of an enemy's capability to employ WMD and under what conditions that enemy is most likely to do so. This advice includes an assessment of the enemy's willingness and intent to employ these weapons. It is important to ensure that high force or materiel concentrations do not provide lucrative targets for enemy WMD.

(b) Known threat of WMD use and associated preparedness against such use are imperative in this environment. The joint force can survive use of WMD by anticipating their employment and taking appropriate offensive and defensive measures. Commanders can protect their forces in a variety of ways, including training, MISO, OPSEC, dispersion of forces or materiel, use of IPE, and proper use of terrain for

Chapter V

shielding against blast and radiation effects. Enhancement of CBRN defense capabilities may reduce incentives for a first strike by an enemy with WMD.

(c) The combination of active and passive defense can reduce the effectiveness or success of an enemy's use of WMD. The JFC may have to conduct offensive operations to neutralize or destroy enemy WMD capabilities before they can be brought to bear. Offensive measures include raids, strikes, and operations designed to locate and neutralize the threat of such weapons. When conducting offensive operations, the JFC must fully understand the collateral effects created by striking or neutralizing enemy WMD capabilities.

(d) JFCs should immediately inform HN authorities, OGAs, IGOs, or NGOs in the operational area of enemy intentions to use WMD. These organizations do not have the same intelligence or decontamination capabilities as military units and need the maximum amount of time available to protect their personnel. In the event WMD are used against nonmilitary targets, JFCs must plan for and prepare to manage the consequences of CBRN incidents to mitigate the effects.

For additional guidance on defensive CBRN measures and countermeasures, refer to JP 3-11, Operations in Chemical, Biological, Radiological, and Nuclear (CBRN) Environments; *JP 3-40,* Combating Weapons of Mass Destruction; *JP 3-41,* Chemical, Biological, Radiological, and Nuclear Consequence Management; *and the* National Military Strategy to Combat Weapons of Mass Destruction.

(3) **Friendly Employment.** When directed by the President and SecDef, CCDRs will plan for the employment of nuclear weapons by US forces in a manner consistent with national policy and strategic guidance. The employment of such weapons signifies an escalation of the war and is a Presidential decision. USSTRATCOM's capabilities to assist in the collaborative planning of all nuclear missions are available to support nuclear weapon employment. If directed to plan for the use of nuclear weapons, JFCs typically have two escalating objectives.

(a) The first is to deter or prevent the enemy from using WMD. To make opponents understand that friendly forces possess and will use such weapons, JFCs may simply communicate that to the enemy, using IO or other means. Regardless, JFCs must implement measures to increase readiness and preserve the option to respond, including the alert and forward positioning, if required, of appropriate systems. Prevention or denial may include targeting and attacking enemy WMD capability by conventional and SO forces.

(b) If deterrence is not an effective option or fails, JFCs will respond appropriately, consistent with national policy and strategic guidance, to enemy aggression while seeking to control the intensity and scope of conflict and destruction. That response may include the employment of conventional, SO, or nuclear forces.

> **JOINT TASK FORCE-CIVIL SUPPORT**
>
> **Joint task force-civil support (JTF-CS) is the nation's only standing chemical, biological, radiological, and nuclear (CBRN) JTF. It is comprised of active, reserve, and National Guard members from the Army, Navy, Air Force, and Marines as well as civilian and contract personnel. Established in October 1999, JTF-CS is assigned to US Northern Command (USNORTHCOM) and focused on CBRN consequence management planning, preparedness, and command and control of Department of Defense (DOD) forces during CBRN incidents. The commander of US Army North serves as the joint force land component commander and has operational control of JTF-CS.**
>
> **When directed, JTF-CS deploys with USNORTHCOM's allocated forces and conducts CBRN response operations in support of civil authorities. JTF-CS coordinates and synchronizes DOD capabilities into the federal, state, local, and tribal response in order to save lives, prevent further injury, and provide temporary critical support to enable community recovery.**
>
> **Various Sources**

16. **Considerations for Stabilization**

    a. **General.** Operations in this phase continue pursuit of the national strategic end state. These operations typically begin with significant military involvement, to include some combat, and then move increasingly toward enabling civil authority as the threat wanes and civil infrastructures are reestablished. As progress is made, military forces will increase their focus on supporting the efforts of HN authorities, OGAs, IGOs, and/or NGOs. National Security Presidential Directive-44, *Management of Interagency Efforts Concerning Reconstruction and Stabilization,* assigns DOS the responsibility to plan and coordinate USG efforts in stabilization and reconstruction. The Secretary of State is responsible to coordinate with SecDef to ensure harmonization with planned and ongoing operations. Military support to stability operations within the JOA are the responsibility of the JFC.

    b. **Several LOOs may be initiated immediately** (e.g., providing FHA, establishing security). In some cases, the scope of the problem set may dictate using other nonmilitary entities which are uniquely suited to address the problems. The goal of these military and civil efforts should be to eliminate root causes or deficiencies that create the problems (e.g., strengthen legitimate civil authority, rebuild government institutions, foster a sense of confidence and well-being, and support the conditions for economic reconstruction). With this in mind, the JFC may need to address how to coordinate CMO with the efforts of participating OGAs, IGOs, NGOs, and HN assets.

For further guidance on CMO, refer to JP 3-57, Civil-Military Operations.

Chapter V

c. **Forces and Capabilities Mix.** The JFC may need to realign forces and capabilities or adjust force structure to begin stability operations in some portions of the operational area even while sustained combat operations still are ongoing in other areas. For example, CA forces and HUMINT capabilities are critical to supporting *stabilize* phase operations and often involve a mix of forces and capabilities far different than those that supported the previous phases. Planning and continuous assessment will reveal the nature and scope of forces and capabilities required. These forces and capabilities may be available within the joint force or may be required from another theater or from the Reserve Component. The JFC should anticipate and request these forces and capabilities in a timely manner to facilitate their opportune employment.

d. **Stability Operations**

(1) As sustained combat operations conclude, military forces will shift their focus to stability operations. Force protection will continue to be important and combat operations might continue, although with less frequency and intensity than in the *dominate* phase. Of particular importance will be CMO, initially conducted to secure and safeguard the populace, reestablish civil law and order, protect or rebuild key infrastructure, and restore public services. US military forces should be prepared to lead the activities necessary to accomplish these tasks and restore Rule of Law when indigenous civil, USG, multinational or international capacity does not exist or is incapable of assuming responsibility. Once legitimate civil authority is prepared to conduct such tasks, US military forces may support such activities as required/necessary.

A US Army soldier, assigned to provide security to a provincial reconstruction team in Afghanistan, greets the foreman of a local construction company during an inspection of a greenhouse project in eastern Afghanistan's Nuristan province.

Security force assistance plays an important part during stability operations by supporting and augmenting the development of the capacity and capability of FSFs and their supporting institutions. Likewise, the JFC's communications strategy will play an important role in providing public information to foreign populations during this period.

For further guidance on SFA, refer to JP 3-22, Foreign Internal Defense.

(2) The military's predominant presence and its ability to command and control forces and logistics under extreme conditions may give it the de facto lead in stability operations normally governed by other agencies that lack such capacities. However, some stability operations likely will be in support of, or transition to support of, US diplomatic, UN, or HN efforts. Integrated civilian and military efforts are key to success and military forces need to work competently in this environment while properly supporting the agency in charge. To be effective, planning and conducting stability operations require a variety of perspectives and expertise and the cooperation and assistance of OGAs, other Services, and alliance or multinational partners. Military forces should be prepared to work in integrated civilian military teams that could include representatives from other US departments and agencies, foreign governments and security forces, IGOs, NGOs, and members of the private sector with relevant skills and expertise. Typical military support includes emergency infrastructure reconstruction, engineering, logistics, law enforcement, HSS, and other activities to restore essential services.

For further guidance on stability operations, refer to JP 3-07, Stability Operations, *and Department of Defense Instruction (DODI) 3000.05,* Stability Operations.

(a) CA forces are organized and trained to perform CA operations that support CMO conducted in conjunction with stability operations. MISO forces will develop, produce, and disseminate products to gain and reinforce popular support for the JFC's objectives. Complementing conventional forces IW efforts, SOF will conduct FID to assess, train, advise, and assist foreign military and paramilitary forces as they develop the capacity to secure their own lands and populations.

For further guidance on SOF, refer to JP 3-05, Special Operations.

(b) **CI activities** safeguard essential elements of friendly information. This is particularly pertinent in countering adversary HUMINT efforts. HN authorities, IGOs, and NGOs working closely with US forces may pass information (knowingly or unknowingly) to adversary elements that enables them to interfere with stability operations. Members of the local populace, who might actually be belligerents, often gain access to US military personnel and their bases by providing services such as laundry and cooking. They can then pass on information gleaned from that interaction in order to seek favor with a belligerent element or to avoid retaliation from belligerents. The JFC must consider these and similar possibilities and take appropriate actions to counter potential compromise. CI personnel develop an estimate of the threat and recommend appropriate actions.

(c) **PA operations** provide command information programs, communication with internal audiences, media and community relations support, and international information programs.

e. During stability operations in the *stabilize* phase, **protection** from virtually any person, element, or group hostile to US interests must be considered. These could include activists, a group opposed to the operation, looters, and terrorists. Forces will have to be even more alert to force protection and security matters after a CBRNE incident. JFCs also should be constantly ready to counter activity that could bring significant harm to units or jeopardize mission accomplishment. **Protection may involve the security of HN authorities and OGA, IGO, and NGO members if authorized by higher authority.** For contractors, the GCC must evaluate the need for force protection support following the guidelines of DODI 3020.41, *Contractor Personnel Authorized to Accompany the US Armed Forces*.

f. Personnel should stay alert even in an operation with little or no perceived risk. **JFCs must take measures to prevent complacency and be ready to counter activity that could bring harm to units or jeopardize the operation.** However, security requirements should be balanced with the military operation's nature and objectives. In some stability operations, the use of certain security measures, such as carrying arms, wearing helmets and protective vests, or using secure communications may cause military forces to appear more threatening than intended, which may degrade the force's legitimacy and hurt relations with the local population.

g. **Restraint.** During the *stabilize* phase, military capability must be applied even more prudently since the support of the local population is essential for success. The actions of military personnel and units are framed by the disciplined application of force, including **specific ROE.** These ROE often will be more restrictive and detailed when compared to those for sustained combat operations due to national policy concerns. Moreover, these rules may change frequently during operations. Restraints on weaponry, tactics, and levels of violence characterize the environment. The use of excessive force could adversely affect efforts to gain or maintain legitimacy and impede the attainment of both short- and long-term goals. The use of nonlethal capabilities should be considered to fill the gap between verbal warnings and deadly force when dealing with unarmed hostile elements and to avoid raising the level of conflict unnecessarily. The JFC must determine early in the planning stage what nonlethal technology is available, how well the force is trained to use it, and how the established ROE authorize its employment. The principle of restraint does not preclude the application of overwhelming force, when appropriate, to display US resolve and commitment. The reasons for the restraint often need to be understood by the individual Service member, because a single act could cause adverse political consequences.

h. **Perseverance.** Some operations may move quickly through the *stabilize* phase and transition smoothly to the *enable civil authority* phase. Other situations may require years of stabilization activities before this transition occurs. Therefore, the patient, resolute, and persistent pursuit of national strategic end state conditions for as long as necessary to achieve them often is the requirement for success.

i. **Legitimacy.** Military activities during the *stabilize* phase should sustain the legitimacy of the operation and of the emerging or host government. During operations where a government does not exist, extreme caution should be used when dealing with individuals and organizations to avoid inadvertently legitimizing them. Implementation of SC-related guidance through the commander's communications strategy can enhance perceptions of the legitimacy of stability operations.

j. **OPSEC.** Although there may be no clearly defined threat, the essential elements of US military operations should be safeguarded. The uncertain nature of the situation, coupled with the potential for rapid change, require that OPSEC be an integral part of stability operations. OPSEC planners must consider the effect of media coverage and the possibility coverage may compromise essential security or disclose critical information.

17. Considerations for Enabling Civil Authority

a. **General.** In this phase, the joint operation normally is terminated when the stated military strategic and/or operational objectives have been met and redeployment of the joint force is accomplished. This should mean that a legitimate civil authority has been enabled to manage the situation without further outside military assistance. In some cases, it may become apparent that the stated objectives fall short of properly enabling civil authority. This situation may require a redesign of the joint operation as a result of an extension of the required stability operations in support of US diplomatic, HN, IGO, and/or NGO efforts.

b. **Peace Building.** The transition from military operations to full civilian control may involve ongoing operations that have a significant combat component, including counterinsurgency operations, antiterrorism, and CT. Even while combat operations are ongoing, the operation will include a large stability component that is essentially a PB mission. PB, transitioning to a DOS led effort, provides the reconstruction and societal rehabilitation that offers hope to the HN populace. Stability measures establish the conditions that enable PB to succeed. PB promotes reconciliation, strengthens and rebuilds civil infrastructures and institutions, builds confidence, and supports economic reconstruction to prevent a return to conflict. The ultimate measure of success in PB is political, not military. Therefore, JFCs seek a clear understanding of the national/coalition strategic end state and how military operations support that end state.

c. **Transfer to Civil Authority.** In many cases, the United States will transfer responsibility for the political and military affairs of the HN to another authority. JFCs may be required to transfer responsibility of operations to another authority (e.g., UN observers, multinational peacekeeping force, or NATO) as the termination criteria. This probably will occur after an extended period of conducting joint or multinational stability operations and PB missions as described above. Overall, transfer likely will occur in stages (e.g., HN sovereignty, PO under UN mandate, termination of all US military participation). Joint force support to this effort may include the following:

Chapter V

(1) **Support to Truce Negotiations.** This support may include providing intelligence, security, transportation and other logistic support, and linguists for all participants.

(2) **Transition to Civil Authority.** This transfer could be to local or HN federal government, to a UN PKO after PEO, or through the UN High Commissioner for Refugees to a NGO in support of dislocated civilians.

d. **Redeployment**

(1) **Conduct.** Redeployment is defined as the transfer of forces and materiel to support another JFC's operational requirements, or to return personnel, equipment, and materiel to home/demobilization stations for reintegration and out-processing. Redeployment normally is conducted in stages—the entire joint force likely will not redeploy in one relatively short period. It may include waste disposal, port operations, closing of contracts and other financial obligations, disposition of contracting records and files, clearing and marking of minefields and other explosive ordnance disposal activities, and ensuring that appropriate units remain in place until their missions are complete. Redeployment must be planned and executed in a manner that facilitates the use of redeploying forces and supplies to meet new missions or crises.

(a) Redeployment planning is the responsibility of the losing supported commander when personnel, equipment, and materiel are redeployed to home or demobilization stations. The gaining supported commander is responsible for this planning when the redeployment is to a new operational area.

(b) Upon redeployment, units or individuals may require refresher training prior to reassuming more traditional roles and missions. Because of this, redeployment planning must be a collaborative and synchronized effort between supported and supporting commanders.

(2) **Redeployment to Other Contingencies.** Due to competing demands for limited forces, the joint force provider may recommend allocating a force from one CCDR to another higher priority mission if the risks warrant. If SecDef approves the recommendation, the allocation will be ordered in a deployment order. Commanders and their staffs should consider how they would extricate forces and ensure that they are prepared for the new contingency. This might include such things as a prioritized redeployment schedule, identification of aerial ports for linking intra- and intertheater airlift, the most recent intelligence assessments and supporting GEOINT products for the new contingency, and some consideration to achieving the national strategic objectives of the original contingency through other means.

(3) **Redeployment in Support of Rotational Requirements.** Due to Service or other rotational requirements, forces may be relieved in place and redeployed to home station for reconstitution or regeneration. Commanders and their staffs must consider security and protective measures during the relief in place between incoming and outgoing forces.

For further information on redeployment, refer to JP 3-35, Deployment and Redeployment Operations. *For further guidance on considerations for termination of operations, refer to JP 5-0,* Joint Operation Planning, *and JP 3-33,* Joint Task Force Headquarters.

Intentionally Blank

APPENDIX A
PRINCIPLES OF JOINT OPERATIONS

1. Introduction

The *principles of joint operations* are formed around the traditional *principles of war.* Three additional principles—*restraint*, *perseverance*, and *legitimacy*—are relevant to how the Armed Forces of the United States use combat power across the range of military operations. These three, added to the original nine, comprise 12 principles of joint operations.

2. Principles of Joint Operations

   a. **Objective**

      (1) The purpose of specifying the objective is to direct every military operation toward a clearly defined, decisive, and achievable goal.

      (2) The purpose of military operations is to achieve the military objectives that support attainment of the overall political goals of the conflict. This frequently involves the destruction of the enemy armed forces' capabilities and their will to fight. The objective of joint operations not involving this destruction might be more difficult to define; nonetheless, it too must be clear from the beginning. Objectives must directly, quickly, and economically contribute to the purpose of the operation. Each operation must contribute to strategic objectives. JFCs should avoid actions that do not contribute directly to achieving the objective(s).

      (3) Additionally, changes to the military objectives may occur because political and military leaders gain a better understanding of the situation, or they may occur because the situation itself changes. **The JFC should anticipate these shifts in political goals necessitating changes in the military objectives.** The changes may be very subtle, but if not made, achievement of the military objectives may no longer support the political goals, legitimacy may be undermined, and force security may be compromised.

   b. **Offensive**

      (1) The purpose of an offensive action is to seize, retain, and exploit the initiative.

      (2) Offensive action is the most effective and decisive way to achieve a clearly defined objective. Offensive operations are the means by which a military force seizes and holds the initiative while maintaining freedom of action and achieving decisive results. The importance of offensive action is fundamentally true across all levels of war.

      (3) Commanders adopt the defensive only as a temporary expedient and must seek every opportunity to seize or regain the initiative. An offensive spirit must be inherent in the conduct of all defensive operations.

c. Mass

(1) The purpose of mass is to concentrate the effects of combat power at the most advantageous place and time to produce decisive results.

(2) In order to achieve mass, appropriate joint force capabilities are integrated and synchronized where they will have a decisive effect in a short period of time. Mass often must be sustained to have the desired effect. Massing effects of combat power, rather than concentrating forces, can enable even numerically inferior forces to produce decisive results and minimize human losses and waste of resources.

d. Maneuver

(1) The purpose of maneuver is to place the enemy in a position of disadvantage through the flexible application of combat power.

(2) Maneuver is the movement of forces in relation to the enemy to secure or retain positional advantage, usually in order to deliver—or threaten delivery of—the direct and indirect fires of the maneuvering force. Effective maneuver keeps the enemy off balance and thus also protects the friendly force. It contributes materially in exploiting successes, preserving freedom of action, and reducing vulnerability by continually posing new problems for the enemy.

e. Economy of Force

(1) The purpose of economy of force is to expend minimum essential combat power on secondary efforts in order to allocate the maximum possible combat power on primary efforts.

(2) Economy of force is the judicious employment and distribution of forces. It is the measured allocation of available combat power to such tasks as limited attacks, defense, delays, deception, or even retrograde operations to achieve mass elsewhere at the decisive point and time.

f. Unity of Command

(1) The purpose of unity of command is to ensure unity of effort under one responsible commander for every objective.

(2) Unity of command means that all forces operate under a single commander with the requisite authority to direct all forces employed in pursuit of a common purpose. During multinational operations and interagency coordination, unity of command may not be possible, but the requirement for unity of effort becomes paramount. Unity of effort—the coordination and cooperation toward common objectives, even if the participants are not necessarily part of the same command or organization—is the product of successful unified action.

g. **Security**

(1) The purpose of security is to prevent the enemy from acquiring unexpected advantage.

(2) Security enhances freedom of action by reducing friendly vulnerability to hostile acts, influence, or surprise. Security results from the measures taken by commanders to protect their forces. Staff planning and an understanding of enemy strategy, tactics, and doctrine enhance security. Risk is inherent in military operations. Application of this principle includes prudent risk management, not undue caution.

h. **Surprise**

(1) The purpose of surprise is to strike at a time or place or in a manner for which the enemy is unprepared.

(2) Surprise can help the commander shift the balance of combat power and thus achieve success well out of proportion to the effort expended. Factors contributing to surprise include speed in decision-making, information sharing, and force movement; effective intelligence; deception; application of unexpected combat power; OPSEC; and variations in tactics and methods of operation.

i. **Simplicity**

(1) The purpose of simplicity is to increase the probability that plans and operations will be executed as intended by preparing clear, uncomplicated plans and concise orders.

(2) Simplicity contributes to successful operations. Simple plans and clear, concise orders minimize misunderstanding and confusion. When other factors are equal, the simplest plan is preferable. Simplicity in plans allows better understanding and execution planning at all echelons. Simplicity and clarity of expression greatly facilitate mission execution in the stress, fatigue, fog of war, and complexities of modern combat, and are especially critical to success in multinational operations.

j. **Restraint**

(1) The purpose of restraint is to limit collateral damage and prevent the unnecessary use of force.

(2) A single act could cause significant military and political consequences; therefore, judicious use of force is necessary. Restraint requires the careful and disciplined balancing of the need for security, the conduct of military operations, and the national strategic end state. For example, the exposure of intelligence gathering activities, such as interrogation of detainees and prisoners of war, could have significant political and military repercussions and should be conducted with sound judgment. Excessive force antagonizes those parties involved, thereby damaging the legitimacy of

Appendix A

the organization that uses it while potentially enhancing the legitimacy of the opposing party.

(3) Commanders at all levels must ensure their personnel are properly trained—including knowing and understanding ROE—and are quickly informed of any changes. Failure to understand and comply with established ROE can result in fratricide, mission failure, and/or national embarrassment. Restraint is best achieved when ROE issued at the beginning of an operation address most anticipated situations that may arise. Since the domestic law of some nations may be more restrictive concerning the use of force than permitted under coalition or allied force ROE, commanders must be aware of national restrictions imposed on force participants.

k. **Perseverance**

(1) The purpose of perseverance is to ensure the commitment necessary to attain the national strategic end state.

(2) Perseverance involves preparation for measured, protracted military operations in pursuit of the national strategic end state. Some joint operations may require years to reach the termination criteria. The underlying causes of the crisis may be elusive, making it difficult to achieve decisive resolution. The patient, resolute, and persistent pursuit of national goals and objectives often is essential to success. This will frequently involve diplomatic, economic, and informational measures to supplement military efforts.

l. **Legitimacy**

(1) The purpose of legitimacy is to maintain legal and moral authority in the conduct of operations.

(2) Legitimacy, which can be a decisive factor in operations, is based on the actual and perceived legality, morality, and rightness of the actions from the various perspectives of interested audiences. These audiences will include our national leadership and domestic population, governments, and civilian populations in the operational area, and nations and organizations around the world.

(3) Committed forces must sustain the legitimacy of the operation and of the host government, where applicable. Security actions must be balanced with legitimacy concerns. All actions must be considered in the light of potentially competing strategic and tactical requirements, and must exhibit fairness in dealing with competing factions where appropriate. Legitimacy may depend on adherence to objectives agreed to by the international community, ensuring the action is appropriate to the situation, and fairness in dealing with various factions. Restricting the use of force, restructuring the type of forces employed, and ensuring the disciplined conduct of the forces involved may reinforce legitimacy.

(4) Another aspect of this principle is the legitimacy bestowed upon a local government through the perception of the populace that it governs. Humanitarian and

civil military operations help develop a sense of legitimacy for the supported government. Because the populace perceives that the government has genuine authority to govern and uses proper agencies for valid purposes, they consider that government as legitimate. During operations in an area where a legitimate government does not exist, extreme caution should be used when dealing with individuals and organizations to avoid inadvertently legitimizing them.

Intentionally Blank

APPENDIX B
REFERENCES

The development of JP 3-0 is based upon the following primary references:

1. General

a. The Goldwater-Nichols Department of Defense Reorganization Act of 1986 (Title 10, USC, Section 161).

b. *The National Security Strategy of the United States of America.*

c. *National Defense Strategy of the United States of America.*

d. *National Defense Authorization Act.*

e. *National Military Strategy.*

f. *The National Military Strategy to Combat Weapons of Mass Destruction.*

g. *The National Military Strategy for Cyberspace Operations.*

h. *National Strategy for Homeland Security.*

i. *The National Strategy to Secure Cyberspace.*

j. *National Response Framework.*

k. *The Quadrennial Defense Review 2010.*

l. *Unified Command Plan.*

m. *Guidance for Employment of the Force.*

n. *Defense Planning and Programming Guidance.*

o. *Joint Strategic Capabilities Plan.*

p. Executive Order 12656, *Assignment of Emergency Preparedness Responsibilities.*

q. National Security Presidential Directive-44, *Management of Interagency Efforts Concerning Reconstruction and Stabilization.*

r. *UN Charter.*

2. DOD Publications

a. DODI 3000.05, *Stability Operations.*

Appendix B

b. DODI 3020.41, *Contractor Personnel Authorized to Accompany the US Armed Forces.*

c. DODD 3025.12, *Military Assistance for Civil Disturbances.*

d. DODD 3025.18, *Defense Support of Civil Authorities.*

e. DODD 5240.1, *DOD Intelligence Activities.*

f. DODD 5525.5, *DOD Cooperation with Civilian Law Enforcement Officials.*

3. **CJCS Publications**

a. CJCSI 3121.01B, *Standing Rules of Engagement/Standing Rules for the Use of Force for US Forces.*

b. CJCSI 3126.01, *Language and Regional Expertise Planning.*

c. CJCSI 3141.01D, *Management and Review of Campaign and Contingency Plans.*

d. CJCSI 5715.01B, *Joint Staff Participation in Interagency Affairs.*

e. CJCSI 5810.01C, *Implementation of the DOD Law of War Program.*

f. CJCS Manual 3122.01A, *Joint Operation Planning and Execution System (JOPES) Volume I (Planning Policies and Procedures).*

g. JP 1, *Doctrine for the Armed Forces of the United States.*

h. JP 2-0, *Joint Intelligence.*

i. JP 2-01.3, *Joint Intelligence Preparation of the Operational Environment.*

j. JP 3-01, *Countering Air and Missile Threats.*

k. JP 3-02, *Amphibious Operations.*

l. JP 3-03, *Joint Interdiction.*

m. JP 3-05, *Special Operations.*

n. JP 3-05.1, *Joint Special Operations Task Force Operations.*

o. JP 3-07, *Stability Operations.*

p. JP 3-07.4, *Joint Counterdrug Operations.*

q. JP 3-08, *Interorganizational Coordination During Joint Operations.*

r. JP 3-09, *Joint Fire Support*.

s. JP 3-10, *Joint Security Operations in Theater*.

t. JP 3-11, *Operations in Chemical, Biological, Radiological, and Nuclear (CBRN) Environments*.

u. JP 3-13, *Information Operations*.

v. JP 3-13.2, *Military Information Support Operations*.

w. JP 3-13.4, *Military Deception*.

x. JP 3-14, *Space Operations*.

y. JP 3-16, *Multinational Operations*.

z. JP 3-18, *Joint Forcible Entry Operations*.

aa. JP 3-24, *Counterinsurgency Operations*.

bb. JP 3-26, *Counterterrorism*.

cc. JP 3-27, *Homeland Defense*.

dd. JP 3-28, *Civil Support*.

ee. JP 3-29, *Foreign Humanitarian Assistance*.

ff. JP 3-30, *Command and Control for Joint Air Operations*.

gg. JP 3-33, *Joint Task Force Headquarter*.

hh. JP 3-41, *Chemical, Biological, Radiological, and Nuclear Consequence Management*.

ii. JP 3-57, *Civil-Military Operations*.

jj. JP 3-60, *Joint Targeting*.

kk. JP 3-61, *Public Affairs*.

ll. JP 3-68, *Noncombatant Evacuation Operations*.

mm. JP 4-0, *Joint Logistics*.

nn. JP 4-10, *Operational Contract Support*.

oo. JP 5-0, *Joint Operation Planning*.

pp. JP 6-0, *Joint Communications System.*

4. Allied Joint Publications

a. AJP-01(D), *Allied Joint Doctrine.*

b. AJP-3(B), *Allied Joint Doctrine for Joint Operations.*

APPENDIX C
ADMINISTRATIVE INSTRUCTIONS

1. User Comments

Users in the field are highly encouraged to submit comments on this publication to: Joint Staff J-7, Deputy Director, Joint and Coalition Warfighting, Joint and Coalition Warfighting Center, ATTN: Joint Doctrine Support Division, 116 Lake View Parkway, Suffolk, VA 23435-2697. These comments should address content (accuracy, usefulness, consistency, and organization), writing, and appearance.

2. Authorship

The lead agent for this publication is the United States Joint Forces Command. The Joint Staff doctrine sponsor for this publication is the Director for Operational Plans and Joint Force Development (J-7).

3. Supersession

This publication supersedes JP 3-0, 17 September 2006, *Doctrine for Joint Operations*, incorporating Change 2, 22 March 2010.

4. Change Recommendations

   a. Recommendations for urgent changes to this publication should be submitted:

   TO: JOINT STAFF WASHINGTON DC//J7-JEDD//

   Routine changes should be submitted electronically to the Deputy Director, Joint and Coalition Warfighting, Joint and Coalition Warfighting Center, Joint Doctrine Support Division and info the lead agent and the Director for Joint Force Development, J-7/JEDD.

   b. When a Joint Staff directorate submits a proposal to the CJCS that would change source document information reflected in this publication, that directorate will include a proposed change to this publication as an enclosure to its proposal. The Services and other organizations are requested to notify the Joint Staff J-7 when changes to source documents reflected in this publication are initiated.

5. Distribution of Publications

Local reproduction is authorized and access to unclassified publications is unrestricted. However, access to and reproduction authorization for classified JPs must be in accordance with DOD 5200.1-R, *Information Security Program*.

Appendix C

6. Distribution of Electronic Publications

a. Joint Staff J-7 will not print copies of JPs for distribution. Electronic versions are available on JDEIS at https://jdeis.js.mil (NIPRNET), and http://jdeis.js.smil.mil (SIPRNET), and on the JEL at http://www.dtic.mil/doctrine (NIPRNET).

b. Only approved JPs and joint test publications are releasable outside the CCMDs, Services, and Joint Staff. Release of any classified JP to foreign governments or foreign nationals must be requested through the local embassy (Defense Attaché Office) to DIA, Defense Foreign Liaison/IE-3, 200 MacDill Blvd., Joint Base Anacostia-Bolling, Washington, DC 20340-5100.

c. JEL CD-ROM. Upon request of a joint doctrine development community member, the Joint Staff J-7 will produce and deliver one CD-ROM with current JPs. This JEL CD-ROM will be updated not less than semi-annually and when received can be locally reproduced for use within the combatant commands and Services.

GLOSSARY
PART I—ABBREVIATIONS AND ACRONYMS

AADC	area air defense commander
ACA	airspace control authority
ACO	airspace control order
ACP	airspace control plan
ACS	airspace control system
AJP	Allied joint publication
AO	area of operations
AOA	amphibious objective area
AOR	area of responsibility
APEX	Adaptive Planning and Execution
C2	command and control
CA	civil affairs
CBRN	chemical, biological, radiological, and nuclear
CBRNE	chemical, biological, radiological, nuclear, and high-yield explosives
CCDR	combatant commander
CCIR	commander's critical information requirement
CCMD	combatant command
CD	counterdrug
CDRUSSOCOM	Commander, United States Special Operations Command
CDRUSSTRATCOM	Commander, United States Strategic Command
C-IED	counter-improvised explosive device
CI	counterintelligence
CID	combat identification
CJCS	Chairman of the Joint Chiefs of Staff
CJCSI	Chairman of the Joint Chiefs of Staff instruction
CJTF	commander, joint task force
CMO	civil-military operations
CMOC	civil-military operations center
CNA	computer network attack
CND	computer network defense
COA	course of action
COCOM	combatant command (command authority)
COG	center of gravity
COIN	counterinsurgency
CONOPS	concept of operations
CONUS	continental United States
COP	common operational picture
CS	civil support
CT	counterterrorism
CTF	counter threat finance

DCA	defensive counterair
DOD	Department of Defense
DODD	Department of Defense directive
DODI	Department of Defense instruction
DOS	Department of State
DSCA	defense support of civil authorities
DSPD	defense support to public diplomacy
EA	electronic attack
EM	electromagnetic
EMS	electromagnetic spectrum
EW	electronic warfare
FCC	functional combatant commander
FDO	flexible deterrent option
FFIR	friendly force information requirement
FHA	foreign humanitarian assistance
FHP	force health protection
FID	foreign internal defense
FLOT	forward line of own troops
FSF	foreign security forces
GCC	geographic combatant commander
GEF	Guidance for Employment of the Force
GEOINT	geospatial intelligence
HD	homeland defense
HN	host nation
HNS	host-nation support
HQ	headquarters
HSS	health service support
HUMINT	human intelligence
IA	information assurance
IED	improvised explosive device
IGO	intergovernmental organization
IM	information management
IO	information operations
IPE	individual protective equipment
ISR	intelligence, surveillance, and reconnaissance
IW	irregular warfare
J-2	intelligence directorate of a joint staff
J-3	operations directorate of a joint staff
J-5	plans directorate of a joint staff
JFACC	joint force air component commander

JFC	joint force commander
JFLCC	joint force land component commander
JFMCC	joint force maritime component commander
JFSOCC	joint force special operations component commander
JIACG	joint interagency coordination group
JIPOE	joint intelligence preparation of the operational environment
JOA	joint operations area
JOPP	joint operation planning process
JP	joint publication
JPEC	joint planning and execution community
JRSOI	joint reception, staging, onward movement, and integration
JSA	joint security area
JSOA	joint special operations area
JSOTF	joint special operations task force
JTCB	joint targeting coordination board
JTF	joint task force
JUO	joint urban operation
LNO	liaison officer
LOC	line of communications
LOO	line of operation
MILDEC	military deception
MISO	military information support operations
MOE	measure of effectiveness
MOP	measure of performance
NATO	North Atlantic Treaty Organization
NEO	noncombatant evacuation operation
NETOPS	network operations
NGA	National Geospatial-Intelligence Agency
NGO	nongovernmental organization
NRF	National Response Framework
NSS	National Security Strategy
OCA	offensive counterair
OEF	Operation ENDURING FREEDOM
OGA	other government agency
OIF	Operation IRAQI FREEDOM
OPCON	operational control
OPLAN	operation plan
OPORD	operation order
OPSEC	operations security
OSINT	open-source intelligence

Glossary

PA	public affairs
PB	peace building
PEO	peace enforcement operations
PIR	priority intelligence requirement
PKO	peacekeeping operations
PM	peacemaking
PMESII	political, military, economic, social, information, and infrastructure
PO	peace operations
PR	personnel recovery
ROE	rules of engagement
SC	strategic communication
SCA	space coordinating authority
SecDef	Secretary of Defense
SFA	security force assistance
SJA	staff judge advocate
SO	special operations
SOF	special operations forces
SOP	standard operating procedure
TACON	tactical control
TCP	theater campaign plan
TF	task force
UCP	Unified Command Plan
UN	United Nations
USC	United States Code
USG	United States Government
USSTRATCOM	United States Strategic Command
WMD	weapons of mass destruction

PART II—TERMS AND DEFINITIONS

accuracy of information. None. (Approved for removal from JP 1-02.)

activity. 1. A unit, organization, or installation performing a function or mission. 2. A function, mission, action, or collection of actions. Also called **ACT**. (Approved for incorporation into JP 1-02.)

adversary. A party acknowledged as potentially hostile to a friendly party and against which the use of force may be envisaged. (JP 1-02. SOURCE: JP 3-0)

air apportionment. The determination and assignment of the total expected effort by percentage and/or by priority that should be devoted to the various air operations for a given period of time. (Approved for incorporation into JP 1-02.)

air interdiction. Air operations conducted to divert, disrupt, delay, or destroy the enemy's military potential before it can be brought to bear effectively against friendly forces, or to otherwise achieve objectives. (Approved for incorporation into JP 1-02.)

air mission. None. (Approved for removal from JP 1-02.)

alliance. The relationship that results from a formal agreement between two or more nations for broad, long-term objectives that further the common interests of the members. (Approved for incorporation into JP 1-02.)

apportionment (air). None. (Approved for removal from JP 1-02.)

area of influence. A geographical area wherein a commander is directly capable of influencing operations by maneuver or fire support systems normally under the commander's command or control. (Approved for incorporation into JP 1-02 with JP 3-0 as the source JP.)

area of interest. That area of concern to the commander, including the area of influence, areas adjacent thereto, and extending into enemy territory. This area also includes areas occupied by enemy forces who could jeopardize the accomplishment of the mission. Also called **AOI**. (Approved for incorporation into JP 1-02.)

area of operations. An operational area defined by the joint force commander for land and maritime forces that should be large enough to accomplish their missions and protect their forces. Also called **AO**. (Approved for incorporation into JP 1-02.)

armed forces. None. (Approved for removal from JP 1-02.)

assessment. 1. A continuous process that measures the overall effectiveness of employing joint force capabilities during military operations. 2. Determination of the progress toward accomplishing a task, creating a condition, or achieving an objective. 3. Analysis of the security, effectiveness, and potential of an existing or planned intelligence activity. 4. Judgment of the motives, qualifications, and characteristics of present or prospective employees or "agents." (Approved for incorporation into JP 1-02.)

assign. 1. To place units or personnel in an organization where such placement is relatively permanent, and/or where such organization controls and administers the units or personnel for the primary function, or greater portion of the functions, of the unit or personnel. 2. To detail individuals to specific duties or functions where such duties or functions are primary and/or relatively permanent. (JP 1-02. SOURCE: JP 3-0)

attach. 1. The placement of units or personnel in an organization where such placement is relatively temporary. 2. The detailing of individuals to specific functions where such functions are secondary or relatively temporary. (Approved for incorporation into JP 1-02.)

attachment. None. (Approved for removal from JP 1-02.)

aviation combat element. None. (Approved for removal from JP 1-02.)

base of operations. None. (Approved for removal from JP 1-02.)

battle damage assessment. The estimate of damage composed of physical and functional damage assessment, as well as target system assessment, resulting from the application of lethal or nonlethal military force. Also called **BDA**. (Approved for incorporation into JP 1-02.)

boundary. A line that delineates surface areas for the purpose of facilitating coordination and deconfliction of operations between adjacent units, formations, or areas. (JP 1-02. SOURCE: JP 3-0)

brigade. None. (Approved for removal from JP 1-02.)

capability. None. (Approved for removal from JP 1-02.)

ceasefire. None. (Approved for removal from JP 1-02.)

center of gravity. The source of power that provides moral or physical strength, freedom of action, or will to act. Also called **COG**. (JP 1-02. SOURCE: JP 3-0)

chain of command. The succession of commanding officers from a superior to a subordinate through which command is exercised. Also called **command channel**. (Approved for incorporation into JP 1-02 with JP 3-0 as the source JP.)

clear. None. (Approved for removal from JP 1-02.)

close air support. Air action by fixed- and rotary-wing aircraft against hostile targets that are in close proximity to friendly forces and that require detailed integration of

Glossary

each air mission with the fire and movement of those forces. Also called **CAS**. (JP 1-02. SOURCE: JP 3-0)

cold war. None. (Approved for removal from JP 1-02.)

combatant commander. A commander of one of the unified or specified combatant commands established by the President. Also called **CCDR**. (JP 1-02. SOURCE: JP 3-0)

combat power. The total means of destructive and/or disruptive force which a military unit/formation can apply against the opponent at a given time. (Approved for incorporation into JP 1-02 with JP 3-0 as the source JP.)

combat service support element. None. (Approved for removal from JP 1-02.)

combat zone. None. (Approved for removal from JP 1-02.)

command channel. None. (Approved for removal from JP 1-02.)

commander's critical information requirement. An information requirement identified by the commander as being critical to facilitating timely decision making. Also called **CCIR**. (Approved for incorporation into JP 1-02.)

commander's estimate of the situation. None. (Approved for removal from JP 1-02.)

commander's intent. A clear and concise expression of the purpose of the operation and the desired military end state that supports mission command, provides focus to the staff, and helps subordinate and supporting commanders act to achieve the commander's desired results without further orders, even when the operation does not unfold as planned. (Approved for incorporation into JP 1-02.)

command guidance. None. (Approved for removal from JP 1-02.)

command post exercise. An exercise in which the forces are simulated, involving the commander, the staff, and communications within and between headquarters. Also called **CPX**. (Approved for incorporation into JP 1-02 with JP 3-0 as the source JP.)

common infrastructure. None. (Approved for removal from JP 1-02.)

common operational picture. A single identical display of relevant information shared by more than one command that facilitates collaborative planning and assists all echelons to achieve situational awareness. Also called **COP**. (Approved for incorporation into JP 1-02.)

communications zone. None. (Approved for removal from JP 1-02.)

condition. 1. Those variables of an operational environment or situation in which a unit, system, or individual is expected to operate and may affect performance. 2. A

Glossary

physical or behavioral state of a system that is required for the achievement of an objective. (Approved for incorporation into JP 1-02.)

conflict. None. (Approved for removal from JP 1-02.)

continuity of operations. The degree or state of being continuous in the conduct of functions, tasks, or duties necessary to accomplish a military action or mission in carrying out the national military strategy. Also called **COOP**. (Approved for incorporation into JP 1-02.)

control. 1. Authority that may be less than full command exercised by a commander over part of the activities of subordinate or other organizations. (JP 1) 2. In mapping, charting, and photogrammetry, a collective term for a system of marks or objects on the Earth or on a map or a photograph, whose positions or elevations (or both) have been or will be determined. (JP 2-03) 3. Physical or psychological pressures exerted with the intent to assure that an agent or group will respond as directed. (JP 3-0) 4. An indicator governing the distribution and use of documents, information, or material. Such indicators are the subject of intelligence community agreement and are specifically defined in appropriate regulations. (JP 2-01) (Approved for incorporation into JP 1-02.)

counterattack. None. (Approved for removal from JP 1-02.)

coup de main. An offensive operation that capitalizes on surprise and simultaneous execution of supporting operations to achieve success in one swift stroke. (JP 1-02. SOURCE: JP 3-0)

crisis. An incident or situation involving a threat to the United States, its citizens, military forces, or vital interests that develops rapidly and creates a condition of such diplomatic, economic, or military importance that commitment of military forces and resources is contemplated to achieve national objectives. (Approved for incorporation into JP 1-02.)

cultivation. None. (Approved for removal from JP 1-02.)

culture. None. (Approved for removal from JP 1-02.)

cyberspace operations. The employment of cyberspace capabilities where the primary purpose is to achieve military objectives or effects in or through cyberspace. (Approved for incorporation into JP 1-02.)

decisive engagement. None. (Approved for removal from JP 1-02.)

decisive point. A geographic place, specific key event, critical factor, or function that, when acted upon, allows commanders to gain a marked advantage over an adversary or contribute materially to achieving success. (JP 1-02. SOURCE: JP 3-0)

defense in depth. None. (Approved for removal from JP 1-02.)

deployable joint task force augmentation cell. None. (Approved for removal from JP 1-02.)

desired effects. None. (Approved for removal from JP 1-02.)

deterrence. The prevention of action by the existence of a credible threat of unacceptable counteraction and/or belief that the cost of action outweighs the perceived benefits. (Approved for incorporation into JP 1-02.)

disarmament. The reduction of a military establishment to some level set by international agreement. (Approved for incorporation into JP 1-02 with JP 3-0 as the source JP.)

economy of force. The judicious employment and distribution of forces so as to expend the minimum essential combat power on secondary efforts in order to allocate the maximum possible combat power on primary efforts. (Approved for inclusion into JP 1-02 with JP 3-0 as the source JP.)

effect. 1. The physical or behavioral state of a system that results from an action, a set of actions, or another effect. 2. The result, outcome, or consequence of an action. 3. A change to a condition, behavior, or degree of freedom. (JP 1-02. SOURCE: JP 3-0)

end state. The set of required conditions that defines achievement of the commander's objectives. (JP 1-02. SOURCE: JP 3-0)

engagement. 1. In air defense, an attack with guns or air-to-air missiles by an interceptor aircraft, or the launch of an air defense missile by air defense artillery and the missile's subsequent travel to intercept. (JP 3-01) 2. A tactical conflict, usually between opposing lower echelons maneuver forces. (JP 3-0) (Approved for incorporation into JP 1-02.)

escalation. None. (Approved for removal from JP 1-02.)

exclusion zone. A zone established by a sanctioning body to prohibit specific activities in a specific geographic area in order to persuade nations or groups to modify their behavior to meet the desires of the sanctioning body or face continued imposition of sanctions, or the use or threat of force. (Approved for incorporation into JP 1-02.)

expedition. None. (Approved for removal from JP 1-02.)

expeditionary force. An armed force organized to achieve a specific objective in a foreign country. (JP 1-02. SOURCE: JP 3-0)

fire support coordination measure. A measure employed by commanders to facilitate the rapid engagement of targets and simultaneously provide safeguards for friendly forces. Also called **FSCM**. (Approved for incorporation into JP 1-02.)

Glossary

first strike. None. (Approved for removal from JP 1-02.)

force projection. The ability to project the military instrument of national power from the United States or another theater, in response to requirements for military operations. (Approved for incorporation into JP 1-02 with JP 3-0 as the source JP.)

force protection. Preventive measures taken to mitigate hostile actions against Department of Defense personnel (to include family members), resources, facilities, and critical information. Also called **FP.** (Approved for incorporation into JP 1-02.)

force structure. None. (Approved for removal from JP 1-02.)

freedom of navigation operations. Operations conducted to protect US navigation, overflight and related interests on, under and over the seas. (Approved for incorporation into JP 1-02.)

friendly force information requirement. Information the commander and staff need to understand the status of friendly force and supporting capabilities. Also called **FFIR.** (JP 1-02. SOURCE: JP 3-0)

full-spectrum superiority. The cumulative effect of dominance in the air, land, maritime, and space domains and information environment (which includes cyberspace) that permits the conduct of joint operations without effective opposition or prohibitive interference. (Approved for incorporation into JP 1-02.)

ground combat element. None. (Approved for removal from JP 1-02.)

hostile. None. (Approved for removal from JP 1-02.)

hostile environment. None. (Approved for removal from JP 1-02.)

hostile force. None. (Approved for removal from JP 1-02.)

incidents. None. (Approved for removal from JP 1-02.)

information management. The function of managing an organization's information resources for the handling of data and information acquired by one or many different systems, individuals, and organizations in a way that optimizes access by all who have a share in that data or a right to that information. Also called **IM.** (Approved for incorporation into JP 1-02.)

innocent passage. None. (Approved for removal from JP 1-02.)

in-place force. None. (Approved for removal from JP 1-02.)

inspection. None. (Approved for removal from JP 1-02.)

interagency coordination. Within the context of Department of Defense involvement, the coordination that occurs between elements of Department of Defense, and engaged US Government agencies and departments for the purpose of achieving an objective. (Approved for incorporation into JP 1-02.)

intervention. None. (Approved for removal from JP 1-02.)

joint fires. Fires delivered during the employment of forces from two or more components in coordinated action to produce desired effects in support of a common objective. (JP 1-02. SOURCE: JP 3-0)

joint fire support. Joint fires that assist air, land, maritime, and special operations forces to move, maneuver, and control territory, populations, airspace, and key waters. (JP 1-02. SOURCE: JP 3-0)

joint force. A general term applied to a force composed of significant elements, assigned or attached, of two or more Military Departments operating under a single joint force commander. (JP 1-02. SOURCE: JP 3-0)

joint force air component commander. The commander within a unified command, subordinate unified command, or joint task force responsible to the establishing commander for recommending the proper employment of assigned, attached, and/or made available for tasking air forces; planning and coordinating air operations; or accomplishing such operational missions as may be assigned. Also called **JFACC**. (Approved for incorporation into JP 1-02.)

joint force land component commander. The commander within a unified command, subordinate unified command, or joint task force responsible to the establishing commander for recommending the proper employment of assigned, attached, and/or made available for tasking land forces; planning and coordinating land operations; or accomplishing such operational missions as may be assigned. Also called **JFLCC**. (Approved for incorporation into JP 1-02.)

joint force maritime component commander. The commander within a unified command, subordinate unified command, or joint task force responsible to the establishing commander for recommending the proper employment of assigned, attached, and/or made available for tasking maritime forces and assets; planning and coordinating maritime operations; or accomplishing such operational missions as may be assigned. Also called **JFMCC**. (Approved for incorporation into JP 1-02.)

joint force special operations component commander. The commander within a unified command, subordinate unified command, or joint task force responsible to the establishing commander for recommending the proper employment of assigned, attached, and/or made available for tasking special operations forces and assets; planning and coordinating special operations; or accomplishing such operational missions as may be assigned. Also called **JFSOCC**. (Approved for incorporation into JP 1-02.)

joint functions. Related capabilities and activities placed into six basic groups of command and control, intelligence, fires, movement and maneuver, protection, and

Glossary

sustainment to help joint force commanders synchronize, integrate, and direct joint operations. (Approved for incorporation into JP 1-02.)

joint operations. A general term to describe military actions conducted by joint forces and those Service forces employed in specified command relationships with each other, which of themselves, do not establish joint forces. (Approved for incorporation into JP 1-02.)

joint operations area. An area of land, sea, and airspace, defined by a geographic combatant commander or subordinate unified commander, in which a joint force commander (normally a joint task force commander) conducts military operations to accomplish a specific mission. Also called **JOA**. (JP 1-02. SOURCE: JP 3-0)

joint readiness. None. (Approved for removal from JP 1-02.)

joint special operations area. An area of land, sea, and airspace assigned by a joint force commander to the commander of a joint special operations force to conduct special operations activities. Also called **JSOA**. (Approved for incorporation into JP 1-02.)

link. 1. A behavioral, physical, or functional relationship between nodes. 2. In communications, a general term used to indicate the existence of communications facilities between two points. 3. A maritime route, other than a coastal or transit route, which links any two or more routes. (JP 1-02. SOURCE: JP 3-0)

main battle area. None. (Approved for removal from JP 1-02.)

major operation. 1. A series of tactical actions (battles, engagements, strikes) conducted by combat forces of a single or several Services, coordinated in time and place, to achieve strategic or operational objectives in an operational area. 2. For noncombat operations, a reference to the relative size and scope of a military operation. (Approved for incorporation into JP 1-02.)

maneuver. 1. A movement to place ships, aircraft, or land forces in a position of advantage over the enemy. 2. A tactical exercise carried out at sea, in the air, on the ground, or on a map in imitation of war. 3. The operation of a ship, aircraft, or vehicle, to cause it to perform desired movements. 4. Employment of forces in the operational area through movement in combination with fires to achieve a position of advantage in respect to the enemy. (Approved for incorporation into JP 1-02.)

Marine air-ground task force. None. (Approved for removal from JP 1-02.)

Marine expeditionary force. None. (Approved for removal from JP 1-02.)

Marine expeditionary unit. None. (Approved for removal from JP 1-02.)

Marine expeditionary unit (special operations capable). None. (Approved for removal from JP 1-02.)

maritime interception operations. Efforts to monitor, query, and board merchant vessels in international waters to enforce sanctions against other nations such as those in support of United Nations Security Council Resolutions and/or prevent the transport of restricted goods. Also called **MIO.** (JP 1-02. SOURCE: JP 3-0)

measure of effectiveness. A criterion used to assess changes in system behavior, capability, or operational environment that is tied to measuring the attainment of an end state, achievement of an objective, or creation of an effect. Also called **MOE.** (JP 1-02. SOURCE: JP 3-0)

measure of performance. A criterion used to assess friendly actions that is tied to measuring task accomplishment. Also called **MOP.** (JP 1-02. SOURCE: JP 3-0)

military capability. None. (Approved for removal from JP 1-02.)

military education. None. (Approved for removal from JP 1-02.)

military engagement. Routine contact and interaction between individuals or elements of the Armed Forces of the United States and those of another nation's armed forces, or foreign and domestic civilian authorities or agencies to build trust and confidence, share information, coordinate mutual activities, and maintain influence. (JP 1-02. SOURCE: JP 3-0)

military intervention. The deliberate act of a nation or a group of nations to introduce its military forces into the course of an existing controversy. (Approved for incorporation into JP 1-02 with JP 3-0 as the source JP.)

military occupation. A condition in which territory is under the effective control of a foreign armed force. (Approved for incorporation into JP 1-02 with JP 3-0 as the source JP.)

mission. 1. The task, together with the purpose, that clearly indicates the action to be taken and the reason therefore. (JP 3-0) 2. In common usage, especially when applied to lower military units, a duty assigned to an individual or unit; a task. (JP 3-0) 3. The dispatching of one or more aircraft to accomplish one particular task. (JP 3-30) (Approved for incorporation into JP 1-02.)

modernization. None. (Approved for removal from JP 1-02.)

nation assistance. Assistance rendered to a nation by foreign forces within that nation's territory based on agreements mutually concluded between nations. (Approved for incorporation into JP 1-02.)

near real time. None. (Approved for removal from JP 1-02.)

neutral. In combat and combat support operations, an identity applied to a track whose characteristics, behavior, origin, or nationality indicate that it is neither supporting nor opposing friendly forces. (Approved for incorporation into JP 1-02 with JP 3-0 as the source JP.)

neutrality. In international law, the attitude of impartiality during periods of war adopted by third states toward a belligerent and subsequently recognized by the belligerent, which creates rights and duties between the impartial states and the belligerent. (Approved for incorporation into JP 1-02.)

neutralize. 1. As pertains to military operations, to render ineffective or unusable. 2. To render enemy personnel or material incapable of interfering with a particular operation. 3. To render safe mines, bombs, missiles, and booby traps. 4. To make harmless anything contaminated with a chemical agent. (Approved for incorporation into JP 1-02 with JP 3-0 as the source JP.)

node. 1. A location in a mobility system where a movement requirement is originated, processed for onward movement, or terminated. (JP 3-17) 2. In communications and computer systems, the physical location that provides terminating, switching, and gateway access services to support information exchange. (JP 6-0) 3. An element of a system that represents a person, place, or physical thing. (JP 1-02. SOURCE: JP 3-0)

normal operations. None. (Approved for removal from JP 1-02.)

operating force. None. (Approved for removal from JP 1-02.)

operation. 1. A series of tactical actions with a common purpose or unifying theme. (JP 1) 2. A military action or the carrying out of a strategic, operational, tactical, service, training, or administrative military mission. (JP 3-0) (Approved for incorporation into JP 1-02.)

operational area. An overarching term encompassing more descriptive terms (such as area of responsibility and joint operations area) for geographic areas in which military operations are conducted. Also called **OA**. (Approved for incorporation into JP 1-02.)

operational art. The cognitive approach by commanders and staffs—supported by their skill, knowledge, experience, creativity, and judgment—to develop strategies, campaigns, and operations to organize and employ military forces by integrating ends, ways, and means. (Approved for incorporation into JP 1-02.)

operational environment. A composite of the conditions, circumstances, and influences that affect the employment of capabilities and bear on the decisions of the commander. (JP 1-02. SOURCE: JP 3-0)

operational level of war. The level of war at which campaigns and major operations are planned, conducted, and sustained to achieve strategic objectives within theaters or other operational areas. (Approved for incorporation into JP 1-02.)

Glossary

operational reach. The distance and duration across which a joint force can successfully employ military capabilities. (Approved for incorporation into JP 1-02.)

overlap. None. (Approved for removal from JP 1-02.)

permissive environment. Operational environment in which host country military and law enforcement agencies have control as well as the intent and capability to assist operations that a unit intends to conduct. (JP 1-02. SOURCE: JP 3-0)

preemptive attack. None. (Approved for removal from JP 1-02.)

preventive diplomacy. None. (Approved for removal from JP 1-02.)

primary interest. None. (Approved for removal from JP 1-02.)

protection. 1. Preservation of the effectiveness and survivability of mission-related military and nonmilitary personnel, equipment, facilities, information, and infrastructure deployed or located within or outside the boundaries of a given operational area. (JP 3-0) 2. In space usage, active and passive defensive measures to ensure that United States and friendly space systems perform as designed by seeking to overcome an adversary's attempts to negate them and to minimize damage if negation is attempted. (JP 3-14) (Approved for incorporation into JP 1-02.)

protection of shipping. The use of proportionate force, when necessary for the protection of US flag vessels and aircraft, US citizens (whether embarked in US or foreign vessels), and their property against unlawful violence. (Approved for incorporation into JP 1-02.)

raid. An operation to temporarily seize an area in order to secure information, confuse an adversary, capture personnel or equipment, or to destroy a capability culminating with a planned withdrawal. (Approved for incorporation into JP 1-02.)

range. None. (Approved for removal from JP 1-02.)

reaction time. None. (Approved for removal from JP 1-02.)

real time. None. (Approved for removal from JP 1-02.)

reinforcing. None. (Approved for removal from JP 1-02.)

risk management. The process of identifying, assessing, and controlling risks arising from operational factors and making decisions that balance risk cost with mission benefits. Also called **RM**. (Approved for incorporation into JP 1-02 with JP 3-0 as the source JP.)

Glossary

sanction enforcement. Operations that employ coercive measures to control the movement of certain types of designated items into or out of a nation or specified area. (Approved for incorporation into JP 1-02.)

sanctuary. None. (Approved for removal from JP 1-02.)

security cooperation activity. None. (Approved for removal from JP 1-02.)

show of force. An operation designed to demonstrate US resolve that involves increased visibility of US deployed forces in an attempt to defuse a specific situation that, if allowed to continue, may be detrimental to US interests or national objectives. (JP 1-02. SOURCE: JP 3-0)

special purpose Marine air-ground task force. None. (Approved for removal from JP 1-02.)

stability operations. An overarching term encompassing various military missions, tasks, and activities conducted outside the United States in coordination with other instruments of national power to maintain or reestablish a safe and secure environment, provide essential governmental services, emergency infrastructure reconstruction, and humanitarian relief. (JP 1-02. SOURCE: JP 3-0)

standing joint force headquarters. A staff organization operating under a flag or general officer providing a combatant commander with a full-time, trained joint command and control element integrated into the combatant commander's staff whose focus is on contingency and crisis action planning. Also called **SJFHQ**. (Approved for incorporation into JP 1-02.)

strategic advantage. None. (Approved for removal from JP 1-02.)

strategic level of war. The level of war at which a nation, often as a member of a group of nations, determines national or multinational (alliance or coalition) strategic security objectives and guidance, then develops and uses national resources to achieve those objectives. (Approved for incorporation into JP 1-02.)

strategy. A prudent idea or set of ideas for employing the instruments of national power in a synchronized and integrated fashion to achieve theater, national, and/or multinational objectives. (JP 1-02. SOURCE: JP 3-0)

strike. An attack to damage or destroy an objective or a capability. (JP 1-02. SOURCE: JP 3-0)

supported commander. 1. The commander having primary responsibility for all aspects of a task assigned by the Joint Strategic Capabilities Plan or other joint operation planning authority. 2. In the context of joint operation planning, the commander who prepares operation plans or operation orders in response to requirements of the Chairman of the Joint Chiefs of Staff. 3. In the context of a support command relationship, the commander who receives assistance from another commander's force or capabilities, and who is responsible for ensuring that the supporting commander understands the assistance required. (Approved for incorporation into JP 1-02.)

supporting commander. 1. A commander who provides augmentation forces or other support to a supported commander or who develops a supporting plan. 2. In the context of a support command relationship, the commander who aids, protects, complements, or sustains another commander's force, and who is responsible for providing the assistance required by the supported commander. (Approved for incorporation into JP 1-02.)

supporting forces. None. (Approved for removal from JP 1-02.)

surveillance. The systematic observation of aerospace, surface, or subsurface areas, places, persons, or things, by visual, aural, electronic, photographic, or other means. (JP 1-02. SOURCE: 3-0)

sustainability. None. (Approved for removal from JP 1-02.)

sustainment. The provision of logistics and personnel services required to maintain and prolong operations until successful mission accomplishment. (JP 1-02. SOURCE: JP 3-0)

system. A functionally, physically, and/or behaviorally related group of regularly interacting or interdependent elements; that group of elements forming a unified whole. (JP 1-02. SOURCE: JP 3-0)

tactical level of war. The level of war at which battles and engagements are planned and executed to achieve military objectives assigned to tactical units or task forces. (Approved for incorporation into JP 1-02.)

tactical unit. None. (Approved for removal from JP 1-02.)

targeting. The process of selecting and prioritizing targets and matching the appropriate response to them, considering operational requirements and capabilities. (JP 1-02. SOURCE: JP 3-0)

termination criteria. The specified standards approved by the President and/or the Secretary of Defense that must be met before a joint operation can be concluded. (JP 1-02. SOURCE: JP 3-0)

theater of operations. An operational area defined by the geographic combatant commander for the conduct or support of specific military operations. Also called **TO**. (Approved for incorporation into JP 1-02.)

theater of war. Defined by the President, Secretary of Defense, or the geographic combatant commander as the area of air, land, and water that is, or may become, directly involved in the conduct of major operations and campaigns involving combat. (Approved for incorporation into JP 1-02.)

theater strategy. An overarching construct outlining a combatant commander's vision for integrating and synchronizing military activities and operations with the other instruments of national power in order to achieve national strategic objectives. (Approved for incorporation into JP 1-02.)

troops. None. (Approved for removal from JP 1-02.)

uncertain environment. Operational environment in which host government forces, whether opposed to or receptive to operations that a unit intends to conduct, do not have totally effective control of the territory and population in the intended operational area. (JP 1-02. SOURCE: JP 3-0)

unit readiness. None. (Approved for removal from JP 1-02.)

unity of command. The operation of all forces under a single responsible commander who has the requisite authority to direct and employ those forces in pursuit of a common purpose. (Approved for incorporation into JP 1-02 with JP 3-0 as the source JP.)

weapon system. A combination of one or more weapons with all related equipment, materials, services, personnel, and means of delivery and deployment (if applicable) required for self-sufficiency. (Approved for incorporation into JP 1-02.)

JOINT DOCTRINE PUBLICATIONS HIERARCHY

JP 1
JOINT DOCTRINE
JP 1-0
PERSONNEL
JP 2-0
INTELLIGENCE
JP 3-0
OPERATIONS
JP 4-0
LOGISTICS
JP 5-0
PLANS
JP 6-0
COMMUNICATIONS SYSTEM

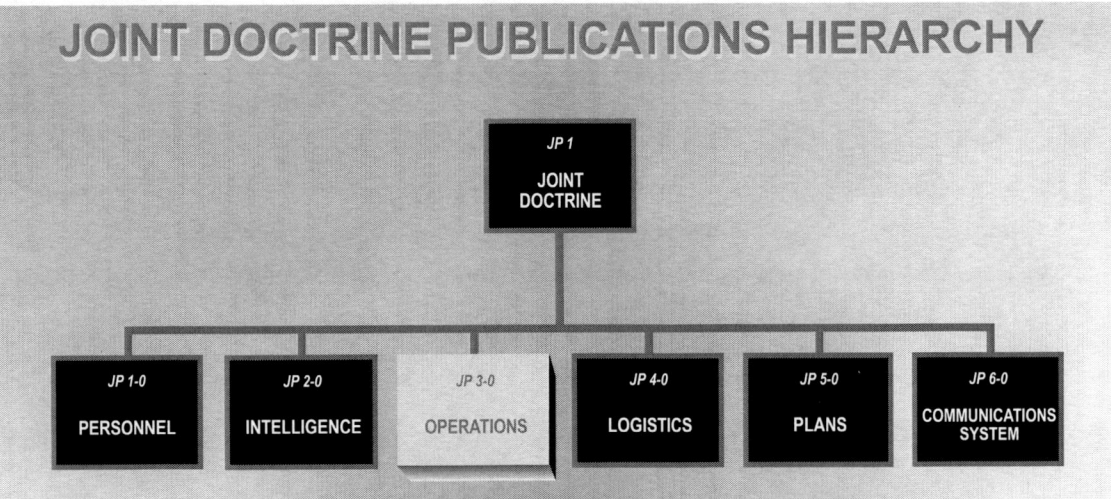

All joint publications are organized into a comprehensive hierarchy as shown in the chart above. **Joint Publication (JP) 3-0** is in the **Operations** series of joint doctrine publications. The diagram below illustrates an overview of the development process:

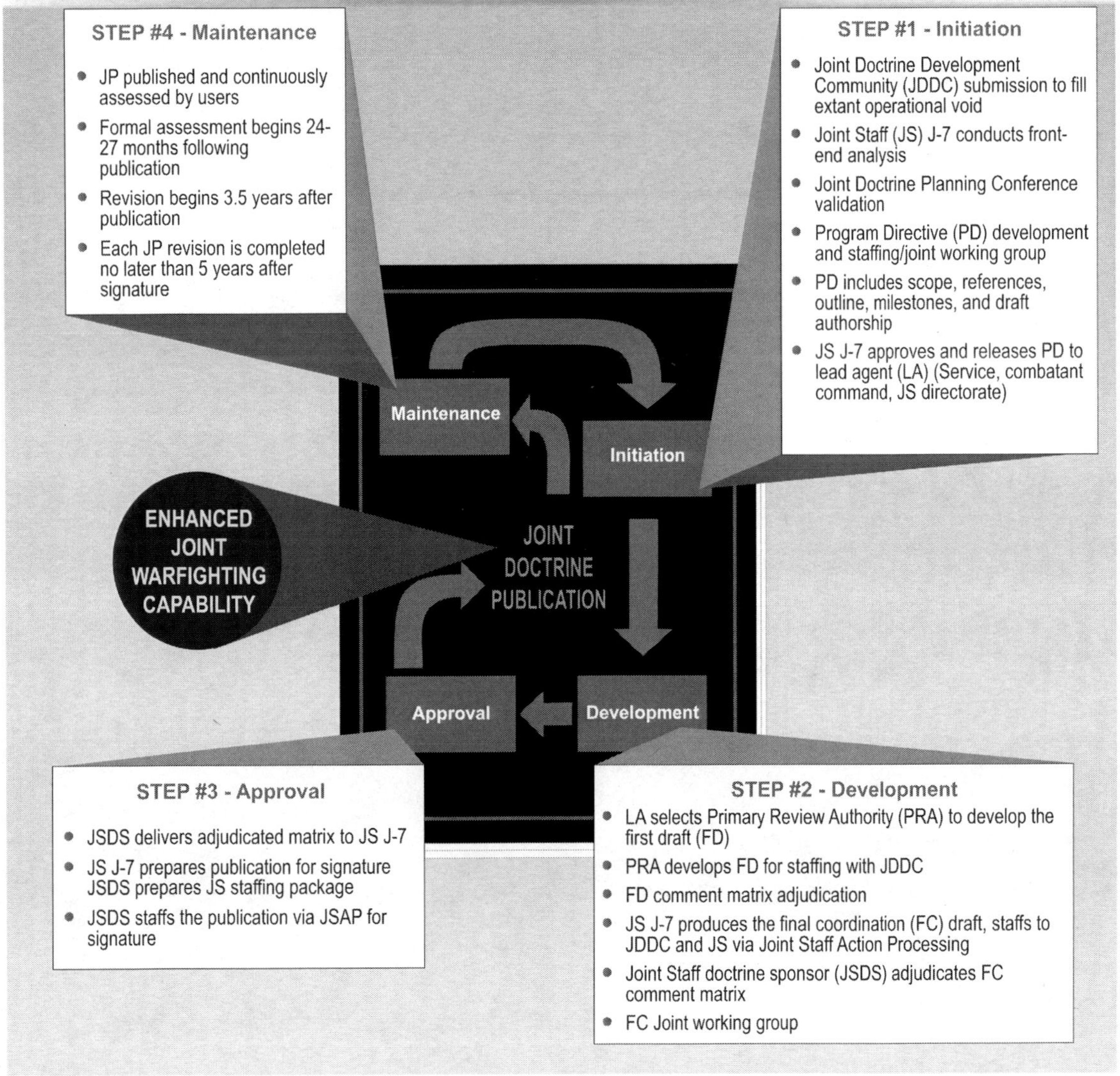

STEP #4 - Maintenance
JP published and continuously assessed by users
Formal assessment begins 24-27 months following publication
Revision begins 3.5 years after publication
Each JP revision is completed no later than 5 years after signature
STEP #1 - Initiation
Joint Doctrine Development Community (JDDC) submission to fill extant operational void
Joint Staff (JS) J-7 conducts front-end analysis
Joint Doctrine Planning Conference validation
Program Directive (PD) development and staffing/joint working group
PD includes scope, references, outline, milestones, and draft authorship
JS J-7 approves and releases PD to lead agent (LA) (Service, combatant command, JS directorate)
Maintenance
Initiation
ENHANCED JOINT WARFIGHTING CAPABILITY
JOINT DOCTRINE PUBLICATION
Approval
Development
STEP #3 - Approval
JSDS delivers adjudicated matrix to JS J-7
JS J-7 prepares publication for signature JSDS prepares JS staffing package
JSDS staffs the publication via JSAP for signature
STEP #2 - Development
LA selects Primary Review Authority (PRA) to develop the first draft (FD)
PRA develops FD for staffing with JDDC
FD comment matrix adjudication
JS J-7 produces the final coordination (FC) draft, staffs to JDDC and JS via Joint Staff Action Processing
Joint Staff doctrine sponsor (JSDS) adjudicates FC comment matrix
FC Joint working group

Made in United States
Cleveland, OH
09 January 2026